Management for the Public Domain

Management for the Public Domain

Enabling the Learning Society

Stewart Ranson

and

John Stewart

St. Martin's Press

First published in Great Britain 1994 by
THE MACMILLAN PRESS LTD
Houndmills, Basingstoke, Hampshire RG21 2XS
and London
Companies and representatives
throughout the world

A catalogue record for this book is available
from the British Library.

ISBN 0–333–49557–8 hardcover
ISBN 0–333–49558–6 paperback

Printed in Hong Kong

First published in the United States of America 1994 by
Scholarly and Reference Division,
ST. MARTIN'S PRESS, INC.,
175 Fifth Avenue,
New York, N.Y. 10010

ISBN 0–312–12284–5

Library of Congress Cataloging-in-Publication Data
Ranson, Stewart.
Management for the public domain : enabling the learning society /
Stewart Ranson and John Stewart.
p. cm.
Includes bibliographical references and index.
ISBN 0–312–12284–5
1. Public administration.   2. Management.   I. Stewart, John
David, 1929– . II. Title.
JF1351.R285 1994
350'.0001—dc20   94–25479
                                                              CIP

Contents

List of Exhibits

Preface

This book has its origins in two articles that we wrote in 1988 of which the first published bore a similar title to this book – 'Management in the Public Domain'. We argued in those articles that analysis of management in the public domain had been conditioned, consciously or unconsciously, by the nature of management in the private sector. Even where differences were recognised, writings on management in the public sector conceptualised it negatively as 'non-market' or 'not-for-profit management', rather than positively as, for example, 'public service management'. Such an approach limited understanding, leading to neglect of the distinctive purposes, conditions and tasks of what we described as the public domain, meaning by that phrase to describe a sphere of activities in which distinctive values are realised and which is governed by its own organising principles.

We showed in the first article (Stewart and Ranson, 1988) that the result of the dominance of the private sector model led either to the neglect of aspects of management that were of importance in the public domain or to a distorted treatment of other aspects. One illustration of neglect was the tendency to ignore the political process which governs activity in the public domain or to treat it as an obstacle to effective management, whereas we argued that management in the public domain should rather be designed to support and express the political processes that govern that domain. An illustration of the distortion that could result from inappropriate application of the private sector model was the introduction of marketing approaches which treated the public solely as customer, ignoring the public as citizen and the reality that many services in the public domain are rationed according to criteria of need rather than supplied according to demand at a given price.

We argued that the private sector model has a different basis from the model of management in the public domain.

Our argument was not that particular approaches could not be developed for the public domain from the private sector. Both can learn particular approaches from each other. Rather our argument was for the development of ways of thinking about management in the public domain which were grounded in the distinctive purposes, conditions and tasks of that domain. There was a need for an analysis of management that was as rigorous as any developed for the private sector, but one which took public purposes, conditions and tasks as its starting point. Approaches to management could be developed from such analysis that could support rather than deny the nature of the public domain.

Since we wrote those articles there has been the development in many countries of what has been called the new public management, which is based to a very large extent upon the private sector model, stressing as it does the use of market mechanisms and competition, and the idea of the public as customer. The development of the new public management has led to the growth of a literature appraising its development. In that literature are to be found both advocates and critics of the development, but whichever stance is taken the starting point is the new public management, rather than the search for an approach to management grounded in the purposes, conditions and tasks of the public domain. The need identified in our article for the development of such an approach has been made more urgent by the advance of the new public management.

It is that task that we have undertaken in this book. It sets out to reconceptualise public management based upon an understanding of its distinctive purposes, conditions and tasks. It is not therefore another textbook on public sector management, but a book that sets out a perspective on public sector management which describes not what is, but points the way to what could be. We hope it will guide both students and practitioners in their thinking. From that perspective can develop, as we show, approaches to management which can strengthen the public domain. From that perspective developments in the new public management can be appraised not on their own terms, but on terms set by a new understanding of the nature of the public domain.

This perspective on public management has grown out of a critical analysis of the social, economic and political changes in the UK since the early 1970s. These changes have suggested that the 'settlement' between the classes after the Second World War to create a more just society was withering away and with it the authority of the polity. Accelerating unemployment together with the fragmenting of communities has often eroded the sense of membership of and participation in the public life of the community. This is particularly disturbing when these and other changes – for example environmental erosion – present problems whose resolution requires by definition collective action informed by some sense of the public good for the community as a whole. It is the principal purpose of the public domain to develop those institutions and values which enable citizens to flourish not only as individuals but also in their contribution to the life and well-being of society. The failure of the polity in this period is to have abandoned this understanding of its purpose, not least because its own legitimacy and thus survival depend upon the authority it derives from public consent. The challenge for the public domain and its management is to rediscover the foundations of democratic citizenship that alone can regenerate the quality of life for the public as a whole.

While the structure of this argument derives from particular experience it leads to a general analysis of wide applicability. The impact upon society of the interaction of the 'post-industrial revolution' and neo-liberal policies which emphasise the individual above society has been experienced in many countries. But this historical juncture should also be taken to illustrate what has been neglected and taken for granted, namely that any society at any time can really only flourish with a public domain that strives to hold in balance the necessary relationship between the private and the public good.

The case study from which we have developed our argument is intended to contribute to a wider international debate about public management.

The argument of the book unfolds in three stages. In Part I we discuss the scope of the public domain, the activities that are governed by it and how the ways of working developed therein have varied over time. We have set out the dominant trends in the

postwar period, placing emphasis upon the social democratic
polity of the immediate postwar period and on the neo-liberal
polity of recent years. We show that both in their different ways
gave expression to a restricted concept of the public domain
which conditioned the nature of management, limiting its role.
We argue that the conditions of our time need a concept of the
public domain that realises its full potential, because it must
support a learning society committed to the development of
communities and individuals. The book aims to show what that
renewal of the public domain means for management, whose role
would then be to enable the learning society. In this part of the
book we draw upon management theory, showing how different
management categories which may provide a common framework
for analysis are given different meanings by the purposes,
conditions and tasks of particular organisational contexts. There
is no generic approach to management; that is why it is necessary
to explore the distinctive nature of the management of the public
domain in the context of the learning society.

Part II explores the nature of the public domain. Because the
learning society requires the development of its full potential, this
part explores its values, which leads to an examination of the
nature of citizenship that is realised in that domain. It is then
argued that the distinctive organising principles of the public
domain are based upon public discourse leading to collective
choice based on public consent. Those principles can best be
realised through institutional reform directed at a renewal of
democracy. Those reformed institutions should realise their
mutual interdependence, resting as they do on a presumption of
cooperation, derived from the organising principle by which all
should be governed.

Part III explores how management can meet the distinctive
purposes and conditions of the public domain derived from its
organising principles. In this way management can enable the
learning society. This part argues that this needs approaches
which permit an enhanced capacity for change and development
in public organisations. The nature of those approaches is
explored in chapters that examine how management can enable
organisational tasks of sustaining public learning, supporting
public choice and public accountability, and empowering a public
culture. In these chapters therefore the nature of management in

the public domain is discussed. These approaches both support and draw upon public discourse and the political processes through which it can be expressed. In exploring the implications new directions can be found for management. The book presents therefore alternatives to both past and prevalent approaches which have too often ignored the necessity of public discourse and of effective political processes for the vitality of the public domain and for its management.

The book concludes with a recognition that management in the public domain has to support and express political judgement, since that judgement tested in public discourse underlies the organisational tasks discussed in Part III. Judgement sustains the learning society and management in the public domain should sustain judgement.

The sources of our interest and concern with management in the public domain are: our continuing work in teaching and research for and in that domain, the many practitioners with whom we have discussed the deep issues all confront in managing in that domain, and our colleagues in the Schools of Education and Public Policy who have challenged our thinking. We are especially grateful to the Local Government Training Board (now the Local Government Management Board) who first gave us the opportunity to reflect on this theme and to Steven Kennedy for his support and considerable patience. We would also like to thank Kathy Bonehill and Jenny Neave for their excellent secretarial support.

The book draws upon ideas and material from various articles and books we have written. In particular it draws upon:

Stewart, J. and S. Ranson (1988) 'Management in the Public Domain', *Public Money and Management*, 8 (1/2), pp. 13–19.

Ranson, S. and J. Stewart (1989) 'Citizenship and Government: The Challenge for Management in the Public Domain', *Political Science*, 37 (1), pp. 5–24.

Ranson, S. (1992) 'Towards the Learning Society', *Education Management and Administration* 20 (2), pp. 68–79.

Stewart, J. and K. Walsh (1992) 'Change in the Management of Public Services', *Public Administration*.

Ranson, S. (1993) 'Markets or Democracy for Education', *British Journal of Educational Studies*, 42 (4), pp. 332–52.

Ranson, S. (1994) *Towards the Learning Society* (London: Cassell).
Stewart, J. and K. Walsh (1994) 'Performance Management When
Performance Can Never be Finally Defined', *Public Money and
Management,* forthcoming.

STEWART RANSON
JOHN STEWART

PART 1

PUBLIC ORGANISATIONS IN QUESTION

1

Transformations and Predicaments

The Beleaguered Public Sector

Although public sector organisations are a significant feature of everyday experience, understanding of their distinctiveness has all but atrophied, a situation which has been accelerated since the late 1970s by what Estrin and Le Grand (1989) call 'an unprecedented barrage of criticism'. Hospitals and surgeries, schools and welfare agencies, local authorities and departments of government provide an array of services, benefits, subsidies and regulations that have formed the context of most people's lives. Nevertheless, for over a decade the public sector has looked beleaguered: its rationale doubted, its effectiveness and efficiency derided and its resources depleted (see Buchanan, 1975; Niskanen, 1971, 1973, 1975). Public organisations have, purportedly, been self-interested and unresponsive to the public and have failed to fulfil the expectations of the postwar years of leading the creation of a fairer, more equal society.

There can be little doubt that some of these criticisms of public organisations are justified. In their own terms some of the large welfare bureaucracies could have been more efficient in their administration and more responsive to differing needs, and it is the case that not all the objectives of eliminating social inequality were fulfilled. Nevertheless, it is also true that there has been considerable exaggeration as Le Grand (1989, p. 194) argues. The administrative costs, for example of state pension schemes or the

National Health Service, take up a much lower proportion of expenditure than comparable private schemes. Most professionals, moreover, are dedicated to serving the needs of their clients and, taken together, the public service organisations in which they work have contributed to the creation of societies that have more overall equality and less poverty than societies without such organisations and services.

It seems clear, however, that the primary focus of the criticisms is less the internal working of public organisations than a challenge to the objectives of public organisation itself. It is the purposes of public organisations, or even the very conception of publicness, which have been brought into question. Thus, the values of the private sector have in recent times come to dominate thinking about every type of organisation. If public organisations were only private, it is contended, then problems of efficiency and bureaucracy would disappear.

The language appropriate to one kind of organisation has now become the currency for all. Underlying most approaches to management are values that thrive in the domain of the private. The values of the public domain are, seemingly, not perceived as relevant to management theories. Organisational models assume the values of the private even when their focus is the public. This has meant that many activities of public bodies are implicitly defined as outside the concern of management: protest, politics, public accountability, citizenship, party conflict, elections, public debate, inter-authority cooperation, and civil rights. The public domain has been simplified. Such public events and processes are even perceived as interferences: 'efficiency has to be sacrificed for democracy', 'the constraints of public accountability', or 'the costs of democracy'.

Yet these dimensions which are conceptualised as constraints upon effective working are arguably qualities of value or constitutive conditions within public organisations. A concept of organisation that encompasses citizens differs from an organisation that knows only customers. The obliteration of significant issues leaves the management of public organisations bereft of concepts that are indispensable to its adequate analysis. There is an urgent need to retrieve an understanding of the distinctive forms of management, for in the public domain any notion of management which cannot encompass the recognition of politics and conflict as constitutive of a public organisation rather than as an obstacle to it is barren.

Interpreting the Significance of the Challenge

The full significance of the challenge to the public sector can only be grasped by locating it in a wider context. Taken separately, the criticisms of public organisations present important matters of concern for their effective working. Together, they represent much more: the most fundamental questioning and analysis of the values and organising principles of the postwar polity. Underlying the arguments about the role and purpose of public organisations has been a debate about the validity of the welfare state and the integrity of postwar social democracy. This has been prompted by the economic, social and political *transformations of our time*, the predicaments of which are generating the re-examination of the postwar polity and its organisational forms. Underlying the scrutiny of the quality of performance in public organisations is a debate about the value and purpose of the public within our society. A dispute about the philosophy and politics of public policy can thus be seen to underlie the arguments about public organisations and their management. An understanding of public sector organisation and management cannot proceed without interpretive analysis of the social and political context which informs it. This will mean an exploration of the dominant ideology of neo-liberal consumerism which has sought to transform the shape and purpose of public organisations. But the flaws of market individualism have only served to illuminate *dilemmas* which, we believe, are intrinsic to the public domain and its management. The distinctiveness of public management is characterised by universal tasks and purposes which distinguish it from all other forms of management. By overemphasising the individual to the exclusion of the needs of the public as a whole, consumerism has neglected the inescapable duality of the public domain which defines its unique management task, that is, the requirement of achieving public purpose that has legitimate authority because it derives from a process of accommodating and reconciling the necessary diversity of interests within society. The defining task of public management is to mediate that duality of democratic citizenship: that citizens are many, yet also members of one community.

The Transformations

The growing intensity of the embattled debate on the public sector and its management has to be understood in the context of a series of changes that had their origin, or at least began to accelerate, in the early 1970s. The transformations are many-sided and often quite independent of each other, yet together they combine to alter fundamentally the world we had become accustomed to and have established new agendas for management in both the public and private domains (see Hirsch, 1977; Ellis and Kumar, 1983; Goodman, 1983). The changes have led to a fundamental questioning of the social and political order which dominated Britain since the Second World War. The period since the mid-1970s has seen a struggle to redefine the polity. For most of this period one perspective – that of the New Right – has imposed its interpretation of reform but there have been alternative programmes which reject their neo-liberalism yet also seek to reform the postwar paradigm. These programmes for the restructuring of the polity each comprise an analysis of as well as proposals for transforming the public sector, the quality of its services and the effectiveness of its management and organisation.

The long postwar period of economic growth and prosperity in Britain came to an end with the 1973 oil crisis, precipitating a recession amongst the Western economies more severe than anything experienced since the 1930s (see Gamble, 1981; Handy, 1984). The recession together with the contraction of production caused accelerating unemployment, with over 3 million registered as unemployed in the early 1980s. The contraction of metal manufacturing and heavy industry in general prompted some to talk of an incipient process of 'de-industrialisation' (see Weiner, 1981; Gershuny, 1978) within the first industrial nation. Harvey (1989) and others (see Massey and Meegan, 1982; Lash and Urry, 1987; Murray, 1989) argue, however, that what is taking place is a broader economic restructuring. The strategy has been to restore profitability by introducing more flexible forms of production, labour market segmentation and organisational arrangement.

These *post-Fordist* forms of 'flexible accumulation' are to be distinguished from the mass production of standardised goods pioneered by Henry Ford that became the paradigm for industrial development in the postwar world and the rigidities of which prevented its smooth adaptation to a changed context. The flexible firm develops a capacity to 'customise' its business, designing quality goods and services to meet the needs and changing fashions of diverse groups (or 'niches') in the market-place. Firms develop flexible production systems to respond to and exploit more specialised markets.

The post-Fordist, flexibly accumulating and service economy is underpinned by the growth of a system of international finance that is increasingly indifferent to the constraints of time or space. Computerised telecommunications allow instantaneous flows of money across the global market for finance and credit which disregard the boundaries of nation states. This trend illustrates a broader shift towards the growing 'compression of our temporal and spacial worlds' (Harvey, 1989).

The degradation of the environment is a consequence of past and present economic forms. The accelerating emission of carbon dioxide into the atmosphere has punctured the ozone layer enough to cause a warming of the globe and, some claim, a shifting of the ice-caps. Added to the plundering of the rain-forests, the steady erosion of top-soil and the destruction of countless rare species, these changes provide a catalogue of grave ecological concern. Locally, the mounting litter and traffic congestion disturb the quality of life. The unintended collective consequences of individual action are becoming apparent, if not well-understood.

The cyclical and structural changes in the economy and the environment stand in complex relationship to equally fundamental changes in society. The differentiation of economic sectors and geographic locations, together with the increasing segmentation of labour markets, is creating greater heterogeneity and diversity of social groupings than traditional class ascriptions allow. Now, when groups of workers organise together, they do so as a means to individual ends rather than to meet the needs of their group or community or class as a whole. Such a calculative orientation to occupational activity for many also reflects the 'decentering' of work (Offe, 1985). Family, the home and leisure pursuits more often preoccupy individuals, shape their identities and provide their lives with meaning than their occupations and careers. Consumption rather than production affords the focus to people's lives. For Hobsbawm (1981) 'the values of consumer-society individualism and the search for private and personal satisfactions' have come to dominate society. The question 'Who am I?' is said to replace the preoccupation of an earlier age, 'Who are we?' (Bauman, 1988). These changes, argues Lukes (1984), reflect the disintegration of traditional moral frameworks in the face of the mechanisms of market seduction. With the unravelling of a moral order, which established a framework of social responsibilities, individuals and groups pursue their interests to exploit their market situation. In the face of seemingly intractable social and economic problems confronting society, individuals quietly retreat from the public domain into the satisfactions of the private sphere. This may be a rational response for the many, who feel they have little sense of control over their destinies, in the face of a public world that is in their perception growing more intractable (see Marshall *et al.*, 1988, p. 8).

A more plural society, expressed in increasingly differentiated lifestyles, is said to reflect the more general emergence of the 'post-modern world' with its preference for difference over uniformity, fragmentation over integration, play and the ephemeral over purpose and form. Yet research shows that there is no evidence for the disappearance or decomposition of class in British society. Both the studies at Oxford (Goldthorpe, 1980) and Essex (Marshall *et al.*, 1988) show that despite complexity and mobility, Britain remains a class society with the service class more advantaged and exploiting opportunities better than the working class. There are deeper structures of disadvantage and discrimination of gender, race and class. The economic growth of the mid-1980s produces opulence for some in the face of continuing anxiety and alienation for those excluded (see Hudson and Williams, 1989). A polarised society emerges (Halsey, 1986).

The transformations of economy and society since the mid-1970s have generated a more political world, as conceptions about ways of resolving the emerging problems have sharpened and fractured the postwar political consensus. A more assertive politics has developed at national and local levels. Yet within the major parties new political perspectives have competed for dominance alongside the more traditional manifestos. Added to the politics of party are the new politics of movements: of parents in education, of the elderly ('grey power'), of consumers, and most significantly, of the green movement campaigning for the protection of the environment.

Re-examining the Postwar Order

The very language now being created to characterise these transformations – 'post-modern' (Lyotard, 1984; Turner, 1990b), 'post-industrial' (Bell, 1974), 'post-Fordist' (Hall and Jacques, 1989) – suggests a historic juncture. Such structural change has provoked questions that further disturb the social and political cohesion of the postwar order. What will be the nature of work in the future and who will be required to work? Do individuals need to work to express their identities, develop their capacities, acquire status and contribute as citizens to the common-wealth of the community in which they live? Will those who remain outside work be regarded as 'members', as 'citizens', by others in the community? Will they be accorded equal rights and status and power in the community?

The trends towards differentiation that characterise post-modern society create space for innovation and change, yet also threaten to undermine the very possibility of 'society'. Social fragmentation threatens the cooperation and trust that define a community and create the possibility of collective action without which any society cannot survive. The most serious 'collective action problem' is the predatory exploitation of the environment with its dramatic consequences. Mounting litter, traffic congestion and the prospect of global warming reveal the unintended collective consequences of our individual choices: self-interest can be self-defeating. The seductive yet ultimately irrational compulsion of some to 'free-ride' presents perhaps the most significant challenge for future society. Parfit succinctly describes the dilemma: 'it can be better for each if he adds to pollution, uses more energy, jumps queues and breaks agreements; but if all do these things that can be worse off for each than if none do. It is very often true, that if each rather than none does what will be better for himself, this will be worse off for everyone' (Parfit, 1984, p. 62).

The question arises whether our society any longer possesses the social conditions to resolve the collective action problems which face it. Yet underlying the quality of social cohesion are political issues. The fragmenting society is reflected in the fracturing of the postwar consensus, as agreement about membership, rights and distributive justice collapsed in the face of the uneven experience of change. Underlying the fiscal crisis (which led to a contraction of public expenditure: see Gough, 1979; Hood and Wright, 1981) was actually a political crisis as the willingness of many tax-payers to support the welfare of others crumbled. Has our society the political resources to create a new framework of justice about rights and duties which acquires legitimate authority across a fragmenting society? Social, economic and political changes have, through the uncertainty they have generated, raised the most fundamental questions for a society to cohere during a period of transition: what is it to be a person? is there any such thing as society? what form should democracy take in the post-modern polity? The effect of these structural changes and the questions to which they have given rise has been to cause a fundamental re-examination of the social democratic polity and the management of the public sector. This questioning has occurred right across the political spectrum – as indicated in the writing for example of David Blunkett (Blunkett and Jackson, 1987) and Hilary Wainwright (1987) on the 'New Left', David Marquand (1988) in the centre, as well as the 'New Right' groups such as the Adam Smith Institute, the Hillgate Group, or the Institute of Economic Affairs. We need to understand the lineages of the postwar world and the styles of management it underwrote before we can proceed beyond it.

Reaching the Limits of the Social Democratic Order

The postwar social democratic state provided opportunities that reflected the requirements of justice, emphasised personal development, rewarded meritocratic achievement, and diffused power within the polity. Yet in spite of the undoubted achievements the crises of the 1970s brought into sharper focus than hitherto the limitations of the democratic order (Mishra, 1984; Offe, 1984). Even those committed to the success of the social democratic project have acknowledged the need for reform. Questions arose about the limits of its achievement, its limited conception (of services/opportunity) and, underlying all, the constraints upon the project imposed by the limits of the polity. Although much had been achieved, the aspirations of social democracy were not sufficiently realised. There still remained poverty, resilient and increasing in the 1970s; equality of opportunity mediated by 'the stubborn resistance of class', with the children of the service class benefiting much more than those of the working class; and the inability to acknowledge and respond to other inequalities in society – of gender, race, disability and sexuality.

The limitations lay in the organising assumptions of the period. The assumptions of professional expertise and standards, reinforced by the orderly controls of rational bureaucracy, were the defining conditions of the welfare and social democratic state (see Perkin, 1989). To question the practice of these professional standards and rules laid down at that time would be to doubt the underlying assumptions of the polity. These were that the charter – as constituted by the settlement – for a just and open society which improved the well-being of all its members, could be *provided* and, as it were, 'handed down' to the public. The good society or an educated public were to be *delivered* by knowledge-able specialists, rather than lived and created by the public with the support of professionals. A passive public in awe of the knowledge and universal rules of the professional bureaucracy would receive the conditions for a new and better world. The idea of 'welfare provision' was thus flawed in conception, because it divided professional and public in what could only be achieved by a shared process of transforming public health or education. It rendered artificial and abstract something which could only have significance through the practice of participation that would have enabled 'services' to be experienced and owned as the public's.

As it was, when the cuts came in the late 1970s and 1980s, the public did not appreciate them as a rationing of 'their' services. The lack of resistance, arguably, reflected not only a lack of attachment to services that were formally constituted as public but a much broader alienation from 'public space'. The litter or the vandalising of public buildings reflect an awareness that the space is not the public's. It is not something over which they believe they have any discretion and thus any sense of responsibility that would allow them to invest anything of themselves in the public space. It is space for which a 'specialist' will take care. The public enters the space of the public domain only on the terms of the

professional and as a means to satisfy individual wants defined by
the professional or welfare bureaucracies.

The Predicament Facing the New Order

The predicament we face, however, is that although the problems
confronting society are public and require a public solution, our
society has developed institutions that are not constituted to encourage an active public domain. The characteristics of structural
change in society (fragmentation, privatism and sectionalism) and
the qualities of the social democratic order (specialisation,
paternalism, passivity) mutually reinforce the erosion of public
life and thus the conditions for personal autonomy as well as
collective well-being. The challenge for the time is to create a new
moral and political order that responds to the needs of a society
undergoing a historic transition and which will inform the society
created through that transition. Such a new order would strive to
create the purpose and conditions of publicness, which proved
impossible within the limited design of social democracy.

The unremitting schedule of reforms to government since the
mid-1970s has been a response to the crisis of change. The state
has been striving to establish the basis of a new social and political
order that would meet the exigencies of a society experiencing a
historic transformation. Two ostensibly alternative strategies for
restructuring the polity – corporatism and consumerism – have
been developed.

The Response of Corporatism

The initial response to the 1970s' 'steering crisis' was to repair the
fractures by centralising power. Pahl (1977) and Winkler (1977)
have described the processes of concentration and rationalisation
which characterise the corporate state (see Panitch, 1980; Cawson,
1978, 1985; Grant, 1985): *unity*, through the collaboration and
cooperation of capital and labour; *order*, to achieve stability and
discipline in industrial relations; *nationalism*, to reinforce indi-
genous interests; and *pragmatism* of ends and purposes to ensure
efficiency. Production replaces consumption as the important
preoccupation of the state, while efficiency becomes the overriding
priority above the previous social democratic goals of equality and

social justice. Economic pragmatism and efficiency are best facilitated by technocratic rational planning within more disciplined, bureaucratic organisational forms. In government these were illustrated by the introduction of new forms of central-local policy planning systems (see Hinings *et al.*, 1983; Rhodes, 1988).

The corporate state developed to meet the exigencies of a declining economy: pragmatism and efficiency were the ends, rationalisation and centralised bureaucracy the means. Local government which had been expanded as the locus of services for the community and the needs of individuals was to be controlled to reflect financial constraints and its services, wherever possible, restructured to facilitate the regeneration of the economy. Most significantly, the centralising thrust of corporatism ensured that it could not resolve the flaws at the centre of the social democratic project – while specialisation and authority of the professional bureaucracy may have undoubtedly improved the quality of services provided to meet client need, it reinforced, at the same time, the passivity of the public whose agency was the essential precondition for achieving the just society to which social democracy was committed.

The vacuum in the postwar polity was the absence of the public. The task for a new generation was to involve the public more than ever before in the life of the polity. Indeed a new consensus may be emerging about the need to empower the public. Yet there is deep disagreement about the method which should be preferred. One manifesto, with its idiosyncratic conception of the public as consumers, came to dominate the next generation.

The New Right and the Challenge of Consumerism

The Conservative Government elected in 1979 inherited and reproduced many of the vestiges of corporatism. But the manifestos and legislative programmes of its second and third terms of office increasingly rejected corporatism in favour of a distinctive strategy of empowering the public as consumers in the market of public services (see Heald, 1983; Levitas, 1986; King, 1987; Jessop *et al.*, 1988; Skidelsky, 1988).

The organising principles of the New Right, espousing the values of individual rights and choice, informed the creation of a neo-liberal polity. 'There are only individual people with their own individual lives', argues Nozick (1974). Individuals are morally self-sufficient and their dignity derives from expressing their unique individuality. What property and skills they possess they are entitled to keep and deploy as they choose. These are natural, inalienable rights, as Locke proposed (1967). The general well-being of society, it is argued, is best served when individuals are allowed to pursue their self-interest. Although individuals only enter society and form associations to further their self-interest, nevertheless, the unintended consequence – guided by a hidden hand – is the general well-being of all in society. When individuals are free to compete with each other in the market-place, they can exchange goods and services to mutual advantage while the efficiency of this allocation secures benefit for all.

Public services will become more accountable when they are made to respond directly to the choices of individual consumers, rather than to the plans of service-producers. As in other forms of market exchange, the products which thrive can only do so because they have the support of consumers. Those products which fail the test of the market-place will lose consumers and go out of business. For consumers to fulfil their allotted role as quality-controllers in the market-place they require the opportunity to choose. If individuals are to acquire the necessary freedom to calculate their interests then government needs to be constrained. For some, such as Nozick, the 'minimal state' should be 'limited to the narrow function of protection against force, fraud, enforcement of contracts, and so on'. Others, however, such as Bentham (see Parekh, 1973), believe that if the market-place is to be protected so that it can work effectively then the state requires extra powers to regulate the deviations of social misfits. The surveillance of the panopticon has its place.

The legitimacy of this moral and political order derives not only from its protection of individual interests, but also because it purports to enable freedom of choice. It is based on an active polity whose members are conceived not as passive, dependent creatures, but as agents reflecting upon and actively developing their interests. Government is made to serve and to account to an active democracy of consumers in the market-place. These values and principles have increasingly shaped the programmes of the Conservative Government. The key themes for public management are (see Stewart and Walsh, 1992; Stewart and Stoker, 1989a; 1994):

● *An emphasis on the public as customer and on customer choice*: the public are conceived as individual customers with rights to choice and quality. They are to choose within a market-place of public and private sector providers.

● *The creation of markets or quasi-markets and the commitment to competition*: single providers are replaced by a plurality of possible providers; an increasing range of services is to be subjected to competitive tendering from the private sector.

● *A greater scope for individual and private sector provision*: individuals are to become more self-reliant and provide for themselves. Voluntary associations are seen as having an expanded role. Private sector provision is set to increase. Public authorities are encouraged to concentrate on those services really 'needed' by the public, abandoning unnecessary functions and allowing scope for individual and private sector provision.

● *The separation of the purchaser role from the provider role*: in all parts of the public service there has been a separation of the role of determining what should be provided from the role of providing a service. The language varies: principal–agent; purchaser–provider; client–contractor.

● *The growth of contractual or semi-contractual arrangements*: traditionally, public sector organisations have been structured for direct hierarchical control or reliance on professionalism; the purchaser–provider developments reveal a new movement towards control through contracts.

● *Performance targets legitimated by the market test*: internally, managers in greater control of resources are required to meet targets and are held accountable for their performance. Externally, as the relationship between paying for and receiving a public service tightens, the accountability of public service increasingly depends upon answerability to consumers in the market-place.

● *Flexibility of pay and conditions*: national scales and conditions are challenged by market conditions and by performance-related pay as the means of motivation.

Together these changes reflect an assumption that the public in the new polity can be and need only be a customer, so that public management can be based on private sector models.

The Value of Responding to the Customer

The neo-liberal polity placed the the customer at the centre, requiring public organisations to respond to their demands. Pure consumerism sees the role of services as being to satisfy their customers. It challenges both bureaucratic and professional orientations in public organisations which have neglected a proper concern for the consumer.

The value of consumerism lies in giving emphasis to the consumer in the management of what had become in the social democratic polity enclosed public organisations. Any organisation can have a tendency to become enclosed in its own necessities. Operational requirements and the routines of administration can become dominant in a way that presents barriers to organisational learning. The enclosed organisation comes to see organisational requirements as primary and the public as clients, whose needs can be defined by the organisation, because: specialist knowledge can be held to be the basis of judging need; there are many clients and interests and a detached collective choice has to be imposed by bureaucratic rule; the clients' views cannot prevail when resources are scarce. Some of the symptoms of the enclosed organisation challenged by consumerism are:

- forms, standard letters, and instructions sent out without market-testing on the public
- buildings constructed without any process of user review after completion
- lack of systematic procedures for learning from the staff who deal with the public
- staff promoted away from dealing with the public and senior staff having no direct contact with the service provided
- lack of procedures inviting the public for views, suggestions and complaints
- no information for the public on the standard of service they are entitled to

The symptoms of enclosure were be found in too many public organisations reflecting the fault-lines in the social democratic polity. 'There is an air of charity about some parts of the NHS where the consumer is made to feel unworthy for demanding additional services or more convenient appointments' (West, 1988, p. 157). A survey of claimants at local DHSS offices conducted for the National Audit Office

> found that claimants expected a prompt service from helpful and knowledgeable staff. They wanted a reasonable environment in which to wait when they visited an office and some privacy when they visited an office and some privacy when they dealt with local office staff ... However, the survey results ... show that a significant proportion of the claimants who had been in contact with a DHSS local office during the preceding 12 months rated the service as poor. (National Audit Office, 1988, p. 9).

Or again, 'Too often people hear about changes in the health service at the last minute when managers divorced from direct use of the service announce their plans' (West, 1988, p. 147). As this quotation from a general manager in the health service shows, there was a growing awareness of the need for public organisations to be responsive to their consumers.

Sir Roy Griffiths stated that 'at the time of the Management Inquiry I placed the subject of the consumer dimension centre stage in the health service' (Griffiths, 1988a, p. 196). The interest in consumerism has led to attempts to improve service for the public. Reception arrangements have been improved in public offices. Surveys have been developed to test out consumer reaction. Suggestions have been invited from the public. Service contracts have set out the standards for the services. The White Paper on the Citizens' Charter can be seen as an expression of consumerism, with its intent to ensure that citizens can expect, for example, openness, information, choice, non-discrimination and accessibility from public services.

The Dilemmas of Public Service

The Limitations of Consumerism

Underlying many of the changes introduced by the Government is a belief in the value of market mechanisms. The development of the internal market in the health services, the extension of

parental choice and opting out in education, and the requirements of compulsory competitive tendering are all examples.
However, the nature of market mechanisms varies in kind and
degree. Sometimes the emphasis is to strengthen competition
between producers, thereby, it is hoped, providing more efficient
and effective services to the public. In other cases the reforms
have been constructed to increase the possibility of consumer
choice directly – as in education. Often what is actually implemented is not the markets conceived in pure theory, but quasi
markets. Even parental choice, far from operating in a free
market, operates under the constraints of a given supply of
schools, themselves limited by the National Curriculum.

Many of the markets introduced are producer rather than
consumer markets. The internal market introduced in the health
services is not a consumer market but one in which doctors,
health authorities or, in some cases, local authorities act on behalf
of the consumer. The nature of the markets introduced by these
changes varies greatly depending on the number and nature of
the purchasers and providers and the relationship between them.
Common, Flynn and Mellor (1992) have concluded from a study
of competitive structures in the public sector:

> It is clear from our analysis of the organisations we have studied
> that they range across the competitive spectrum. At one end
> there is no competition at all, rather an arms length relationship
> between a purchaser and a provider. At the most competitive
> end, while politics still has influence (in the form of government
> ownership, enabling legislation and so on), an organisation may
> face both public and private sector competitors and supply its
> products and services to a range of organisations. So it is ap-
> parent already that introducing 'markets' to former public sector
> monopolies has a wide range of meanings. (p. 33)

It cannot be assumed that these markets will operate as if there
were perfect competition. One is dealing with structured markets
or quasi markets and it cannot be assumed that a quasi market is
guided by an invisible hand to an optimum solution. The
outcome is influenced by the market's structure. Thus the use of
market mechanisms should be seen as a policy instrument whose
design, monitoring and control remains a responsibility of the
public sector, subject to public accountability.

The flaw is to assume the universal validity and applicability of market mechanisms. A decade or more of accelerating implementation has provided growing experience of their effect upon public services (see Ranson, 1988; Jonathon, 1990; Elster, 1992). The assumption is made that all goods and services are discrete products which can be purchased in the market. Yet the market can actually change certain goods. If I purchase a chocolate bar or take out an Austen novel from my library my 'purchase' has no effect on the product although pressure may be placed upon production or delivery. But my preference for a school, privately expressed, together with the unwitting choices of others, will transform the product. A small school grows in scale with inevitable consequences for learning style and administrative process. The distinctive ethos which was the reason for the choice may be altered by the choice. Some of the most important writing in the human sciences is preoccupied with the unintended consequences of private decision-making: with the growing realisation, especially in many public services, that self-interest can be self-defeating. It is likely in education, moreover, that choice will not only change the product but eliminate it. Choice implies surplus places, but if market forces fill some schools and close others then choice evaporates leaving only a hierarchy of esteem with little choice for many.

The Inadequate Language of Consumerism

Consumerism provides an incomplete and ultimately inadequate language for the public domain. Its emphasis is upon the individual in receipt of a service, rather than on the citizen as an active participant in the polity. The emphasis on the customer of public service has the merit of forcing public organisations to look outward to those who use and receive their services. The flaw is that the language of consumerism cannot encompass the scope of public action. For a public service such as education the proper scope of policy is the community as a whole, not just parents, for example, as specific consumers.

There are limits, moreover, to the extent to which public services can regard those affected by the service as customers whose wishes are to be met. Public organisations have the distinctive task of exercising the powers of the state. Sometimes they have to order, inspect and control; it is not helpful to treat as customers those who are required to take action by a public organisation. Public bodies providing free services may well have to ration services, determining who will receive them. In other instances public bodies have to decide between competing interests as when local residents object to a home for the mentally handicapped being sited in their area. In the public domain, public purposes have to be realised which may not conform to the wishes of individual members of the public. Public purposes can set limits to responsiveness to the customer. The language of consumerism has a contribution to make to the public domain, but a more appropriate language has to be developed to express the complexity of public purpose.

The Dilemma

The challenge for our time, of restoring the public to the polity, remains. Despite the purposes of policy individual consumers are not empowered by the market which serves to deny most individuals their preferred choices. The dilemma facing any polity searching for legitimacy, therefore, is one of achieving public purpose which reconciles individual and collective interests.

This dilemma is reflected, in particular, in the provision of public services which consumerism has not been able to resolve. Public services strive to realise public purpose as determined by collective choice, but they are also intended to meet the needs of the individual members of the public. Purposes set by collective choice may not necessarily meet the needs as seen by individual members of the public. Matching public purpose based on collective choice and service for individuals can be problematic. In the postwar welfare state the dilemma was often ignored because the determination of public purpose could not accommodate the wishes of individual citizens. This was largely because the public were perceived as 'clients' whose needs were best interpreted by professionals and provided for according to the uniform provision of standard services. If judgement was required it was not that of the clients but that of the professional. In the neo-liberal polity, however, the dilemma is also ignored because the individual is emphasised at the expense of the needs of the public as a whole. This is because the public were seen merely as customers, as required by the language of consumerism.

The dilemma posed by public service has been neglected. One aspect or another of the duality of publicness has been ignored in the postwar polities of the welfare and neo-liberal states. Public services have their own conditions which reflect the necessary dualities of the public domain.

Diversity and collectivity: Public purpose has too often been translated into standard services, enforced by rules or professional judgement, when the actual nature of public purpose has not required it. It has been assumed too readily that public purpose requires uniformity and that a diversity of practice undermines it. As a result it has been assumed that individual choice can only be provided in the market.

In fact a moment's thought will show that public purpose can not merely encompass but encourage variety. Public purpose can, and in some cases does, provide choice. Libraries are provided in which the public are given a wide variety of books to choose from. If libraries were organised like some public services, then the books to be read by library-users would be determined by the professional judgement of the librarian or by political decision! In old people's homes meals are provided, but a menu can provide choice without undermining public purpose. If one can – admittedly with difficulty – choose a doctor, there may be no reason why clients cannot choose a social worker.

Not merely can a public service encompass variety, but it should do so. Citizens have a diversity of needs and aspirations which public services can meet. Indeed, in meeting diversity, learning can grow. Far from being in conflict with it, responsiveness in service can enhance public purpose. Of course the space for responsiveness in action will and should vary from service to service. What is required is that public purpose should be specified in no more detail than is required to achieve that purpose.

Each public service has to be analysed. The requirements of public purpose will vary in the extent to which they permit responsiveness and choice. They may be encouraged in certain aspects, but not in others. In the 1988 Education Reform Act public purpose was expressed in the specification of the National Curriculum. The scope for parental choice was extended at least in theory, but only within that purpose. Whether public purpose was defined too widely or too narrowly is an issue that can be contested.

The point is that the limits of public purpose within which responsiveness of service can develop should be considered. In that way public purpose and responsiveness of service can be reconciled and the dilemma of public service resolved. If, however, the dilemma is to be resolved in practice, ways have to be found of breaking out of the enclosed organisation, not only in discourse, but in action.

Individual and public purpose: The language of consumerism cannot encompass all the relations involved in public services. For public services the customer, if one tries to use that language, may be the community at large. There is no individual customer for defence, for smoke control or for environmental health. Such 'collective action problems' can only be resolved through public choice providing the necessary 'public goods' and services. It follows that there are concerns beyond those of the individual consumer. Indeed, it may be difficult to define the consumer. Certainly it would be difficult to define the consumer in the public domain as the private sector defines the customer. When a private sector firm sells a service in the market it knows who its customer is – the individual or organisation that buys that service. It is not so easy to define the customers of a public service because the service may be provided not merely to meet the needs of the immediate consumers, but the needs of others. Who are the customers of the education service? The child is the immediate consumer, but the parents, future employers, the local community or the public at large all have a legitimate interest, which is recognised in the constitution of governing bodies. In public services it cannot be assumed there is only one 'customer'. That is one reason why services are subject to collective choice – to balance the interests of different 'customers' – for it cannot be assumed that all those affected by a service will necessarily share the same interest. Neighbouring families may resist the conversion of a house into a children's home, even though it is suitable for those children. Local people may resist the siting of a new prison in their locality, even though it meets the needs of the wider community.

Conclusion

The public domain is at any moment in time characterised by dilemmas which are, it has been argued, especially acute at this moment in time. This chapter has argued that transformations of the present have illuminated the limits of the postwar era of social democracy: the vacuum in the postwar polity – the absence of the public, or the presence of a passive public. Whereas 1970s corporatism believed that a centralised strategy could repair the flaws of the liberal democratic state's age of professional bureaucracy, it reinforced the position of the passive subject. The 1980s have seen the emergence of a new consensus across the political spectrum promoting the view that the central task for the polity in repairing the past and providing the conditions for a new post-industrial order lies in regenerating an active public able to participate in and influence the working of a new polity. The consensus, however, is divided about how the public is to be conceived: whether as the aggregate of separate individuals ('there is no such thing as society') or as the inescapable collectivity of any social community. For more than a decade the dominant strategy for empowering the public has emphasised the need to provide choice for the individual consumer of public services as far as possible in replicas of the private sector market. Public choice as customer choice would enhance the effectiveness of public services by making them responsive and accountable to the customer.

The limitations and contradictions of the consumerist model of management have become increasingly apparent. It assumes that there is a single model of management for all purposes and contexts. Public organisations carry out a wide range of activities that are subject to very different conditions. The irony is that the challenge provided by the New Right to a uniform model of public sector management that assumed direct control and provision within organisations structured by hierarchical control has substituted a new simplistic uniformity of the market. There are distinctive purposes and tasks in the public domain which cannot be fulfilled by the mechanisms of the market. 'Exit' cannot replace 'voice' as the principal mechanism, nor can the self-interest of the customer replace the citizen's search for justice in the common-wealth. There is a need for a more appropriate vision of the public domain and a more discriminating theory of its management.

The challenge for the new era is to discover the moral and political principles which are appropriate to the public domain facing the transformations of our time. Only a different conception of the public domain and its management – one which grasps the creative duality of citizenship within the public domain – can reconcile individual and public purpose. The public is a citizen both as a participant in public discourse leading to collective choice and as an individual entitled to public service.

This task of reconstruction can be realised more effectively than hitherto if it is based upon foundations of theoretical knowledge as well as understanding derived from historical narrative. A theory is required which articulates the relationship of organisation and management to the designing purposes and tasks that constitute different organisations. Knowledge of the rationale and conditions for effective public organisation will provide a more secure ground for the constituting of citizenship and government in the new era. Only theoretical analysis will deepen understanding of the social mechanisms that explain why public organisations develop their distinctive form and characteristic mode of management and how that development can and should proceed. It is, therefore, to this theoretical task that we now turn before setting out in Part II our interpretation of the purposes and conditions for the public domain.

2

Towards a Theory of Public Management

The challenge to the management of public service organisations should be understood as part of a wider critique of the postwar polity. The changing purposes and beliefs about the the role of the polity have revised conceptions of managing public organisations. The creation of a new and distinctive public management has stimulated a burgeoning literature in recent years, reviving a debate about whether there is any significant difference between management in the public and private sectors. Conceptual clarification will prepare the ground for theoretical analysis, the task of which is to enable explanation of managing public organisations in their changing social and political context.

Rediscovering Public Management

This question of the relationship between public and private organisation was the focus of a lively debate in an earlier period (see Millett, 1961; Self, 1965; Keeling, 1972) with the public administration case for difference emerging better from the argument than the organisation theory case for similarity. Yet by 1982 Dunsire was able to argue that because changes in practice had blurred the boundaries any preoccupation with the public and private distinction was increasingly a 'distraction and an irrelevance'. The growth of a new style of management since the 1970s has been described by Pollitt (1990) as a distinct set of beliefs and practices developed across all kinds of organisations both in America and in the UK as a strategy for improving their performance. 'Managerialism' as a new ideology was promoted, as Pollitt shows, by politicians as well as by management consultants and academics: 'it is managers and management that make institutions perform' (Drucker, 1974); 'efficient management is the key to national revival ... And the management ethos must run right through our national life – private and public companies'(Michael Heseltine, 1980).

The Government's reconstituting of public sector organisations in the image of the private sector has served to reinforce Dunsire's conclusion. The differences between private and public management became increasingly blurred. Nevertheless, the restructuring has prompted a major rediscovery of the study of public management. Much of the writing has sought to analyse and critically evaluate the distinctive constellation of ideas that characterise 'the rise of the new public management' shaped by the Government's market-oriented political values (see Hood, 1990; Flynn, 1990; Pollitt, 1990). The distinguishing features of the new public management, described in Chapter 1, have involved a change in the culture of public organisations: 'Without changing the values, beliefs and expectations of those working in the public services, managers cannot achieve the objectives set for them' (Farnham and Horton, 1993).

Performance in the public sector can only be improved, the Government claims, by making public organisations and their management look as much like the private sector as possible. Good managers have the same tasks and qualities whatever sector they are in. Indeed, the accelerating introduction of market-like competition to organise the provision of public services is intended to dissolve the boundary between public and private provision. Between the ideal types of private and public organisation are a number of hybrid forms such as public services that are 'contracted out' or include administered market competition. Private organisations on the other hand may incorporate state sponsorship or even an element of state ownership.

It is clear, however, that although the differences between public and private organisations may have diminished, important distinctions remain and continue to require explanatory and normative analysis. Questions continue to be asked about the distinctions between public and private and whether a reformed context and polity constituted by alternative values reshape a very different public domain. A number of studies have sought to clarify the elusive but ineluctable distinction between public and private sectors (see Perry and Kraemar, 1983; Smith Ring and Perry, 1985; Kooiman and Eliassen, 1987; Perry and Rainey, 1988; Metcalfe and Richards, 1987). Whereas private organisations serve particular interests, public organisations, it is argued, are created to serve the needs of society as a whole and, as such, are constituted within a statutory framework which imposes legal obligations (Pollitt and Harrison, 1992). The founding *public purposes*, therefore, are distinguished by a concern to identify needs rather than demand, and to serve rather than accumulate profit. It means that the tasks of public organisations are often unique when taken individually or together. The 'goods' which a public organisation is expected to deliver are frequently both abstract and comprehensive in reach – 'public health' or 'an educated democracy'. The specificity of private interest contrasts, as Willcocks and Harrow (1992) argue, with the indeterminateness and yet comprehensiveness of public purpose. Public administration is *intrinsically political* in nature, driven by multiple values and the need to reconcile the priorities of diverse publics:

> A distinguishing feature of public administration, then, is the political character of its services. The content and level of such services is determined by qualitative judgements, and by a publicly defensible compromise between competing values, rather than by any single criterion such as profitability. The demand to meet business criteria of 'efficiency' is itself a political demand which has consequences for the nature and level of the service provided. Public administration is thus not a matter of carrying out goals set by the politician in the most cost-efficient manner. It is a matter of administering policy in accordance with the values which have determined it, among which considerations of cost-efficiency may have a smaller or a larger place. Ends and means interconnect, in other words policy and its administration are not rigidly separable.
> (Beetham, 1987, p. 36)

Whereas the practice of adherence to rules within private organisations is designed to secure efficiency but which, if necessary, can be set aside in the interests of flexibility, in public administration rule-keeping expresses an essential political value of equity, in treating like cases alike. Bureaucracy in public organisations is the organisational vehicle of justice as fairness.

The intrinsically political nature of public organisations determines the principles which shape decision-making as well as criteria by which it can be judged. Decisions in the public domain are based upon judgements of value, so that goods and services are allocated to the public by budget choices. In the private domain decisions are, in the last resort, based upon calculations of cost-efficiency and the distribution of goods and services is determined by price in relation to market demand. Whereas clear quantitative criteria exist to judge the performance of organisations in the private sector, it is more difficult to evaluate the activities of public organisations. Even judging what is to count as an output is sometimes difficult to determine, let alone to measure. How is 'an education' to be assessed? Recent studies have shown how difficult it is to make sense of this service's most quantifiable indicator of performance – examination results. Any adequate judgement must take account both of the background of the students and the contribution of the school to their academic progress. Even if sophisticated statistical analysis manages to produce the necessary 'value-added' data, an education is always intended to imply more than cognitive development alone. Do young people leave school more creative, skilful, sensitive, socially-concerned members of society than they were before they began? Are the health and social services to be judged by the diseases and family breakdowns they have prevented or cured? Decisions about what kind or level of service is to be offered and what criteria should be applied to evaluate its performance are inescapably value-laden. Thus what is to count as efficiency and effectiveness is itself a political judgement.

In the last resort the significant test for a public organisation is the ballot box where the performance of public services is finally evaluated. An election can result in the ultimate 'governors' of public organisations – local councillors or Members of Parliament – being ousted in favour of an alternative party. Representatives and officials are stewards of the public interest. Public organisations are thus accountable to the electorate in a way that has no equivalent in the private sector (see Day and Klein, 1987; Pollitt and Harrison, 1992). Services are expected to be open to the public not only in providing information about decisions and the manner in which they were reached, but also in providing public access, on many occasions, to the decision-making process. Where this is not possible or feasible, the visibility of public administration is protected by institutionalising scrutiny on behalf of the public: by establishing independent review or audit commissions, or by enabling citizens to have recourse to an ombudsman as well as the courts. What is peculiar to public admininstration, however, is the realisation that anything (the decision and the process of making it) *can* 'go public' (Beetham, 1987, p. 38).

While modern organisations, therefore, may have a number of characteristics in common, the argument for recognising fundamental distinctions has been well-made. The public domain has unique qualities which require patterns of organisation and management that cannot be found elsewhere. In developing this analysis the prolific growth in recent years of writing on public sector management has made significant advances. We believe, however, that there remains the need for theoretical development which provides a framework to interpret and explain both essential distinctions and the historical variations between public and private management.

The Need for Theory

Three distinct achievements can be identified in the present literature on public sector management. First, studies have enhanced conceptual understanding of distinctions between public and private management (see Golembiewski, 1985; Gunn, 1987; Friedmann, 1987). The progress is illustrated in the confident conclusion of Pollitt and Harrison (1992) that the distinctively different purposes, tasks and processes of public management can be identified: they

shape both the management behaviour and the management culture of every major public service, and do so to a degree that is quite foreign to other kinds of organisation such as say Sainsbury's, Ford or ICI. This does not make public-service management *totally* different ... but it does imply that many of

the prescriptions of generic management will require considerable adaptation before they will fit in this distinctive context.
(p. 2)

A second development is the delineation of the rise of the new
public management. This work is impressive in its interpretive
and critical analysis of a particular system of public management
during a historical period: distinctive values and beliefs about
policy development, to be sustained by programmes of institutional forms and ethos of public management, are clarified and
located in their chronological moment (see Walsh, 1989; Hood,
1990; Pollitt, 1990; Common *et al.*, 1992).

A third development is the incipient trend to elucidate the
different 'models and approaches' which can be used to understand the public sector where Lane (1985, 1987 and 1993) and
Willcocks and Harrow (1992) are perhaps the most important
contributions. Lane (1993) begins with the predicament facing
the science of public administration that it had 'lost an empire
and not yet found a role' (Hood, 1990):

> Replacing it there is now a proliferation of concepts, frame-
> works and theories. Public sector processes of decision-making
> and implementation in the modern state are approached
> through a variety of models from such different fields as public
> policy, policy implementation, management and evaluation as
> well as the public choice approach and neo-institutionalism.
> (Lane, 1993, p. vii)

Lane's book illustrates this multiplicity of approaches to the
public sector and its management. What emerges is an exemplary
overview of the separate perspectives without any attempt to
create any concluding synthesis. Arguably, however, an integrating framework is now what the study of public sector management
urgently requires. The field is fragmented along the fault-lines of
separate academic disciplines. Public administration meticulously
describes and classifies the differences of organisational type,
while organisational analysts and management consultants con-
ceptualise what processes and structures all organisations have in
common, economists (public choice theorists) have theorised the
relationship between market institutions and public sector efficiency, and historians have illuminated a notion of time and

period. Each discipline provides its own questions, concepts and analytical perspectives when analysis of the subject of public management would benefit from a multi-disciplinary approach.

Such a multi-disciplinary approach can provide the missing integrating framework and repair the theoretical limitations in the present understanding of public sector management. The discussion of public and private organisations begins an essential process of clarifying the meaning of key concepts. It seems evident at this level of 'linguistic analysis' that it is possible to define dimensions both of similarity and distinctive difference between public and private. At the level of meaning public is different in kind from private. Whether public and private organisations are actually different in practice, or to what degree they differ, is an empirical question and explaining why variations of difference occur requires theoretical analysis. The previous chapter shows that the purpose and characteristics of public organisations have altered over time, and that the current reforms of government are designed to recreate public organisations in the image of the private. Theory can clarify the conceptual distinctions between public and private organisations and explain the underlying processes and social mechanisms which produce and reproduce distinctive forms of public organisation. A theory, it is hoped, can account for the changing direction of public purpose and organisation during the transformations of our time. This analysis will prepare the basis for developing a theory of management in the public domain. To accomplish these tasks we propose to create a theoretical framework in four parts:

1. A conceptual framework which clarifies what public and private organisations have in common and how they differ.
2. An approach to explanation which begins by relating the systems of management, and the way they can vary, to the values, purposes and interests of the groups which control them. Public management varies according to the purposes which inform it.
3. A theory which interprets these purposes of management in the context of the social and political characteristics of a particular historical period. The purposes of public management vary over time according to the changing structure of the polity.

4.   A normative analysis which strives to find values and purposes that can inform a public domain appropriate to the challenges of our time. (This is the subject of Part II.)

Conceptualising Management

The discussion of the issues involved in the challenge to public organisations over the past decade and more can provide a foundation for understanding the nature and principles of management in general and also what is distinctive in management in specific situations and, in particular, in management in the public domain (see Pettigrew, Ferlie and McKee, 1992).

The prevalence of 'management' within public as well as private sectors should not, however, be taken for granted. Traditionally, a distinction was made between (public) administration and (private) management and these distinctions were embodied in different academic disciplines: public administration and management theory. Administration was the public responsibility of civil servants and local government officials charged with the efficient delivery of public services as prescribed by legislation. The task for public administrators was to adhere to the rules, established in law, in their dealings with the public, ensuring that meticulous records were maintained of their equitable administration of public services and treatment of individual clients. Professionals exercised discretion in the interpretation of the rules. Yet tensions could arise even within this sphere, as Beetham (1987) points out:

> Public administration, in fact, is a combination of two competing practices, law and management: the effective delivery of a 'product', and the interpretation and application of legal rules. The precise balance between the two will differ according to the nature of the service (policing, welfare provision, water supply). But tensions between the two practices are not always easy to reconcile, and they constitute a typical source of those charged with 'red tape', to which public administration is characteristically more prone than private industry. (p. 37)

The tensions within the model of public administration between the assumption of the political choice of policy and the administrative, rule-governed implementation of policy came to be exposed increasingly both within research (see Dunsire, 1978; Self, 1985; Hood, 1986) and by practitioners themselves.

The necessary processes, within public organisations, of clarifying choices and direction for policy as resources become more constrained increasingly encouraged an understanding of the importance of management within the public as well as the private domain. All organisations needed managing. Administration will always play a necessary role of routine and efficient implementation of policy, but management has come to assume an inescapable place in the process of organisational working. Yet what management is and how it is practised are still to be defined, while the significance and explanation of variations between forms of management remain to be analysed. Our discussion of the changing forms of management during the postwar period has left implicit what is common to any form of management and what must be identified as unique or distinctively different. Our framework proposes a way of analysing this similarity and variety.

The Common Ground of Management: Purposive Decision in Action

If organisations are constituted for *distinctive purposes* – perhaps to provide services, proffer advice, manufacture goods, or even as in the public domain to realise values – then management is the activity which strives to develop and to realise those purposes in practice. Management, therefore, is *a process*, the starting point for which is *strategic choice* of priority amongst purposes and the best means of achieving them. This process of strategic decision-making defines the way in which a number of *tasks*, inherent in management, are to be interpreted, together with the *conditions* that are essential for these tasks to be delivered effectively. These processes of management are, moreover, always located within and have to respond to a particular institutional and environmental *context*. This suggests a conception of the key dimensions of management.

The purposes of management. Management is driven by purposes. In the social democratic polity the constituting purpose was to deliver the established standard of service to the public, while within corporatism the defining purposes became the unity of an organisation in its management of a changing and complex environment, and within the neo-liberal polity the purposes focus upon realising competitive supremacy within the mechanism of the market. A debate about management necessarily begins with an analysis of the purposes which constitute its rationale. It is not possible to evaluate the efficiency or performance of an organisation without an understanding of its purposes. Under one set of purposes, the objectives of 'accountability', or 'public debate' or 'democracy' itself are time-wasting interferences, while under another set of purposes they constitute the very rationale and value of the organisation, defining the nature of management.

The defining quality of management is thus the process of *strategic choice*: choosing how these defining purposes are to be elaborated as well as clarifying which means will best achieve them. Strategy, Chandler (1962) has argued, is 'the determination of the basic long term goals and objectives of an enterprise, and the adoption of courses of action and the allocation of resources necessary for carrying out these goals'. Once guiding values have been formed, priorities have to be established amongst purposes about how to carry them into practice: which services or products, which audiences or markets, and with what implications for organisation and management? Strategic choice determines the significant changes in direction which an organisation needs to make in relation to a changing environment. The management of strategic choice, therefore, strives for clarity of direction in a context of uncertainty.

The tasks of management.   The process of determining strategic choices is dependent upon a number of management tasks:

(i)   *Policy planning*   Strategic choice has to be based upon analysis of the changes and issues facing the organisation, identifying the possible courses of action given available resources. Such a process will require information *systems* as well as a capacity for policy analysis. Strategic choices about objectives will lead to processes of planning and programming.

(ii)   *Staff motivation, communication and development*   The quality of choice and the achievement of purpose will depend upon the commitment and *skills* of staff within the organisation. This requires management processes which ensure staff both contribute to and understand purposes and decisions, and which recognise the value of the staff, develop their potential and draw upon their experience and skills.

(iii) *Organisational development* Whether an organisation can clarify strategic choices will depend upon its capacity to develop structures that are appropriate to its objectives and purposes. Defining how work is to be organised, what the pattern of roles and functions will be, where authority will lie and who will take decisions are all characteristics of an organisation that directly impinge upon the quality of its strategic choices. Clarifying responsibilities for action and holding managers accountable for their actions are a central tasks of management design.

(iv) *Relations with the public* No organisation is enclosed: it relates to a public by selling products for a particular market of consumers, by providing services for clients with particular needs or, as in the case of the public domain, enabling citizens to express their demands directly or indirectly through elected representatives.

(v) *Review and evaluation* The quality of choices about the future will depend upon the capacity of management to monitor and evaluate the quality of its past activity. Has the organisation actually delivered the services or products which it promised, have standards of service been achieved, have resources been used efficiently, and are the customers satisfied with the goods and services delivered, or has the voice of citizens been heard in the policy process?

The conditions for management. The values and purposes of an organisation define the appropriate conditions as well as the tasks of management. These can be internal as well as external to the organisation. *Internally*, the effectiveness of the management process depends upon an important degree of cohesion between the internal systems – of planning, staff and organisational development – and the objectives which they are designed to realise. The possibility of an organisation possessing, for example, the staff skills or financial resources to accomplish its objectives can depend upon a number of *external conditions* such as the quality of the national education and training systems or the state of the economy. More significantly, organisations, whether public or private, depend upon the integrity or recognition of legal rules if they are to carry out their purposes. Private sector businesses depend upon the effective working of the market and the law of contract if they are to flourish, while public service organisations depend upon the legitimacy and accountability of government if the consent of citizens is to be granted.

We argue, therefore, that there are a number of dimensions which are defining qualities of management in every kind of organisation. Management, in this understanding, is a purposive process of clarifying strategic choice, that defines the character of a number of key tasks and the required conditions so that its chosen aims and purposes can be realised. Yet, our earlier account of the changing patterns of management in the public domain suggests that there are distinctive differences in management which require analysis: do the variations lie at the surface or are they indicative of more fundamental differences and what is the relationship between the unity and the variety of management?

The Variety of Systems of Management

The dimensions of management need to be perceived as *a system of management*: the parts are interdependent, the coherence of the whole defined by the nature of the originating purposes. In any organisation a system emerges that defines a uniquely differentiated form of management. The meaning of the parts will be shaped by the whole. The management of a particular service such as health or education, or of a sector – private, voluntary or public – will have its own purposes, conditions and tasks. It can only be understood in terms of those purposes and in those conditions. Management thinking therefore has no universal principles that can be applied to each and every situation. There are no standard packages. Rather, management approaches in any situation have to reflect organisational purposes and conditions. Those purposes and conditions are not peripheral to management, rather they define the management task. The processes of management within the voluntary charity or the manufacturing combine or the community service will vary with the way the purposes are defined. Thus the (professional) values which emphasise the boundary around a client are very different from the (corporate) values which seek to weaken that boundary in favour of wider needs. Very different management processes follow from those originating values and purposes.

There is, therefore, no universal package of management. The meaning given to the purposes, tasks and conditions of management will be very different according to very different constitutive values. Management has therefore to be understood in its context. The purposes and conditions of that context and the tasks to be carried out determine the unique nature of a management system and the criteria for its evaluation. If management structure, processes and style do not reflect the purposes and conditions of the tasks to be carried out, then management is ineffective. Why do the systems of management vary, however? Are the purposes, conditions and tasks somehow 'given' or are they chosen? An explanatory framework is needed to account for the variations in management.

Explaining the Variety of Management Systems

Systems of management have varied radically in their purposes and have altered significantly over time. The classical account of bureaucracy, for example, written at the turn of the century to make sense of trends towards the rationalisation of modernity, became for an era the dominant mode of interpreting the effectiveness of organisational arrangements, yet it now appears a particularly inappropriate approach to resolve many of the problems confronted by organisations towards the close of the century. Hierarchies of authority, divisions of labour, adherence to rules and spans of control are now regarded as denying the flexibility and responsiveness that provide the necessary conditions for effective management.

A perspective is needed which enables analysis of the way values and purposes are constituted to define the rationale of different systems of management and organisation in different contexts and historical periods. One such theoretical model which can begin the process of explaining variations in systems of management is *action theory* (see Pettigrew, 1973; Ranson *et al.*, 1980; Rhodes, 1988). This seeks to make sense of the differences in management by relating the purposes which define the system to

the values and interests of the groups that control an organisation. Different groups will want the decisions, policies or plans
to reflect their particular values and objectives. To get their way
they may have to come into conflict with other groups and the
outcome of the struggle will depend upon the relative power of
those involved. These processes can relate to transactions external
to an organisation as well to internal processes of decision-
making. The key elements in this 'politics of decision-making
model' are:

(i)   *The actors* These will typically involve defined groups:
       professionals, administrators, elected representatives, entre-
       preneurs, parents, communities and so on. Within the
       private sector, marketing executives may vie with produc-
       tion directors while both may strive to influence investors
       or capture new market niches. In the world of local govern-
       ment, elected councillors relate to officers and advisers,
       who may strive to win agreement for policies with parti-
       cular professional associations as well as serve the needs of
       diverse communities.

(ii)   *Motivation and purpose* Each group may bring to the deci-
       sion process distinctively different motivations and perspect-
       ives. Each pursues particular aims and objectives, striving to
       ensure that the relevant decisions or choices embody its
       values and reflect its interests. We define *values* as those
       desired ends or preferences which constitute actors' motiva-
       tions: for some actors these may include seeking equal
       opportunities, for others the right to individual choice. We
       define *interests* as the tendency of actors to maintain and
       enhance their distribution of scarce resources: these may
       include finance, authority, expertise, information, access,
       status and many more (Rhodes, 1981; Jones, 1979).

(iii) *Exchange and transactions* The various groups interact with
       each other to realise their chosen values and purposes.
       Only by transacting with the other parties will they be able
       to gain influence and get their way.

(iv)   *Conflict and power* The divergent purposes and interests of
       groups may bring them into conflict which can only be
       resolved in the struggle by those who have more resources
       and can therefore exert more influence over the decision

process. Success in strategic management reflects relative power. Blau (1964) and Archer (1979) have articulated the conditions necessary for successful accumulation of power: the possession of strategic resources which others may desire; ensuring that they are scarce and unavailable elsewhere; forming alliances and being organised; promoting sectional interests and being indifferent to the resources possessed by others.

(v) *Changing context* While the analytical categories of action and power are central to any adequate explanation of varying forms of management, the danger of such a perspective alone is to overestimate the social construction of organisations. Actors in the constituting of management do not exist in a vacuum. It is always necessary to understand the way in which groups are located in, and limited by, *some* environmental constraints which provide the milieu of obstacles and opportunities for their choice-making. The management of organisations is 'inescapably bound up with the conditions of their environment' so that a complete understanding requires a grasp of the 'ecology of the organisation' (Pfeffer and Salancik, 1978). Such an ecology is social and political as much as physical and environmental. Much comparative research has also shown that what is to count as effectiveness in management varies according to the 'contingencies' which the organisation faces (Child, 1972). A large organisation has to be managed in a very different way from a small one, routine technologies may require more structured forms of management than organisations coping with uncertain technologies.

This action theory, therefore, makes sense of strategic decision-making by setting the system of management in the context of a political process of decision-making: identifying combatants, their competing value systems, different bases of power and searching to understand the way dominant groups respond to as well as shape the changing context in which they are located. The strength of this theoretical model is that it strives to illuminate the agency which lies behind the creation and recreation of systems of management. As Gouldner (1955) encouraged us to perceive, organisations are human constructions. The social mechanisms provided by action theory lie close to the surface; the analysis it reveals of purposively interested actors reflects our everyday experience. It illustrates the bustle and noise in the immediate activity of decision-making and the struggle to provide a sense of direction.

Yet, the systems of management which have been identified as constituting the post war narrative have not been shifting, evanescent patterns of management. They have had considerable temporal durability: the dominant purposes became institutionalised over time, so that for a period the expressed values became taken-for-granted assumptions. As Brown (1978) suggested: '"making decisions" is not the most important exercise of organisational power. Instead, this power is most strategically deployed in the design and imposition of paradigmatic frameworks within which the very meaning of such actions as "making decisions" is defined.'

The theory needs to be further developed to reveal the deeper social structures of value and power that have enabled systems of organisation and management to endure over time. A theory of (public) management systems needs to be informed by political theory. To understand the changing patterns of postwar public management requires an analysis of the polity, the social and political order of the time, which legitimated those forms of management (both public and private) and provided them with their distinguishing meaning and purposes. A system of management cannot escape the defining assumptions of an era.

Constituting Systems of Management: The Social and Political Order

The elements of analysis can be set out in a model which describes the constituting of a social and political order:

This mode of analysis can provide the presuppositions for a theory of public organisation and management in a changing society. The coordinates of the theory propose that all social and political forms are constituted by *common dimensions of action* (values, power and organisation) which find expression at different levels or *spheres of society*. Each level, therefore, of practice (day-to-day interactions), of institutional domains (organisational forms) and of society and culture, expresses a distinctive pattern

FIGURE 2.1
Framework of analysis

		Dimensions of Action		
		Values	Power	Organisation
	Social Order			
Spheres of Society	Institutional Domain			
	Practices			

of values and beliefs which both legitimates an order of power and defines organisational arrangements that are designed to secure their perpetuation. Where this distinctive pattern persists through time it is appropriate to call it *an authoritative or dominant order* which has been constituted in such a way that it acquires the consent of its members, whose day-by-day practices become an expression of those assumptions which underlie the wider social and political order their actions have helped to form. Conflicting values and interests can fracture any settled cohesion of this order and lead to change, just as the unintended consequences of action can generate the conditions for the transforming of stable social and political forms.

To illustrate the working of this theoretical model we take each of the dimensions of action and discuss the way they are constituted within the different spheres as practices, institutional conditions and as an order of belief and power.

From Values to Interpretive Schemes

Human action is typically purposive, oriented to realising chosen ends. Yet this process works in different ways according to the particular sphere of practice, institution or society. At the level of practice within management, purposes are expressed in more explicit values or interests. Values can be said to articulate desired ends or preferences which become the subject of explicit argument and conflict. One group of protagonists will promote the values of 'comprehensive' as against 'selective' education, or in the health service, the value of 'care in the community' will be advanced against the 'institutionalisation' of the sick or infirm. Sometimes such commitments express *interests*: these refer both to the distribution of scarce resources and to the ineluctable orientation of members to advance their sectional claims. The subjective nature of 'interested' action derives from a perceived distribution of wealth, status or authority, and a motivation to protect or improve a resource position. As with values, however, members strive to secure their sectional claims within the very structure of the organisation which then serves to reproduce those interests.

Some management values and interests become institutionalised so as to take on the form of *domain assumptions* (Gouldner, 1971). These reveal entrenched 'frames' of orientation which operate in every encounter as shared assumptions about the way to approach and proceed in the situation. The values of 'professionalism' or of 'profit' illustrate institutionalised domain assumptions. The public service professional expresses the value of service to clients based upon expert knowledge, grounded in specialist training. The authority deriving from specialist knowledge often leads to the claim to autonomy from lay judgement, whether it be from clients, politicians or different specialisms. Within the private sector, management profit becomes the overarching domain assumption, articulating a value which defines the criteria of what it is to be an effective organisation, and thus how actions are to be evaluated.

Some values become so fundamental to the identity of communities that they define the very process of interpreting and constituting meaning. Such '*interpretive schema*' inform the practical values and domain assumptions so as to define the essential character of a moral and political order. Interpretive schemes refer to the indispensable cognitive schema that map our experience of the world, identifying its constituents and relevances and how we are to know and understand them (Giddens, 1976, 1984). Such frames typically remain taken for granted and incorporate both evaluative sentiments about the relative worth of things and implicit 'stocks of knowledge' and systems of belief 'which serve as my reference schema for my explication of the world' (Schutz and Luckmann, 1973).

In this way interpretive schema help us to understand the structuring of interactive patterns within organisations and society. At this level we might identify the values of 'privacy' and 'publicness', or of the 'individual' and 'community', or of 'rationality' itself, as illustrating some of the typically taken-for-granted schema that cognitively organise our world and enable us to understand our experience as meaningful.

Dependencies of Power

Organisations and societies are constituted by their members. More accurately, however, structuring is typically the privilege of *powerful* members. The meanings that shape social forms are as often the source of cleavage as of consensus, bringing members into conflict. Power is manifested in different forms according to the sphere of action (see Lukes, 1974). At the level of practice within management, power is revealed in the capacity to determine the 'decisions' or the 'outcomes' within the organisation, a capacity grounded in differential access to resources such as information, finance or authority. Power can be visible in conflicts over the construction of a motorway, or the closure of a school sixth form, or the loss of a rural bridleway.

Advantage is most effective however when power over decision-making is institutionalised in the roles, rules and authority relations of organisational management or within a community. The organisation itself and its management processes become an expression of the values and interests of the dominant group. The powerful can influence the scope of decision-making, determining which 'issues' enter the decision arena. Yet power is most effective and insidious in its consequences when issues do not arise because actors remain unaware of their sectional claims; power-holders have constituted their purposes in the very assumptions which define relations within an organisation or society (see Brown, 1978, p. 376).

The interpenetration of power and assumptive frames is of the greatest consequence for social structures. This interdependence of power and meaning is best conceptualised in Weber's (1978) terms as 'order of legitimate domination'. The postwar polity of social democracy constituted forms of power that became taken for granted: the legitimacy of the state and its rulers depended upon the beneficial use of power to create the conditions for a just and meritocratic society. An interventionist welfare state and rising public expenditure became the dominant order. Yet through the 1980s a very different set of values and power relations has constituted an alternative order of legitimacy that institutionalises the market and the power of the entrepreneurial organisation.

Organisational Structures

The concept of organisation is usually understood to imply a configuration of structured activities that is characteristically enduring and persistent. Accounts of management structure have typically focused upon very different aspects of such patterned regularity. Some have identified the substructure of practice and interaction while others have emphasised the institutionalising of structure in roles, procedures and authority relations. At a further level we can identify generalised norms of organisation that are influential across society as a whole.

For the interactionists it is only by examining the regularities of day-to-day transactions, the 'informal structure' or 'substructure' of what people actually do, that we can arrive at a fundamental understanding of structuring. Much research has indicated the way in which emergent patterns of interaction are not prescribed by organisations. The work of Bittner (1965), Garfinkel (1967), Douglas (1971) and Zimmerman (1971) suggests that the 'rational' panoply of roles, rules and procedures which make up organisational design is not pregiven by managers but is the skilled, practical and retrospective accomplishment of organisational members. For our purposes in the understanding of public management, this perspective would suggest the need to examine how members of public service organisations actually define their roles in relation to clients and members of the community: whether they use procedures and files to distance their organisations from the public, or to make a management 'decision' appear a more technical process than it really is. There is a need, moreover, to understand whether the rhetoric of collaborative working between professionals masks the maintaining of boundaries reproduced to protect autonomy and budgetary interests.

Yet, any subversion of organisation roles or amplifying of rules that occurs in the practice of day-to-day management takes place within *some* framework of organisation. Analysis of the institutionalising of forms of organisation is needed to complement interpretive understanding of actual transactions. The notion of formal structure focuses on the different positions, formulation of rules, and prescription of authority, the explicit purpose of which is to achieve more predictable control of organisational performance. Organisational arrangements have taken distinctive forms within the institutional realm of the public domain. For example the development of the 'segmented bureaucracy' in government established strong boundaries between formally differentiated services to maintain the distinctiveness of specialist professional knowledge.

At the most abstract level a society is characterised by norms of organisation. At this level patterns of structure reveal dominant ideas and expectations about organisation. Patterns of interaction and formal structures coalesce in deep cultural assumptions about organisation. For Weber (1978), 'bureaucracy' was the organisational expression of values which constituted the modern order – the principles of legality and rationality. For us, one focus of analysis is to ask why a particular conception of organisation – dominant in the private sector – has come to hold sway over organisations of every kind however different they are.

A Typology of Management

Distinctively different orders of domination have developed during the postwar period expressing values that have constituted unique structures of power and organisation. These patterns of domination when made explicit in a formal typology can further clarify our understanding of the altered forms of public organisation and the conditions for future change. There has been no single pattern of public organisation and management: its nature and purpose have varied over time.

Public Management as Social Democracy

During the era of social democracy from the 1950s to the early 1970s many public organisations were shaped by 'the mantle of professionalism' (Burns, 1977). Such was the dominance of professionals and their values in the postwar period that Perkin (1989) has called it the high point in an 'age of professionalism'. The post-Enlightenment world, striving to free itself from dependence upon the scarcity of nature and emancipate itself from the myths of tradition, places its faith in knowledge and reason to establish more rational forms of thought and organisation. The professional mantle provided the modern world with an interpretive schema to express the values of universalism and knowledge.

Discrete elements of the professional mantle are frequently articulated as particular values and interests: hence the notion of a sense of 'vocation' which is committed to 'public service' and checked by a 'code of ethics' that is monitored by the peer group. Public values merge into sectional interests as professions compete for scarce public resources that underwrite their employment and preferment. The constituting of the political order as a 'meritocracy' expresses the values of a society that believes in the importance of knowledge for rational reconstruction and opens itself to those with 'talents'. Yet the dissolving of one social boundary – ascribed status – leads to the substitution of another – the qualification. The very instrument of openness is at the same time an instrument of closure.

The purposes of professionals express their values of service but also reinforce the bases of power that can ensure their survival through time. The domain assumptions of professionalism can define and generate resources which create relations of autonomy and dependence. While 'specialist knowledge' can respond to the needs of clients, it can also deny their beliefs the status of knowledge. The claim to 'autonomy' based upon specialist knowledge and training is also a claim to detach knowledge from critical evaluation; autonomy is the value which legitimates the raising of a boundary around a profession and its practice: only peers with similar knowledge and training can assess the quality of a decision. Those beyond the boundary of knowledge, clients, the public or even other professions cannot question a professional judgement. The professional qualification is the credential that legitimates access to practice, and yet it is also the instrument of exclusion, and thus of closure: the laity, because they are 'not qualified' do not 'know' and therefore cannot 'practise'. The beliefs and practice of professionalism lead directly to relations of power and dependency that were perceived as legitimate for a generation and more through the postwar period. The public consented, implicitly, to be ruled by the carriers of knowledge.

Distinct patterns of organisation and management provided the setting for the forming and reforming of the age of professionalism. Yet this period of professionalism was allied to the ways of bureaucracy, expressing the application of the rules defining the welfare state. We will call the typical form of this alliance the 'segmented bureaucracy'. The claim to autonomy leads to the creation of highly differentiated organisations whose divisions provide the setting for the nurturing of specialised services.

Public Management as Corporatism

With the deepening economic crises of the 1970s the state became increasingly preoccupied with re-examining the bases of economy–polity–social-system relationships searching to redefine points of control. Habermas (1976) has argued that such crises create 'steering problems' for social systems, if they are to maintain control and integration. To protect and restore system integration, the state responds by progressively extending its boundaries, its tentacles of political leverage, into the economic and social subsystems. The public domain expands its reach into civil society. The extension of steering capacity, however, presupposes the emergence of new modes of rationality, 'new technically utilisable knowledge about subsystems' and their operation.

Blau and Schoenherr (1971) suggested that new forms of power were emerging which relied less on the exercise of personal command and more on indirect forms of control – for example, financial procedures. Offe (1975) extended the argument. The state, in order to maintain its function of system integration, is increasingly driven to develop new forms of intervention. The traditional rules, adequate for the purposes of legislating the system's broad inputs and boundary rules, become inappropriate and have to be replaced by decision rules which determine policy formation itself. This new mode of intervention calls for 'stricter controls of objectives, outputs and outcomes by such techniques as program budgeting, cost–benefit analysis and social indicators'. To ensure system maintenance and the development of infrastructures the state is driven into progressively detailed planning of public service activities. Instrumental rationality dominates, leading to the pervasive application of calculable decision processes, rooted in formal and technical procedures, the determining criterion of which is economic efficiency.

Public management reflected and was shaped by the age of corporatism. Technocratic rational planning and disciplined bureaucracy were the means. The response to the steering crisis was to retrench and concentrate power at the centre in order to establish a more pragmatic social order that would ensure social efficiency and discipline. The corporate state sought to stratify opportunity through a system that would tie the public domain to the requirements of the labour market.

Public Management as Neo-Liberalism

If public management in the era of corporatism sought to plan its way out of the economic crisis, the new era of neo-liberalism sought to control finance and leave outcomes to market forces. An emergent economic orthodoxy of monetarism proposed tight control of the money supply as the strategy for controlling inflation and protecting investment and property values. Inflation had purportedly been caused by the profligate expansion of public services beyond the financial means of the state, thus burdening the public sector borrowing requirement and draining resources from profitable private sector investment. A free market would encourage more stringent and effective deployment of resources. Heald (1983) describes this attack upon the assumptions of postwar welfare democracy:

> as part of the rolling back of the state in favour of the market some of the underlying premises of the social democratic state were challenged. There began unprecedented questioning of public provision in areas such as housing and health which have been central pillars of the welfare state. Public intervention in industry was reduced with the nationalised industries being the subject of extensive privatised schemes. The emphasis which the 1979 Conservative government placed upon restoring the operation of the free market stands in vivid contrast to the policies of its post war Conservative predecessors. (p. 3)

The new economic perspectives reflected a new spectrum of values – of freedom rather than equality, individualism rather than community, efficiency rather than justice, and competition rather than cooperation as the key to an effective public domain.

Conclusion

Management has to be understood in terms of the purposes which define its tasks and conditions. Because these change over time management can only be grasped in the context of the social and political structures which shape its emerging forms. These structures and the purposes they serve may vary over different historical periods as organisations meet the needs of the time.

For a decade or more the polity has sought to erode the distinctive purposes of public organisation and make the purposes of the private sector the organising principles for all organisations. But the market has not been ideally suited to the needs of public services. Markets cannot by themselves provide what is needed for society. The unintended consequences which follow from individuals acting in isolation ensure that self-interest is often self-defeating. More importantly, markets are formally neutral but substantively biased. Under the guise of neutrality the market actively confirms and reinforces the preexisting social order of wealth and privilege. Markets are, therefore, the supreme institution of winners and losers, with the winners imposing their power on the losers without redress, because of the structure of social selection: markets produce survivals and extinctions in a Darwinian zero-sum game. Markets, therefore, are political, that is, a way of making decisions about power in society, and they ensure that the already powerful win decisively. Whereas the postwar state sought to construct a public domain which diminished the effects of class advantage, the neo-liberal state constructed a public domain which released and reinforced class division and advantage through the market mechanism.

The problems we face derive from the transformations of the time: the restructuring of work; environmental erosion; the fragmentation of society. These transformations raise questions about what it is to be a person, what is the nature of the community, what kind of polity we need to secure the future well-being of all. These questions present issues of identity, well-being, rights, liberty, opportunity, and justice. The predicaments that confront us cannot be resolved by individuals acting in isolation, nor by 'exit' because we cannot stand outside them. Markets by themselves can only exacerbate these problems.

The predicaments we face are collective or public in nature and require public action to resolve them. Only the public domain can solve the physical problems of the environment – the conditions for which lie in collective action – or solve the moral and social problems facing our society. Yet if such issues are to be confronted, it will imply not only public action, but a reconstituting of the organising principles of the public domain in the context of a reformed polity.

PART II

THE PUBLIC DOMAIN: PURPOSES AND CONDITIONS

3

The Dualities of Citizenship

Public and private describe significant boundaries in social life, defining membership or exclusion and thus the very way we see and interpret ourselves in relation to others – the constituting of the 'I' and the 'we' in society. Some historical periods have drawn strong boundaries between public and private while others have weakened the boundaries (see Barrington Moore, 1985).

Though we wish to distinguish between the public domain and the private domain, we do not wish to suggest that the boundary is clear-cut. We shall, however, describe the public domain as a constituted domain, that is, a domain constituted separately from the private domain, expressing distinctive political, social and moral values, which requires distinctive conditions and practices for its effective working. The public and private domains are interdependent. The private depends upon the public and the public gains from its impact upon the private domain. The rationale of the public domain is found in its distinctive values, conditions and practices.

There are many layers in the lexicon of 'public' and 'publicness'. The analysis which follows will disclose in stages our understanding of these levels. Though we begin with the idea of public as defining the collective characteristics of any society, we proceed to explore the necessary duality in publicness which expresses 'the many' as well as 'the whole'. It is this duality that, for us, captures the values and purposes of the public domain and its characteristic principles of citizenship which we seek to make explicit during the chapter.

The Distinctive Purposes of the Public Domain

The Public as Collective Tasks and Purpose

Initially we define public as collectivity, while publicness refers to the members of a community or society as a whole, the interests which they may hold in common and the activities which they undertake together. Publicness defines the inescapable collectivity of any society as against the privateness of particular individuals and their associations.

Publicness can refer to 'any person' within a society: the public park, the public meeting or being out in public denoting a context which is open to anybody. Public, however, can define everyone inclusively: hence the public holiday, the public rules which define that motorists should drive on the left. Privateness in contrast is distinguished because, as Bentham argued, 'an assignable individual is such and such an individual to the exclusion of every other' (see Barry, 1965; Benn and Gauss, 1983). Publicness refers also to the interests which all hold in common. Thus the 'public interest' indicates a matter of collective concern for a society as a whole (Miller, 1962). A society can share a common concern for basic provision and shelter or a shared interest in safety and protection. Barry (1967) defines those policies which are in the public interest as those which 'treat everyone affected in exactly the same way', while Rousseau believed that the 'general will' would benefit me in common with everyone else rather than me at the expense of everyone else. Thus the public or collective interest is often seen as opposed to narrow sectional interests and can be used to override a private interest of particular individuals or groups.

A further distinctive characteristic of publicness is something which is open to public display or scrutiny as against private which is closed, concealed or secluded. The public document is open for all to peruse, while the public inquiry describes the opening of activities to general scrutiny, and the public meeting is accessible for all to attend.

The distinctive purpose of the public domain, therefore, which follows from these understandings of publicness is to support and develop our collective life. The institutional settings of the public domain are constituted to undertake tasks which individuals cannot carry out alone, but only together; or conversely, those activities which a society cannot do individually but only as a collectivity. The scope of the public domain is the whole community or society. The responsibility of the public domain is the health of those activities which are distinctively and inescapably collective and public in scope. What are these distinctively collective tasks of the public domain?

Providing public goods and services. The public domain will value and choose to provide those goods and services which are regarded as essential to the community as a whole. They are 'collective goods' because they meet the needs of all and because they are provided following a collective choice and financed by collective funds. Public goods possess distinctive characteristics which, as Hood says, 'do not fit into the normal assumption in law that property rights are exclusive and transferable or the normal assumption in economics that goods and services can be provided by voluntary market exchanges' (Hood, 1986). Public goods are defined by economists as possessing, first, 'non-excludability' (Brown and Jackson, 1986; Foster, Jackman and Perlman, 1980). It is impossible, inefficient or impracticable to exclude consumers from the benefits of the goods and services once they are provided. It is therefore not possible to charge for them (for example, street lighting). Second, public goods possess 'non-rivalness'. The consumption of a good is said to be non-rival when the marginal cost of additional consumption is zero. Non-rivalness arises because of indivisibility of the product: adding an extra consumer does not detract from the benefit of another (the classic example of this is crossing a bridge) .

Public goods, therefore, are collective goods. Provided for one, they are necessarily provided for all. The public domain will take responsibility for providing those goods and services which individuals cannot (or will not) provide and which are regarded as essential to maintaining the 'common-wealth'. It may be defending the boundaries of the realm, or regulating hygiene and thus public health, or producing the physical infrastructure of roads and street lighting that are chosen as activities of such significance for the whole community that responsibility for undertaking them should be a collective endeavour. The public domain might provide a number of welfare benefits – for example, unemployment insurance – because private markets would not do it or would do it ineffectively (Barr, 1983).

Although these defining characteristics of public goods appear clear, deciding whether a good has these characteristics, and whether to provide it, are value-laden, necessarily political choices. A number of goods or services are what Laver (1986) calls 'hybrid'; they have both private and public characteristics. Health care and education are consumed by individuals and are services which can be charged for, while additional consumption raises marginal costs. Yet inoculating against infectious diseases or creating an educated democracy can be defined as public goods because the benefits are non-excludable, indivisible and jointly consumed. Thus

> though the characteristics defining public goods are quite precise the goods which possess these characteristics may not be clearly defined until some agreement is reached as to the benefits they provide ... The decision about which goods are public goods may be dependent on a judgement about the value of the benefits to others: it may thus be a 'political decision'. (Foster *et al.*, 1980, p. 41)

The 'technical' definition of what is to count as a public good can conceal the necessity of collective judgement. What is a public good, which ones are needed in society and how they should be distributed to ensure fairness and equity are intrinsically political decisions and can only be decided collectively.

Establishing collective efficiency.   The value placed upon an efficient context for individual or private transactions will lead to another set of public choices about goods and services which should be provided collectively. Even if we are all in agreement about the purposes which should shape our society, the unintended consequences of our mutual interdependence point to the rationality of collective decision-making. A factory exuding waste chemicals into a nearby river or poisonous fumes into the air, or an individual casting aside chip papers on returning home from the pub can illustrate the public consequences of private actions for the environment we all have to share. These collective action problems, or 'spillovers' as Laver (1983, 1986) chooses to call them, arise because our individual wants can result in mutual frustration.

A number of writers, including philosophers such as Parfit (1984), economists such as Sen (1987, 1990), as well as political scientists like Elster (1979, 1983, 1987), have become increasingly preoccupied with the paradox which collective action problems present to individuals: self-interest can be self-defeating. On many occasions the rational solution for each individual is to act collectively, for it is only by acting together that individuals can improve their individual welfare. The paradox is reinforced by a number of familiar illustrations:

● '*The tragedy of the commons*': A peasant village borders a river. Each peasant owns a plot of land, part of which is used for cultivating crops and part as an orchard. As each family grows in size trees are felled to allow more land to be tilled. But the trees have also fulfilled the function of binding the soil. The process of felling causes soil to slip into the river, gradually eroding the banks not only of the orchard but also of the arable land. Thus each family seeking to gain more land will end up with less. If, however, trees were felled on every second plot of land the general acreage of arable could be increased and the banks protected. The actions which are rational for each family are in fact irrational. Only if the families act together can they take decisions which improve their own welfare.

● '*The prisoners' dilemma*': Two prisoners are to be taken to trial for a crime which they both committed but for which the prosecution does not have enough evidence to convict them. Knowing that the prisoners are guilty of a minor crime, each is asked separately whether he will confess. The dilemma arises because each has to make a difficult calculation. If both confess they know they will receive a reduced sentence of ten years. If neither of them confesses they will be tried for the minor crime and receive two years each. If one confesses but not the other then the 'virtuous' criminal goes free while the other receives twenty years. Given their situation each chooses to confess. Yet if they had been able to collaborate they would both have been better off.

● '*The contributor's dilemma*': It may be the case that I continue to pay subscriptions to my trade union or professional association knowing that only a small portion of the benefits will return to me. Yet I could calculate taking a 'free ride', withdrawing my subscription while continuing to enjoy the benefits won by the remaining collective effort. But if all acted in this way each would be worse off.

The need to act collectively in order to make the social context more amenable to our separate purposes is a significant lesson. Yet the dominating assumptions remain individualistic. Collective action, it seems, remains a necessary burden in which all individuals must engage, though with reluctance, in order to improve the efficiency of social transactions. Yet many, however, argue that the good produced by common endeavour in collective decision-making can be more than a means designed to serve the ends of private individuals. For Mills (1959) the social task of reason is to discover the ends and purposes which can shape the development of society according to some agreed understanding of the common good. Decisions about collective efficiency lead inevitably to political (that is, collective) choices about social structure and purpose.

Constituting collective rules and purpose: The collective responsibilities of the public domain are, in the last resort, much more deep-seated than producing public goods and services or dissolving the harmful unintended consequences of individual transactions. This is because they depend upon understandings – about what is public – which in the end cannot be taken for granted but have themselves to be articulated and decided upon. The fundamental purpose of the public domain is to constitute the social and political preconditions that make society possible: to create those agreements which enable social life to proceed and develop. Those constitutive agreements establish the framework of political purpose, process and structure that provide the necessary conditions for individual and social relationships. Who is to be a member and what are the defining qualities? What are to be their rights and duties towards each other? What are the rules for determining the distribution of status and opportunity? Decisions about such matters have implications for every individual. They determine the bases of individual identity, their well-being and the nature of their social ties. Yet these considerations of membership, of rights and duties, of ownership and obligation can only be determined collectively.

The public domain has to constitute the process by which such decisions are taken. Who is to be involved, how will they participate and when? These questions about the very process and structure of the polity cannot be determined by individuals independently but only collectively. The ultimate purpose of the public domain is to constitute those conditions which presuppose agreements about the most fundamental concerns in any society: the collective conditions for common well-being but also individual dignity. The public domain has the responsibility for constituting a community or society as a political community, that is, a public, which has the capacity to assume such responsibilities and make such collective choices. By enabling agreement about the constitutive framework for any society, it establishes the conditions which make social relations and individual development possible at all. Indeed without these political preconditions we should not know what 'private' was, what constituted acceptable private ownership or fair rules of exchange in the market-place. The paradox of privacy is that it depends upon public rules and agreements.

Political Choice as Public Choice

It follows from this analysis that the collective choices which have to be made – about services, efficiency or constitutive rules – are necessarily political choices. They are political choices because it is likely, given the issues, that choice has to be made from a number of competing claims. There will be arguments about needs, spillovers, rights and obligations. Collective choice is political because these disagreements and conflicts of interest have to be resolved before social life can proceed. Collective conflict has to lead into collective choice. The significance of the political process is that it has to clarify public choice about collective tasks, made on behalf and in the interests of the public as a whole. The scope for public choice pervades the whole community and necessitates a judgement about what is the collective or public interest out of the contending claims. The public choice will acquire authority if it is perceived as legitimate by the public, because it strives to secure the interests and well-being of all rather than some.

The essential task of the public domain can now be interpreted as enabling authoritative public choice about collective activity and purpose. In short, it is about clarifying, constituting and achieving public purpose. It has the ultimate responsibility for constituting a society as a political community which has the capacity to make public choices. Producing 'a public' which is able to enter into a dialogue and decide about the needs of the community as a whole is the uniquely demanding challenge facing the public domain (see Dewey, 1915, 1939; Keane, 1984). When Arendt (1958, 1973) asks what it is that properly belongs to the public domain her answer identifies those matters which can be debated, which form and test our opinions; and which require judgement; those matters, that is, about which we seek to persuade each other through public argumentation. The proper subject of the public domain, however, is not public debate and persuasion as an end in itself. It is clarifying and negotiating the constitutive framework of public purpose which establishes the very preconditions for individual development, social relations and economic transaction.

The duality of publicness.   The challenge for the public domain in constituting public choice and purpose can best be accomplished if it gives recognition to an inherent duality in the concept of publicness (Ranson and Stewart, 1989). We began by defining public as collectivity but this understanding masks the necessary two-sidedness in the concept of publicness – the many and the whole. Public means not only 'the public as collectivity' (the whole) but also 'the public as plurality' (the many). The notion of 'a citizen', which is central to the public domain, perfectly expresses this duality. The citizen is both an individual and a member of the collectivity. Indeed, citizen has to be understood as 'individual-as-a-member-of' the public as a political community.

   Publicness, moreover, expresses a relationship between plurality and collectivity which can be strongly or weakly defined. The public domain can seek to emphasise the regular contribution which citizens and groups can make to collective life, or it can reduce participation to periodic occasions through significant events such as voting in elections. Publicness can also denote a process of creating or strengthening unity out of diversity. The public domain can reinforce the importance of shared interests or activities, undertaken in common, or it can seek to reduce the sphere of public and collective life. Whatever the scope of the public, however, what is significant is the relationship between the public as plurality and as collectivity.

Renewing the Public Domain

The postwar social democratic polity emphasised a passive public, taking its lead from professional experts and distant elected representatives. While much was achieved, excluding the public from participating in the development of society led in time to a withering of identification and support. The vacuum in the polity was the absence of public engagement. Public consent and legitimacy have atrophied as a result. Understanding of this predicament has been widespread but differences surround the appropriate response. For a decade and more the market has provided a strategy for empowering the public conceived as consumers. This agenda has found appeal across the spectrum: in the New Right (Hayek, 1976; Friedman, 1962; Pirie, 1992) but also amongst Fabian Socialists (Miller, 1989; Le Grand and Estrin, 1989) and Marxists (Roemer, 1983; Elster and Moene, 1989).

The strategy of empowering the public through market consumerism cannot, as we have argued, achieve its desired end. It is not just that markets are a Darwinian zero-sum game of some winners and many losers. It is that the very organising principles of consumerism are inappropriate to resolving the issues which confront societies as they approach the year 2000. The predicaments of our time – whether in understanding how to sustain the environment or to reconcile the rights and well-being of diverse communities – cannot be determined by individuals or groups in isolation, nor by 'exit' because we cannot stand outside them. The predicaments of our time are faced by communities and societies as a whole: 'they are urgent problems for human beings together and in common …. If we are so much as to survive as a species … we clearly need to think about well-being and justice internationally, and together' (Nussbaum, 1990). What each individual or group experiences as separate concerns has actually to be faced together and can only be tackled through public institutions that enable us to share understanding and act together: 'facing the obscure and extravagantly complicated challenges of the human future our most urgent common need at present is to learn how to act together more effectively' (Dunn, 1992).

The public domain provides the key to realising this sense of common purpose and shared understanding required to meet the challenge of a changing society. If this ambition is to be realised, however, there is an urgent need to rethink and renew the purposes, tasks and conditions of the public domain in our time. We begin with a discussion of the distinctive values and conditions of the public domain constituted to express the duality of publicness: plurality of public expression but also public choice and purpose. This establishes the tasks for management in the public domain as well as the criteria for its evaluation.

The Distinctive Values of the Public Domain

The dual nature of the social, moral and political relations that are needed to constitute the public domain is expressed in and reinforced by four juxtapositions of public values which celebrate: autonomy and *civitas* in moral identity, private and public virtue, justice and rights in society, and discourse and public choice in politics and government. The values hold in tension the duality between the individual and the collective virtues of the public domain.

This duality values both the separateness of each person as a fundamental ethical fact and their membership of the community. The individuality *and* interdependence of each is recognised as an indispensable feature of living within the public domain. The duality provides reciprocal responsibilities: of the citizen, endowed with rights and privileges but also duties towards the community, and of the community towards each citizen member, respecting the liberty of each and their equal right both to self-development and to share in the responsibilities of the public domain. As Pericles expressed it in his Funeral Oration:

> Here each individual is interested not only in his own affairs but in the affairs of the state as well: even those who are mostly occupied with their own business are extremely well-informed on general politics ... we do not say that a man who takes no interest in politics is a man who minds his own business; we say that he has no business here at all. (Thucydides, 1954)

A key idea, therefore, is self-determination, both as an individual (in the private sphere) and collectively as a community (in the public sphere). Citizens are to share equally in liberty, being ruled and ruling in turn. They may have different economic or social backgrounds, but citizens are equal in the community.

A Public Ethos of Autonomy and Civitas

Autonomy defines the capacity for citizens to express their mind and advance ideals, while *civitas* expresses the civic virtues of cooperation and friendship which are intrinsic values but also a condition for autonomy. The interdependence of autonomy and cooperation can form the moral and social ties which help to integrate society and make it a community.

Raz (1986) has made autonomy the centre of 'the morality of freedom'. The positive freedom of autonomy concerns individuals being able to shape and plan a life. Yet for Raz, the quality of autonomy depends upon public virtues. The conditions which allow individuals to express their autonomy are a public and collective good: 'the provision of many collective goods is constitutive of the very possibility of autonomy'. This understanding of the dependence of individual expression and development upon the quality of the public domain has more often been articulated in feminist writing (Elshtain, 1982; O'Neill, 1984). Elshtain argues that if women are to develop their autonomy and to contribute to the public domain, then the rigid distinction between public and private needs to disappear and the particularity of private life understood and supported. If individuals are to express their autonomy then public virtues of *civitas* are required to ensure the well-being of the public domain.

Civitas expresses the civic virtue of community as against self-interest and personal avarice. Selfishness is not only morally degrading because corrosive and divisive of the common welfare; it is frequently irrational because self-defeating. *Civitas* should lead not to expediency but to a concern for the equal value of all citizens and the value of fraternity between citizens. For Halsey (1978), as well for Tawney (1931), fraternity is the value which provides the 'creed and code of conduct' that can morally integrate the community, encouraging a sense of belonging as well as social and moral ties.

> I mean [fraternal institutions] to denote social groups whose members share the same essential ideals of conduct – recognition of and care for, the needs of others ... I take the notion of fraternity in political discourse to be metaphorical reference to this idea of a moral community. (Halsey, 1978, p. 160)

For Aristotle, the idea of 'civic friendship' – of sharing a life in common – was the only possibility for creating and sustaining life in the city (see MacIntyre, 1981). Without it, without the possibility of identifying, sharing and cooperating with others, a public domain cannot be realised. Taylor (1984, 1986) argues that forms of knowing and understanding as well as a shared moral order are the necessary basis of civic virtue.

The value of ordinary people serving the needs of others in the community in which they live and work may often take the form of voluntary activity. Simey (1985) and Titmuss (1971) recognise that the importance of voluntary service in the community lies in the expression and reinforcement of responsible citizenship, of citizens taking greater ownership of the shape and direction of their lives. The principle of voluntarism strengthens the polity as well as the common welfare of all.

Private and Public Virtue

It is often claimed that the ancients had a concept of freedom which neglected individual rights and that they emphasised the public above the private. But the Athenians believed in individual liberty as much as we do. They grasped, however, what we may be in danger of forgetting: the mutual dependence and benefit of private and public. The Athenians can teach us about the dual relationship between values that are necessary for human development. To be *a good person* and to be *a good citizen* were one and the same: to pursue excellence or 'human flourishing' (the good, complete, life) for *all.* This process of development involved learning how to live a valuable life over the whole span of a life, a struggle which could only be worked out with and through others in a moral community. The civic virtue of cooperation helps to unfold our own qualities of character as well as enrich the life of the community which sustains us all. The Athenian way of life thus encouraged individuals to take responsibility to serve and develop 'the public good'.

The contemporary world, by contrast, is in danger of stressing the autonomy of each individual at the expense of their shared membership, interdependence and responsibility. Moreover, 'the good' is regarded as a private matter for each individual and firmly outside the remit of the public domain. The modern liberal order has been neutral about the good. Because society comprises a plurality of groups which may hold incommensurable values and beliefs, their allegiance depends upon the state restricting its agency to the framework of rules and rights that govern their relationship to each other. Morals have been left as a matter for private reflection and choice and the state has eschewed any prescription of virtue in the public domain. There could, it was claimed, be no single conception of the good about which groups in any modern society would be able to agree. Rawls (1982) expressed this liberal perspective forcefully:

> The presupposition of liberalism ... as represented by Locke, Kant and J. S. Mill, is that there are many conflicting and incommensurable conceptions of the good, each compatible with the full autonomy and rationality of human persons. Liberalism assumes, as a consequence of this presupposition, that it is a natural condition of a free democratic culture that a plurality of conceptions of the good is pursued by its citizens...
>
> The consequence [of this liberal presupposition] is that the unity of society and the allegiance of its citizens to their common institutions rests not on their espousing one rational conception of the good, but on an agreement as to what is just for free and equal moral persons with different and opposing conceptions of the good. This conception of justice is independent of and prior to the notion of goodness in the sense that its principles limit conceptions of the good which are admissable in a just society. (Rawls, 1982, p. 160)

It can be argued, however, that not only does this liberal perspective mistake the degree to which the 'neutral' rules of justice as fairness themselves imply a conception of the good but also that the efficacy of the rules requires members of society to espouse them as shared moral values. The liberal values of autonomy depend upon their being agreed as virtues of the public domain. The good, therefore, is prior to and informs justice. We argue that what Rawls presupposes and what modern society has increasingly taken for granted – an agreed framework of moral and political values that is indispensable for any society to cohere at all – now urgently needs to be recovered. Unless a larger area of living is informed and enriched by common values then even the skeletal infrastructure of agreed procedures is at risk. The challenge for the public domain is precisely the task of creating a shared conception of the good, which is at the same time consistent with a diversity of values. Realising agreement can only emerge from processes of discourse and practice that are enabled by the public domain. The virtues grow out of the reflected practices of members within and between communities.

Once more we can learn from the Athenians for whom 'the good' (human flourishing) was a public concern – indeed, the defining purpose of the polity. If Athenian citizens had responsibilities to the community, then it had obligations in turn towards them. The polity was defined by its moral purpose to enable the distinctive capacities of each citizen to develop.

> The best polity is that ... in which anyone whatsoever might do best and live a flourishing life :
>
> A just polis allows man's best qualities to flourish. (Aristotle)

This was done by providing the conditions – material (for example, clean public water), institutional (for example, the polity), and moral (civic ethic) – which offer the possibility for all to become excellent. The *polis* aims at producing the capabilities for choosing: the choice is left to citizens (Aristotle; see Nussbaum, 1990).

Justice and Rights in the Distribution of Public Goods

A cohesive society depends upon agreement about the distribution of rights and duties as well as opportunities for *all* members of the community. Justice secures the foundation for the polity's moral purpose. Citizens respect and obey the law because they are equal before it and because it expresses the moral values of their community, especially justice.

The sense of responsibility for others and commitment to strengthen the ties of cooperation within the community may vary with the extent to which society is willing to accord individuals rights and treat them fairly. If free and equal individuals are to retain their dignity as moral agents then, Rawls (1971) argues, the institutions of society need to be founded on a public principle of justice as fairness. If the rights of all are to be protected, then the basic structure of society needs to distribute the primary goods – basic liberties, opportunities, wealth, self-respect – so that 'all citizens in a well ordered society have the same basic liberties and enjoy fair equality of opportunity'. The public domain will seek a foundation charter based upon the values of justice, so that rights and duties are assigned fairly, as would be the distribution of benefits and burdens from social cooperation.

Given the overriding value embodied in the public domain – of citizens gathering together to participate in and take responsibility for the government of the community – public choice may emphasise fair distribution in order to meet the needs of the public as citizens. If members of the community are to retain self-respect and to develop their powers and capacities in order to participate as citizens in the polity, their rights need to be supported by public institutions which express justice. 'Taking rights seriously', as Dworkin (1977) argues, presupposes just systems of distribution. Poverty, ignorance through inadequate education and the idleness of enforced unemployment may all disable citizens from contributing to the life and quality of the public domain.

How rights and justice are to be reconciled is likely to be 'essentially contested'. Part of the deliberation within the polity will inevitably focus upon those collective goods and services which are considered to be a precondition for the life and vitality of the public as a whole. The public domain has to determine which activities are essential to maintain and develop the 'common-wealth'. It may be defending the boundaries of the realm, developing the efficient infrastructures for private transactions, or more actively pursuing the public purpose of an active citizenship. There may be considerable differences within the public domain about which principles should have priority in determining the scale and distribution of public resources (Ryan, 1984; Dunn, 1984). Some will argue that individuals have an inalienable right to possession of property and skill which cannot be invaded by the public domain. Bentham and Nozick set narrow limits to the arena of public choice: law and order, contract and defence. Individuals are morally self-sufficient and are entitled to determine the use of their property as they choose. The public is best served when individuals are able to express their self-interest. An alternative conception, however, equally begins with the inviolability of persons whose rights cannot be set aside by some calculus of social welfare. Differences of value and principle can only be resolved through the duality of politics and government.

The Politics of Discourse and Government in Public Choice

The differences of language, culture and experience which are endemic to society can lead to conflict. For some this is a sign of failure, but for others such disagreements are inescapable and even a sign of vitality: the issue is rather the process of resolving conflict. For Aristotle the only effective process is politics, the *polis* being the only arena in which contending interests and classes can transcend their disputes.

> Politics arises then ... in organised states which recognise themselves to be an aggregate of many members not a single tribe, religion, interest or tradition. Politics arises from accepting the fact of simultaneous existence of different groups, hence different traditions within a territorial unit under common rule ... What matters is that its social structure unlike some primitive societies is sufficiently complex and divided to make politics a plausible response to the problem of governing it, the problem of maintaining order at all ... The establishing of political order is not just any order at all: it marks the birth, or the recognition of freedom. For politics represents at least some tolerance of differing truths, some recognition that government is possible, indeed best conducted, amid the open canvassing of rival interests. Politics are the public actions of free men. (Crick, 1964, pp. 17–18)

The process of politics is one which brings together diverse interests and perspectives within a society. Politics is the process by which groups meet, deliberate and decide the differences between them. Deliberation must resolve in collective decision.

The politics of collective choice provides the central value and rationale of the public domain. Its essential purpose is to give expression to the duality of publicness as the only way of resolving the political struggle which is intrinsic to public choice. Its dual task is to encourage the politics of participation and voice and also the value of collective choice and government. The value of politics lies in the collective process of public discussion in which differences of purpose can be negotiated and resolved. Disagreement can be a sign of vitality. What is important for our analysis is the understanding that politics is necessarily a process of public argument, of open debate. The political process is one in which groups are necessarily enjoined 'to make public' their claims and challenges, although contending groups will be expected to listen as well as articulate their views.

At the centre of such a public sphere lies the value of reason in public discourse. Diverse interests are encouraged to reason with each other in order to reach mutual understanding and agreement. Habermas's (1981) concept of 'communicative rationality' is explicitly a project to rescue the concept of public reason embodied in the Enlightenment. The more the patterns of life are based upon conscious, argued-out, adducement of reasons the greater is the possibility of establishing an accountable dialogue between different views, making politics a particularly practical activity of speaking, listening and compromising. The public sphere thus extends the scope of reason.

The open, public discourse which is politics also forms and defines 'a public' as a political community. The idea of a public formed by and promoting critical political discourse has been central to a number of twentieth-century writers who believe that such 'a public' is now seriously at risk. For Dewey (1915, 1939) a public fosters debate, discussion and dialogue by enabling its members to interact freely with one another. Publics enable 'the participation of every human being in the formulation of the values that regulate the living of men together' (1939). For Wright Mills (1959) publics create a space conducive to the free ebb and flow of discussion, a place where authority is grounded in discussion, where people have an effective voice in the making of those decisions which vitally affect them, where the power to make those decisions is publicly legitimated and where those who exercise power are publicly accountable. The process of reasoning in public discourse helps to discover common ends and thus transform different groups into sharing a sense of community: in effect, to become a public.

Thus the politics of public discourse must lead to collective choice and to the processes of government as part of the necessary duality of publicness: 'politics is the art of reaching decisions by public discussion and then obeying those decisions as a necessary condition of civilised existence' (Finley, 1985). The public domain has to lead from conflict and argument into decision and action by government, if necessary in the absence of agreement. Consent derives from the legitimacy of a procedure of discourse and decision as much as agreement with a substantive decision. Having made policies and decisions about the purposes which will shape the polity, it is the task of government to make authoritative allocation of values and to secure their implementation through law-making and regulation. Through the politics of expression and the government of decision, the public domain secures the authority and legitimacy of public choice in society.

The dual values of the public domain outlined – of autonomy and *civitas*, of public and private virtue, of justice and rights, of discourse and government – are distinctive in themselves, yet they are drawn together in the unifying principle of citizenship which becomes the overarching purpose and value of the public sphere.

For Citizenship in the Public Domain

The idea of citizenship has moved to the centre of social and political thought during the 1980s (see Roche, 1987, 1992; Barbalet, 1988; Turner, 1990a and b, 1993; Plant and Barry, 1990; Mouffe, 1992). This is, arguably, only to have been expected. Fundamental questions have been raised about what it is to be a person, about the nature of society and the polity. The answers any society gives to these questions express its beliefs about *citizenship*, for to be a citizen defines a conception of human agency, an understanding of relations in society, and of political association. We define citizenship, drawing upon Held (1984), as: 'granting the status of *membership* of a (national) community which thereby bestows upon all individuals equally reciprocal rights and duties, liberties and constraints, powers and responsibilities. Citizens express the right as well as the obligation to participate in determining the purposes and form of community and thus the conditions of their own association.'

Citizenship, in this way, expresses a conception of the conditions for human agency within the community in which individuals are to live. To be a citizen defines:

- what it is to be a person, as a member of the community, and whose identity acquires meaning only through the essential

agency of developing the self with and through relations with others
- how citizens are expected to relate to each other in society, and indeed how society is to be conceived through ties and obligations to the community as well as rights upon the community
- what responsibilities citizens are to have, and how they are to participate in the decision-making of the polity

Thus citizenship defines the boundaries of social and political life (the public domain) and a conception of human agency, and of the conditions for agency, within society.

the structures in which citizens participate in their collective affairs have ...implications for the organisation of society as a whole. Thus a ... question raised by the practice of citizenship concerns the consequences of advances in citizenship rights, especially for the social relations of citizens (and non-citizens) and for the social and economic institutions in which they live and work. In particular, disadvantaged groups in society might struggle for citizenship rights in order to improve their conditions. The question immediately arises of whether an expansion of citizenship participation can reduce class inequality, or affect the structure of relations between persons of different sex or race. (Barbalet, 1988, p. 1)

The substance of such a vision can vary. Beliefs and institutional arrangements – values, power, organisation – of citizenship have varied and developed over time. The most important analysis of this historical unfolding of citizenship is that of Marshall (1977). His formative essay, *Citizenship and Social Class*, argued that citizenship has three dimensions – civil, political and social – each of which has had its characteristic formative period since the eighteenth century.

Civil Rights

The civil dimension of citizenship, the achievement of the eighteenth century, comprises legal rights which establish the equality of all individuals before the law, their right to own property and to enter into contracts, their right to liberty of the person and to freedom of speech, thought and faith as well as the right to choose where and how to live consistent with the freedom of others. The institutional condition for these legal rights were the rule of law, the courts and the judiciary. The new rights were conferred upon *individuals* who, freed from their feudal ties to place, status and occupation, could enter into contracts as equals to exchange their property – whether capital or labour – in the market.

Civil rights created new freedoms, but these emerged not in opposition to but in support of the rise of capitalism from the seventeenth and eighteenth centuries.

> civil rights bestow on those who have them the capacity to enter market exchanges as independent and self-sufficient agents. Owners of property and labour are indistinguishable in having the same right to contract freely with each other. (Barbalet 1988, p. 8).

Marshall (1977) knew that civil rights 'were indispensable to a competitive market economy' (p. 96) and were therefore 'necessary to the maintenance of a particular form of inequality' (p. 96) because the freeing of the market-place from the constraints of feudal custom and obligation enabled owners of property freely to compete and appropriate. The paradox of civil rights therefore was that 'the single uniform status of citizenship provided the foundation of equality on which the [modern] structure of inequality could be built' (p. 96).

The formal equality of legally constituted rights does not ensure that all share the substantive capacity to exercise these rights. It is this realisation which generated the struggle on the part of disadvantaged classes to extend their rights and conditions to secure the initial promise of civil equality.

As Giddens (1982) says: 'civil freedoms were essentially an end process in the dissolution of the remnants of feudal society. They were the necessary foundation for the emergence of political rights: for only if the individual is recognised as a capable, autonomous agent does it become either possible or sensible to recognise that individual as politically responsible' (pp. 168–9).

Political Rights

Political rights refer to the right to participate in the exercise of political power – 'as a member of a body invested with political authority or as an elector of the members of such a body'. Marshall charts the growing assertion of political rights during the nineteenth century and early twentieth century, beginning with the Reform Acts of 1832 and 1867 which extended the right of men to vote in elections although it was not until 1928 that the universal right to political citizenship was finally achieved.

Political rights are fought for to strengthen, and give reality to, the emerging freedoms for individuals. The victory which civil rights achieves for liberty remains empty unless individuals have the right to participate in the political process that will determine the conditions in which they will live out their lives. While civil rights establish the principle of liberty, political participation provides the possibility of determining the conditions for all to live out their lives in freedom.

For Marshall the enfranchising of the working class deflected the full potential danger of the class system. It diffused conflict and exposed the political inexperience of the working class to exploit their new rights effectively. Yet Marshall argues that although the working class was unable to mobilise political power towards the end of the nineteenth century it did create trade unionism as 'a secondary system of industrial citizenship parallel with and supplementary to the system of political citizenship' (Marshall, 1977, p. 104). Trade unionism and the collective bargaining with employers it permitted became a means by which the economic and social status of organised workers was raised. In other words the collective exercise of rights by members of the working class in creating and using trade unionism established 'the claim that they, as citizens, were entitled to certain social rights' (ibid., p. 103).

Social Rights

The social element of citizenship is composed of a right 'to a modicum of economic welfare and security to the right ... to live the life of a civilised being according to the prevailing standard of life and the social heritage of society' (Marshall, 1977, p. 78). These entitlements have been developed through the twentieth century and especially in the postwar welfare state. Members of society could realise their civil and political rights only if their powers and capacities were developed as citizens. A fairer, more just distribution of opportunities and life chances would be needed to underpin the realisation of a modern citizenship.

The political strength of the working class enabled it to establish a contract for justice that would ensure equality of welfare and educational opportunity as rights that would make equality of life chances as well as freedom a reality in modern citizenship. The state promotion of social justice would aim to modify the working of market forces in society. It was designed to ensure much greater equality of access to the market. The principle of a market society was not being abolished; rather the state was constituting the conditions for all to compete equally within the market by trying to ensure that all had the same starting conditions of good health, housing and education that would enable all to develop their talents and to do justice to them as they entered the labour market.

For some, like Ossowski (1963), the advances of citizenship rights has ensured the retreat of class divisions in society: 'class conflicts give way to other forms of social antagonism'. Marshall believed that although citizenship had led to the 'abatement' of social class, nevertheless class and citizenship tend to stand in a continual relation of tension. The economic institutions of capitalism and the political institutions of citizenship continually confront each other with competing principles.

This way of seeing the rights of citizenship has been further developed in our own time by Ignatieff (1984a, b, 1989), Dahrendorf (1987a, b, 1988, 1990) and Plant (1988, 1990). If an active public is to be (re)created then their social rights will need to be restored for, as Dahrendorf argues, it is their social rights (shared entitlements and public services) which enable citizens to make use of the other two sets of rights:

> Social rights liberate people from insecurity, and that is why the new debate about citizenship must begin with such unambiguous social rights as the right not to fall below a certain level of income and the right to an education... There are obligations of citizenship, such as compliance with the law, assuming it has come about in a legitimate manner, and paying one's taxes... The key point about the obligations of citizenship is not so much that they should be kept to a minimum, but that they have no trade-off relationship with citizenship rights. Rights are absolute. We accept that every 18 year old has the right to vote. Period. (Dahrendorf, 1990)

Social rights are thus a precondition for exercising the others. Without health, or capacities developed by education, or independence provided by employment and income, members of society will be unlikely to become active citizens able to exercise their legal rights or influence in the polity. The 'growth of semi-citizens or second class citizens who are marginalised and who cannot defend themselves is a most serious development. It undermines the principle of citizenship, which is intrinsically universal' (ibid.).

Ignatieff, Plant and Dahrendorf argue that maximising private freedom without providing the means to enable citizens to be free is both incoherent and likely to threaten the freedom it strives to expand. Only a shared foundation grounded upon a citizenship of entitlement can make freedom possible. This depends, for Ignatieff, upon recognising 'the structural dependence of private freedom upon public provision'. The conditions for each individual to flourish are public and collective. There is an 'indissoluble interdependence of the private and the public'. A free society depends upon the polity providing the means. Plant argues that 'if we are interested in empowering all people in society' the market will have a place but 'we will still require state-provided or state-guaranteed services'. For Dahrendorf this requires a new social contract that will restore the necessary connection between entitlements and provision of services to ensure that life chances are secured for all. His liberal political agenda strives to renew the life chances of the underclass of the poor and unemployed created by the 1980s market society. Only such a new settlement can provide a stake in society for those it has summarily excluded. A contract for citizenship will provide membership, identity and participation in shared opportunities.

The Limits to an Entitlement Citizenship

Marshall's paper written to understand and to chart the course for the postwar welfare state has always been admired. In the 1980s it has become the focus of debate used by social and political theorists as the principal statement that forms the foundation for any further analysis (see Giddens, 1982; Held, 1984). Their critique argues that Marshall's analysis neglects the extent to which citizenship rights have developed through *struggle* rather than natural evolution, and that any future development of citizenship must accommodate the diversity of struggles in society rather than just the class struggle. These struggles will need to be acted out through the polity. There is a need to build upon the work of Marshall and shape a new theory of citizenship.

Those who have tried to develop and modernise Marshall's framework have made an important but limited contribution. The argument for shoring up contemporary citizenship by restoring entitlement to the social conditions that enable citizens to exercise their rights is an important correction to neo-liberal strategies for empowering the public as customers. Nevertheless it provides too limited an analysis. Ignatieff, for example, having diagnosed the problem – the passivity of social democracy – fails to present a solution which addresses this predicament. To reassert the value of entitlements entrenched in a 'contract' takes us back to where we were before, with the limits of social democracy unresolved. Parekh (1988) has argued, moreover, that Dahrendorf does not go beyond provisions and entitlement to address the deeper cultural malaise and moral shortcomings of our society. The task is not to find better management of existing political paradigms but to reconstruct the paradigm. The task is not to give better *answers* to neo-liberal questions but to ask better *questions* which alter the agenda of the polity. There is a need to move beyond individualism towards a new moral and political vocabulary.

A new theory of citizenship will need to embrace obligations as well as rights and emphasise political participation as a central part of those civic responsibilities (see Barber, 1984). Any contemporary elaboration of citizenship needs to be enriched by a moral dimension concerned to clarify and pursue an idea of the common good (see Jordan, 1989; Taylor, 1991; Skinner, 1992).

Such a revised, integrated theory of citizenship – embracing the civil, political, social and moral principles of active citizenship, – is provided, we argue, in the concept of the learning society. If the achievement of the eighteenth century was civic citizenship, the nineteenth political citizenship and the twentieth social citizenship, then the challenge as we move towards the year 2000 is to reinterpret the purposes of citizenship in the public domain so that they express the values of the learning society (Ranson, 1992).

The Learning Society

This sketch for a theory of the learning society builds upon the ideas and practice being developed in local communities. Reforms do not begin *de novo*, they have their origins in the publics which are discovering solutions to dilemmas they confront. Our task is to develop understanding of underlying principles in order to create the basis for their more general application.

Key Components of the Theory of the Learning Society

The theory builds upon three axes: of presupposition, principles and purposes: The *presupposition* establishes an overarching proposition about the need for and purpose of the learning society; the *principles* establish the primary organising characteristics of the theory; while *purposes and conditions* establish the agenda for change that can create the values and conditions for a learning society.

Presupposition. There is a need for the creation of a learning society as the constitutive condition of a new moral and political order. Learning is the understanding which develops following reflection upon some puzzle in our experience about people, events or processes. The discovery reveals the reasons why things are as they are and how they might change. Learning is most secure when we learn to learn, continually questioning our received beliefs about experience so as to further develop our understanding. The learning society is one which strives to place these values and processes of learning at the centre of the public domain, so that the conditions can be established for all to develop their capacities, for insititutions to respond openly and imaginatively to a period of change and for the differences between communities to become a source of reflective understanding. The dilemmas faced in society require the valuing of and commitment to learning both individual and collective; as the boundaries between languages and cultures begin to dissolve, as new skills and knowledge are expected within the world of work and, most significantly, as new generations, rejecting passivity in favour of more active participation, require to be encouraged to exercise such qualities of discourse in the public domain. A

learning society, therefore, needs to celebrate the qualities of
being open to new ideas, listening to as well as expressing
perspectives, reflecting on and inquiring into solutions to new
dilemmas, learning from experience, cooperating in the practice
of change and critically reviewing it.

Principles.   Two organising principles provide the framework for
the learning society:

(a)   *Citizenship establishes the ontology, the mode of being, in the
       learning society.*   The notion of being a citizen ideally ex-
       presses our inescapably dual identity as both individual and
       member of the whole, the public; our duality as autonom-
       ous persons who bear responsibilities within the public
       domain. Citizenship establishes the right to the conditions
       for self-and collective development but also a responsibility
       that the emerging powers should serve the well-being of the
       common-wealth. By encouraging the orientation of mem-
       bers of a community to one another, citizenship encourages
       the possibility of mutual understanding and therefore
       learning.

(b)   *Practical reason establishes the epistemology, the mode of knowing
       and acting, of the citizen in the learning society.*   Practical wisdom
       (or what Aristotle called 'phronesis'), describes a number
       of qualities which enable us to understand the duality of
       citizenship in the learning society: knowing what is required
       and how to judge or act in particular situations; and know-
       ing which virtues should be called upon. Practical reason,
       therefore, presents a comprehensive moral capacity because
       it involves seeing the particular in the light of the universal,
       of a general understanding of what good is required as well
       as what proper ends might be pursued in the particular
       circumstances. Practical reason, thus, involves deliberation,
       judgement and action as the defining qualities of the learn-
       ing society: *deliberation* upon experience to develop under-
       standing of the situation, or the other person; *judgement* to
       determine the appropriate ends and course of action, which
       presupposes a community based upon sensitivity and tact;
       and learning through *action* to realise the good in practice.

Purposes, values and conditions. To provide such purposes and conditions, new values and conceptions of learning are valued within the public domain at the level of *the self* (a quest of self-discovery), at the level of *society* (in the learning of mutuality within a moral order), and at the level of the *polity* (in learning the qualities of a participative democracy). The challenge for policy-makers is to promote the conditions for the learning society; this should enable parents to become as committed to their own continuing development as they are to that of their children; men and women should be able to assert their right to learn as well as to support the family; learning cooperatives should be formed at work and in community centres; and the preoccupation with learning should result in extensive public dialogue about reform.

Conditions for a Learning Self

At the centre of the learning society is a belief in the power of agency: only an active self or public provides the purpose and conditions for learning and development. Three conditions are proposed for developing purpose within the self: a sense of agency; a revived conception of discovery through a life perceived as a unity; and an acknowledgment of the self in relation to others:

(i)   *The self as agent.*   Learning requires individuals to progress from the post war tradition of passivity, of the self as spectator to the action on a distant stage, to a conception of the self as agent both in personal development and in active participation within the public domain. Such a transformation requires a new understanding from self-development for occupation to self-development for auto-nomy, choice and responsibility across all spheres of experience. The change also presupposes moving from our prevailing preoccupation with cognitive growth to a proper concern for development of the person as a whole – feeling, imagination and practical/social skills as much as the life of the mind. An empowering of the image of the self presupposes unfolding capacities over (a life-) time.

(ii) *The unity of a life.*   We need to recover the Aristotelian conception of what it is to be and to develop as a person over the whole of a life and of a life as it can be led (see MacIntyre, 1981). This has a number of constituent developments: first, perceiving the life as a whole, the self as developing over a lifetime; second, therefore, a conception of life as a quest with learning at the centre of the quest to discover the identity which defines the self; third, seeing the unity of a life as consisting in the quest for value, each person seeking to reach beyond the self to create something of value, which is valued; fourth, developing as a person towards the excellences, perfecting a life which is inescapably a struggle, an experience of failure as well as success; fifth, accepting that the struggle needs to be guided by virtues which support the development of the self, dispositions which strengthen and uplift (character); and last, acknowledging that the most important virtue is that of deliberation, a life of questioning and inquiry committed to revising both beliefs and action. Learning, from being a means, becomes the end in itself, the defining purpose creatively shaping the whole of a life.

(iii)   *The self in relation to others.*   But we can only develop as persons with and through others – the conception of the self presupposes an understanding of how we live a life with each other, of the relationship of the self to others; the conditions in which the self develops and flourishes are social and political. The self can only find its moral identity in and through others and membership of communities. Self-learning needs to be confirmed, given meaning by others, the wider community. What is of value will be contested; therefore we need to agree with others what is to be considered valuable, to deliberate, argue, provide reasons. It is that process which constitutes the learning society.

The Social Conditions for Learning

The unfolding of the self depends upon developing the necessary social conditions which can provide a sense of purpose within society both for the self and others.

Virtues of civitas: the virtues of recognising and valuing others, of civic friendship.   The conditions for the unfolding self are social and political: my space requires your recognition and your capacities demand my support (and vice versa). Jordan (1989) emphasises the importance of mutual responsibility in developing conditions for all individuals to develop their unique qualities. It recalls Aristotle's celebration of civic friendship – of sharing a life in common – as being the only possible route for creating and sustaining life in the city. Such values are now to be found within feminist literature which emphasises an ethic of caring and responsibility in the family and community, and the dissolution of the public as a separate (male) sphere (see Gilligan, 1986; Pateman, 1987; Okin, 1991). It is only in the context of such understanding and support that mutual identities can be formed and the distinctive qualities of each person can be nurtured and asserted with confidence.

Creating a moral community. The post war world was silent about the good, holding it to be a matter for private discretion rather than public discourse. But the unfolding of a learning society will depend upon the creation of a more strenuous moral order. The values of learning as much as the values which provide the conditions for learning (according dignity and respecting capacity) are actually moral values that express a set of virtues required of the self but also of others in relationship with the self. The values of caring or responsibility upon which can depend the confidence to learn derive any influence they may have from the authority of an underlying moral and social order. The civic virtues, as MacIntyre (1981) analyses, establish standards against which individuals can evaluate their actions (as well as their longer 'quest'); yet particular virtues derive meaning and force from their location within an overall moral framework (what MacIntyre calls a 'tradition'). A moral framework is needed to order relationships because it is the standards accepted by the moral community which provide the values by which each person is enabled to develop.

Yet a moral order is a public creation and requires to be lived and recreated by all members of the community. Each person depends upon the quality of the moral order for the quality of his or her personal development and the vitality of that order depends upon the vitality of the public life of the community. For the Athenian, the virtuous person and the good citizen were the same because the goods which inform a life were public virtues. But the authority of a moral order for the modern world will only grow if it is an open morality rather than a socialisation into a tradition. The development of a moral community has to be a creative and collaborative process of agreeing the values of learning which are to guide and sustain life in the community. Simey (1985) and Titmuss (1971) have recorded the emergence of communal virtues which reflect the process of citizens taking ownership and responsibility for their lives.

Interpretive understanding: learning to widen horizons.   Taylor (1984) has argued that the forms of knowing and understanding, as much as or at least as part of, a shared moral order, are the necessary basis of civic virtue. Historically conditioned prejudices about capacity, reinforced by institutions of discrimination, set the present context for society. The possibility of mutuality in support of personal development will depend upon generating interpretive understanding, that is, on hermeneutic skills which can create the conditions for learning in society: in relationships within the family, in the community and at work. In society we are confronted by different perspectives, alternative life-forms and views of the world. The key to the transformation of prejudice lies in what Gadamer (1975) calls '*the dialogic character of understanding*': through genuine conversation the participants are led beyond their initial positions, to take account of others, and move towards a richer, more comprehensive view, a 'fusion of horizons', a shared understanding of what is true or valid. Discourse lies at the heart of learning: learners are listeners as well as speakers.

The presupposition of such agreement is *openness*: we have to learn to be open to difference, to allow our pre judgements to be challenged; in so doing we learn how to amend our assumptions, and develop an enriched understanding of others. It is precisely in confronting other beliefs and presuppositions that we are led to see the inadequacies of our own and transcend them. Rationality, in this perspective, is the willingness to admit the existence of better options, to be aware that one's knowledge is always open to refutation or modification from the vantage point of a different perspective. For Gadamer, the concept of '*bildung*' describes the process through which individuals and communities enter a more and more widely defined community – they learn through dialogue to take a wider, more differentiated view, and thus acquire sensitivity, subtlety and capacity for judgement.

Reason emerges through dialogue with others: through which we learn not necessarily 'facts' but rather a capacity for learning, for new ways of thinking, speaking, and acting. It is Habermas (1984) who articulates the conditions for such communicative rationality as being 'ideal speech contexts' in which the participants feel able to speak freely, truly, sincerely. The conditions for this depend upon the creation of arenas for public discourse – the final and most significant condition for the creation of the learning society.

Conditions in the Polity

The conditions for a learning society are, in the last resort, essentially political, requiring the creation of a polity which provides the fundamental conditions for individuals and the communities in which they live to develop their capabilities and to flourish. This is the moral purpose of the polity as articulated by Aristotle (see Nussbaum, 1990, 1993). The personal and social conditions, described above, will be hollow unless bedded in a conception of a reformed, more accountable, and thus more legitimate, political order that empowers the public. The connection between individual well-being and the vitality of the moral community is made in the public domain of the polity: the good (learning) person is a good citizen. Without political structures which bring together communities of discourse, the conditions for learning will not exist: it is not possible to create the virtues of learning without the forms of life and institutions which sustain them. The preconditions of the good polity are justice, participative democracy and public action.

Justice: a contract for the basic structure. The conditions for agency of self and society depend upon agreement about its value as well as about allocating the means for private and public self-determination. Freedom rests upon justice (see Rawls, 1971, 1993; Barry, 1989; Nagel, 1991). But this makes the most rigorous demands upon the polity which has to determine the very conditions on which life can be lived at all: membership, the distribution of rights and duties, the allocation of scarce resources, the ends to be pursued. The good polity must strive to establish the conditions for virtue in all its citizens. These issues are intrinsically political and will be intensely contested, especially in a period of transformation that disturbs traditions and conventions.

If decisions about such fundamental issues are to acquire the consent of the public then the procedures for arriving at those decisions will be considered of the greatest significance for legitimate authority of the polity. The process of making the decisions – who is to be involved and how the disagreements that will inexorably arise are to be resolved – will be as important as the content of the decisions themselves.

Participative democracy.   Basing the new order upon the presupposition of agency leads to the principle of equal rights of citizens both to participate in determining what conditions the expansion of their powers and to share responsibility for the common good. The ancient Athenians believed, moreover, that every citizen could take part in the democratic process because the art of political judgement (without which there could be no civilised society) was a capacity which all could express. Politics could not be for specialists alone.

The political task of our time is to develop the polity as a vehicle for the active involvement of all citizens, enabling them to make their contribution to the development of the learning society. There is a need to fashion a stronger, more active democracy than the post war period has allowed (see Pateman, 1970; Keane, 1988; Green, 1985; Hirst, 1990; Dunn, 1992; Held, 1993; Phillips, 1991, 1993).

The principle which constituted classical democracy, of 'proper discussions' – of free and unrestricted discourse, with all guaranteed a right to contribute – needs to be restored in a form appropriate to the modern world. The aim would be to enable all to contribute to public discourse, the purpose of which is to ground decisions in the force of the better argument. The challenge is to restore a culture which values the practice of public discussion and the open giving and taking of reasons as grounds for conclusions (see Dunn, 1992).

The constitutive conditions for citizenship within a more active democracy is a polity that enables the public to participate and express their voice, but also a polity that will permit public choice and government (Ranson and Stewart, 1989; and this volume). How to combine the politics of public expression and the government of choice and action is the challenge for the new polity. Within such a polity the procedures for involving the public and for negotiating decisions will be important (see Habermas, 1981; Haydon, 1987; Hampshire, 1989). Citizens need to acquire a disposition for listening and taking into account as well as of asserting their view:

> The deliberative process of democratic decision-making requires that each participant not only permit the others to express their views and offer their judgements but take others' views seriously into account in arriving at his or her own judgement. Clearly this does not require agreement with the views of others, but rather serious attention to, and respect for, their views. Such reciprocal respect also presupposes that disagreements be tolerated and not suppressed. (Gould, 1988)

By providing forums for participation the new polity can create the conditions for public discourse and for mutual accountability so that citizens can take each other's needs and claims into account and will learn to create the conditions for each other's development. Learning as discourse must underpin the learning society as the defining condition of the public domain.

Public action. A more active citizenship, Mill believed, would be a civilising force in society. Through participation citizens would be educated in intellect, in virtue and in practical activity. The upshot of participation should now be public action based upon deeper consent than that obtained from earlier generations. For Sen (1990; Dreze and Sen, 1989) the possibility of producing a fairer world, one which will enrich the capacities and entitlements of all citizens, depends upon the vitality of public, democratic action. The creation of a learning society expresses a belief in the virtue of the public domain and will depend upon the vitality of public action for its realisation.

Empowering the Voices of Different Citizens

The reform of the political process within the public domain is a fundamental condition for the learning society. It is only by elaborating democracy so as to allow citizens to participate, through fair rules of discourse, that they can all articulate and gain recognition for the needs and aspirations which they believe to define what they wish for themselves and the communities in which they live.

Discourse, free of distorted power (with some groups imposing their will on others) enables a fair politics through which different values and interests can be heard and negotiated. A just polity will empower different citizens (for example, women or the minority communities, or the disabled) whose voices have often not been heard until their experience is so unfair or painful that they have to shout; even then they have typically not been listened to (Lukes, 1974; Saunders, 1979). An open, involving public domain will encourage learning, through listening to and taking account of others so that public policies and the distribution of resources are made more responsive than in the past to significant differences that enrich rather than diminish society (Phillips, 1991, 1993). In this way citizens have an equal opportunity to constitute the conditions for living a life in which they can flourish because their identity is acknowledged, their values understood and their welfare sustained.

Conclusion

The predicaments of the time are those which can only be faced by communities in common. Those anxieties which individuals experience separately about the restructuring of work, the decay of the environment, or the fragmentation of the communities in which they live, can only be faced together with and through public institutions that encourage shared understanding of these issues and enable the appropriate action on behalf of the whole community. The urgent task of the present, as Dunn (1992) has argued, 'is to learn how to act together more effectively'.

If this task is to be realised and the eroded roots of public consent are to be restored, then a polity is needed for our time which expresses a new vision of the public domain: in which the public are conceived neither as passive clients, nor as competing consumers, but as citizens encouraged to contribute to and take a shared responsibility in the development of their society – a learning society which grasps the value of opening itself to reflective understanding of the diversity of culture within as much as to the issues which press in upon it from without.

The role of this polity is to develop the conditions for such a learning society to unfold. Its responsibility is not to distance itself from society but to provide the conditions for citizens to flourish as active and creative members of their communities. The quality of individual capacity as much as the quality of life for all will depend upon our relearning the duality of publicness, that mutual dependence of individual and community. It will depend upon renewing and developing the institutions of the public domain as the condition for the learning society. It is to this task that we now turn.

4
Organising Principles

The public domain constitutes a distinctive form of rule, values and beliefs which legitimate a particular distribution of power and organisation. The principles of its institutional organisation establish the relationship members of society have to the polity, how conflicts are resolved and collective choices formulated. The public domain has organising principles that link its unique purposes to distinctive conditions and tasks distinguishing it from other domains: the integrating theme is public discourse leading to collective choice based on public consent. This concept underlies and legitimates the working of organisations in the public domain, even when they themselves give imperfect expression to it as in the diminished public domain of the neo-liberal democracy. It expresses the perfect model of action in the public domain as perfect competition expresses the model of action in the market. The reality may be a restricted discourse and an uncertain consent as in the market the reality may be limited or imperfect competition. To enable the learning society the following organising principles, we argue, will need to constitute the purposes, conditions and tasks of the public domain.

An Unbounded Area of Public Concern

The realm of public concern is in principle unbounded. The scope of the public is the whole of the community and the purpose of institutions that constitute the public domain is the well-being of all the citizens in the common-wealth. There are 'few

88

limits on those who can get involved in the decision-making process, who can work on it, or who can speak about it' (Perry and Kraemer, 1983, p. 20) and not merely are there few limits, but there should be few limits in the public domain. Issues and concerns can be raised that are at present beyond the boundaries of public concern. In the arena of public discourse those boundaries can be contested as aspirations, knowledge and conditions change. An emerging concern for the environment has extended the understanding of the public good and the boundaries of public action through public pressure and protest.

Any activity undertaken in the public domain can be challenged in the public arena both by those directly affected and those indirectly affected. This means that all interests, whether of organisations or individuals, can raise issues and that there are no fixed boundaries to these issues or to the criteria that can be applied in their judgement. In the arena of public discourse the judgement of public action cannot be limited to the concerns of those for whom the service is provided or based only on the achievement of the immediate purposes for which the service is provided. A private sector organisation can limit its concerns. If homes are provided by developers which are beyond the reach of many of those requiring accommodation, it need be of no concern to the private firm that there is a growing problem of homelessness. A private medical insurance scheme may exclude certain diseases or client groups. It need not be of concern to the private firm that there are patients whose needs they do not meet. In the public domain, those issues cannot be excluded. They may be of concern precisely because of neglect in the private sector. If the building of a new private housing estate imposes costs on the community, that is not of concern to the private firm. A private firm can have concerns beyond its customers and beyond its internal organisational concerns. It may take account of social or of environmental considerations. The point is that it need not do so, but in the arena of public discourse there can be no boundaries. All can contend and urge their reasons:

> What makes public management so hard – and so interesting –
> is that all these players act simultaneously with few clear lines of
> authority, constantly changing public mandates and frequent
> turnover of people. Getting the garbage picked up, a child

treated for lead poisoning, a subway to the station on time, or an elderly person a social security cheque may not seem Herculean tasks. But when they are multiplied hundreds of times over, and their execution occurs in the context of the manager's environment, the real challenge of government becomes clear. The tasks can be done, and done well, by public managers who master this world; but such tasks can easily elude managers who are befuddled by the politics around them, disconcerted by the mixed signals they hear and unsure of their own agenda and purpose. (Chase and Reveal, 1983, pp. 15–16)

Many issues which have to be confronted in the public domain, moreover, are those for which there are typically no simple solutions. That is why they fall to be resolved in the public domain. They often present dilemmas because the ensuing choice will have to weigh the balance of benefit and disadvantage for the well-being of the many and of all. Establishing the balance between inflation and employment in pursuit of economic development, or the level of control of private actions required to protect the environment in the interests of all, or the balance of private and public interest in the provision of health or education, all present intractable predicaments for society.

The problems of inner-city areas are as difficult to define as they are to solve. Instead of well-defined criteria of effectiveness, there are great difficulties in formulating problems. Instead of a controllable process of implementation, widespread support has to be mobilized and maintained. Resources are not abundant. Problems, objectives and resources may all vary during the course of the project. (Metcalfe and Richards, 1987, p. 153)

These are obstinate problems which are not easily defined and have no clear criteria by which they can be resolved. They inescapably present themselves for decision-making in the public domain because they can only be resolved by collective action. The depletion of the rain-forests or the fracturing of the ozone layer are problems which cannot be resolved, by individual action. Uncertainty, ambiguity and conflict are thus inescapably 'givens' for organisations in the public domain. Criteria can never be established objectively and different groups are likely to bring a variety of perspectives to the interpretation of issues and the decisions which they believe appropriate. Collective choice is typically the focus for challenge and debate. The responsibility of the public domain is to seek criteria (values), enable all the voices to be heard (discourse) and mediate their claims (politics).

Public Discourse

The ambiguities of the public domain can only be clarified, the controversies confronted, the differences given their due place and criteria, through public discourse. Members cannot 'exit' the public domain. The policies of the past decade have created the illusion that the public can realise choices and improve the quality of services by withdrawing from them. If some do, it can only be at the expense of others. The quality and the degree of collective choice available to all can only be determined by the public as a whole. This is why 'voice' – the articulation of perspectives, claims and grievances – is inescapably the means of realising choice and quality for all. Voice and *a right to voice* is a condition of the public domain. Citizenship provides the basis for voice in the arena of public discourse informing collective choice, with the potential to mould public services in their provision. The customer in the market mainly uses the exit option:

> some customers stop buying the firm's products or some members leave the organisation: this is the *exit option*. As a result, revenues drop, membership declines, and management is impelled to search for ways and means to correct whatever faults have led to exit. (Hirschman, 1970, p. 4)

The customer in the market cannot directly shape the choices available. The citizen who may be the direct consumer of the public services, but need not be, can use the voice option:

> The firm's customers or the organisation's members express their dissatisfaction directly to management or to some other authority to which management is subordinate or through general protest addressed to anyone who cares to listen: this is the *voice option*. As a result management once again engages in a search for the causes and possible cures of customers' and members' dissatisfaction. (Hirschman, ibid.)

Voice can be exercised in the market, but it is not its dominant mode. Voice is the dominant mode in the public domain and has the potential to shape the nature of the services available. That potential may not be realised – the point is that it exists. Citizenship can be an active process as opposed to consumerism which can be regarded 'as essentially a passive process. It presumes that at some "higher" level decisions or "pre-choices" are being made' (Morrison, 1988, p. 212). Offe has argued the potential of active citizenship for what would be otherwise mere consumers in the public domain:

> Citizens become the final and decisive executive organ of state policy wherever the existing tasks of politics and administration are such that they cannot be solved with the classical means of the threat of punishment or the distribution of goods, that is, through positive and negative sanctions. Instead, state policies require a task-specific mobilization of the 'base' and its willingness to co-operate. Examples which reveal this dependency-relationship of the administration include such problems as: the improvement of traffic safety; the expansion of a preventive system of health care; the responsiveness and standardization of the educational process; the transformation of local city traffic into mass transit; the enhancement of environmental protection; the preservation of monetary stability, and so on. In all of those areas of public administration, a 'politically supportive' role definition of vehicle drivers, patients, the elderly, pupils, students, transportation users, income recipients and consumers decides the success, costs, and timing of administrative policy, the individual measures and decisions of which must be 'sold' to the respective segments of the public. (Offe, 1985, p. 311)

Public pressure and protest, therefore, rather than being something to be regretted, as they often are, can actually provide an essential contribution to political discourse, illuminating new ways of looking at public issues and providing information for their understanding and resolution. But mechanisms should be provided that can transform pressure and protest into discussion.

It is only through open and comprehensive discourse that a plural society can reach the consent necessary to legitimate the polity. *Public discourse provides both the source for and the test of action in the public domain*: in public discourse voice is given expression in public arenas which are the settings to which government responds. The organising principle of public discourse leading to collective action requires ready access to arenas for those who have problems to raise, actions to contest, aspirations to express, issues to pursue and comments to make. The effectiveness of these arenas depends upon undistorted discourse which in turn requires the free flow of information in the public domain, so that choices may be tested by debate and discussion, and by pressure and protest should they be required.

Public discourse sets the conditions for collective choice: public discourse alone cannot determine collective choice where views differ and agreement cannot be reached in discussion. Then action in the public domain will be determined within public institutions or taken directly by the public in voting. Collective choice cannot necessarily represent the choice of each and every individual, but the basic organising principle requires that it be taken after full public discussion.

> Public discussion is an essential prelude to any discussion about public action. The purpose of a discussion open to all adults is to inform public decisions with the multiplicity of perspectives in the citizenry. Such discussion does not aim at, nor need it be characterised by an egalitarian airing of any and all viewpoints that might be brought to an issue. Rather it aims to find a perspective persuasive to all and thereby a decision for action (or inaction) deemed judicious by all. (Adams *et al.*, 1990, p. 229)

If the diverse interests are allowed their voice and given undistorted conditions, the integrity of the most effectively reasoned argument can prevail. Habermass' 'communicative rationality' – in which through unfettered dialogue actors can explore the integrity of their reasons and the basis for agreement on shared understanding – should be a basic condition of the public domain.

Consent through Accountability

In the final resort the authority or legitimacy of public choice rests upon consent. Consent is not given to each and every act, but is given to public organisations in their capacity to act. Where consent is continuously and generally denied the public domain is itself threatened, because the condition upon which legitimate collective action rests is weakened and eroded.

Consent to the exercise of authority rests upon the processes through which decisions are taken and the quality of public discourse. Consent may usually be given where the processes are accepted even though a particular decision may not be supported. Consent is tested and confirmed through public accountability. Organisations in the public domain are required to account for their actions in the public arena of discourse and there has to be a means by which they are held to account by the public on whose behalf they act. That is the ultimate test of consent.

One of the unique characteristics of the public domain is the scrutiny to which it is subjected. Public accountability can constitute the necessary conditions for the duality of publicness. It can help to institutionalise both an active citizenship and the processes of collective choice in government. This requires openness from public organisations, for without openness communication is distorted. If openness is the condition of undistorted discourse, organisations in the public domain should not merely accept openness, but should extend it as a condition of discourse. The enclosure that belongs to the private sector has no place in the public domain. It has to be realised that:

> the fishbowl environment presents both opportunities and problems for the public manager. (Perry and Kraemer, 1983, p. 18)

> Possibly the most difficult adjustment a businessman has to make is learning to live with a far more complex decision-making process, in which just about everyone wants to have his say, and which he can influence but not control. (Blumenthal, 1983, p. 29)

Openness is a condition which has to be fulfilled for public accountability and consent in the public domain. It presupposes extending the political process so as to develop participation and public discourse within the system of representative democracy. As participation develops so will the ties between discourse, decision, openness and public accountability.

Political Process and Collective Choice

In the realm of public discourse all can contend and urge their reasons. Such diversity makes political process an indispensable and defining institution of the public domain, enabling difficult decisions to be made amongst competing objectives. Politics thus organises the resolution of differences within society. It institutionalises the necessary processes of mediating conflicting interests and values in stages of discourse, argument and bargaining through to the forming of a judgement enacted in collective choice. The ambiguities and uncertainties of the political process are not to be regretted but seen as a necessary part of the search for criteria inherent in the predicament of choice and which are explored in the arena of public discourse.

Realising values. Not one but many values are sought in the public domain. There are no single objectives, but a multiplicity of objectives expressing differing values and supported by differing individuals and groups in the arena of public discourse. This means that decisions cannot be automatically derived from technical objectives or determined by singular values; values have to be balanced and interests reconciled. As one American businessman said, reflecting on experience in government: 'What impresses me about the government is the fact that the people there have to amalgamate a number of diverse points of view and that they actually succeed in doing so. This is really the essence of the difficulty of government: to take into account the problems that the air carriers face, the travelling public, the business community, the manufacturers and so on' (Weiss, 1983, p. 48).

Balancing interests. In the management of public service the interests of different customers have to be balanced along with those of others concerned with the service and of the community at large. Values can be sought as an expression of that wider interest:

> the resources of the public sector are finite and limited, and distributed as an act of political will. This creates an immediate dilemma for the pure application of consumer principles. On the one hand, the nature of public services suggest they are of the utmost importance to those consumers who want to use them; on the other hand the interest of individual consumers must constantly be juggled against the interest of the community as a whole, and of other groups who make up the community. (Potter, 1988, p. 151)

If a public service were to be provided solely to meet the wishes of those for whom it is provided, collective concerns that justify public provision may be neglected. In education, both the views of parents and of children are important, but those are not the only factors relevant to the determination of the curriculum. Rochefort and Boyer, writing on the use of opinion polls in health care, have called for

> a judicious sense of balance... what opinion polls provide is less a set of precise and pre-emptory directives than a general indicator of prominent social concerns, preferences and values not all of them in harmony or especially articulate. (Rochefort and Boyer, 1988, p. 157)

The decision to provide public services is an act of collective choice, which expresses values, interests and concerns beyond that of the individual consumer. It will express a search for the public interest.

Choice expressing multiple criteria.   There are no clear criteria to guide choice. Criteria are not given in the public domain as they are in the market. Organisations in the public domain have to arrive at authoritative collective choices in the absence of clear criteria.

> Multiple criteria of success are inherent in the government of any political or social unit, however small. For the multiple needs and diverse standards of expectation of people bring together in a place, interact with and limit each other in ways which cannot be ignored. Functional organisation can ignore problems which they set for each other; and when in doubt they can simplify their choices by referring to their function as defining their primary responsibility. But general organisations, even the smallest, have no built-in priorities to guide them in their multi-valued choices. They must decide not only what to do but what more exactly what to value most in the concrete situation of every decision. They must define and redefine the unacceptable, not in one dimension alone but in many. (Vickers, 1972, p. 134).

It is not sufficient to judge a public service by customer satisfaction alone. This is partly because there are other values and interests at stake than those of the immediate consumer. In addition, because the service may well be provided free of charge satisfaction cannot be deduced from continuing provision as it might be deduced from sales. Finally, certain criteria are particular to the public domain of which the most important is equity. Potter, building on previous work by Maxwell (1984) has argued that

> services should be: *appropriate* and *relevant* (to meet individual and community preferences, wishes and needs); *available* and *accessible* (to everyone, or to those groups/individuals given explicit priority); *equitable* (that is, fair in the treatment of individuals or groups of people in similar circumstances); *acceptable* in terms of the quality of services provided (this criterion incorporates a number of others, including whether services are approachable, convenient, pleasant to use, reliable, timely, prompt, responsive and humane); *economic* and *efficient* (from the viewpoint of service users, those who pay for services through rates and taxes, and to the community as a whole); and *effective* in turns of the benefits to users and the community. (Potter, 1988, p. 155)

Public services necessarily have to be judged by multiple criteria.

Collective choice rests on public consent.   Collective choice acquires authority the more it is grounded in public consent. That does not mean that each choice requires public consent but that the process rests upon a mode of working that has public consent. Public consent is expressed in elections, but that by itself is a limited consent. Consent depends upon the effectiveness of public discourse which requires that choice is tested in discussion and that the voice of many perspectives is heard and listened to.

Yet although the political process may conclude with a collective choice based upon and enabling public consent the process will not rest there. In the public domain the purposes and criteria that should guide both choice and action can never be finally resolved. They remain *essentially contested*. The criteria and the weight to be attached to them can always be challenged in the arena of public discourse. The market provides its own criteria of success, but in the public organisation the criteria must always be sought and once found can never be assumed to be final. It is a condition of the public domain that organisations within it are *criteria-seeking* rather than conditioned by predetermined criteria. The only final criterion is the public interest and this can always be redefined in public discourse.

Political Process as the Condition for Public Management

Political processes provide the vehicle for reconciling the dilemmas of the public domain and are constitutive conditions of its management. This means that management should not merely recognise political reality but should support and express political processes. The mistake is often made of regarding the nature of management and of politics as opposed. Management can, however, be developed to support the building of consensus through the political process and yet to recognise the necessary conflict within that process. The mistake is to assume that management in the public domain can have any meaning apart from political processes since they constitute the basis for action in the public domain. There is a tendency for officials to say:

- 'That is mere electioneering'
- 'Public protest stands in the way of effective action'
- 'Fortunately in health authorities we are protected from the political process'
- 'The politicians are at it again, working out a deal, without regard to all the work we have done'
- 'The charade of party politics has nothing to do with the real problems'

Such remarks reflect a concept of the officer's role opposed to the reality of the public domain and more seriously to its constitutive conditions. They reflect a stance which represents not merely an unreal dream that politics will disappear, but a failure to understand the rationale of action in the public domain. Public pressure and protest are part of public discourse. Bargaining is part of the balancing of interests which provide a basis for collective choice. The regard that politicians have for their electoral interest expresses the necessity of generating public consent. These aspects of the political process are not to be regretted, but seen as supporting the organising principles that govern the public domain. Management should be grounded in those conditions, strengthening them and working with them, rather than against them.

Not every expression of the political process has to be accepted uncritically as the only possible basis of action in the public domain. The reform of the political process can and should be discussed, and we contribute to the discussion of institutional change in Chapter 5, but such discussion should be based on an understanding of the organising principles.

The argument that management must support and express the political process can be seen most clearly in central government and in local authorities. To many organisations in the public domain, however, the political process may seem at one remove. Some see that as being the purpose of creating Next Steps agencies. Health authorities, the Arts Council and the Housing Corporation are all organisations subject to control by appointed boards rather than by elected politicians and can too easily see themselves as protected from the political process. The frameworks within which these bodies function are, however, governed by the organising principles and are subject to the conditions of the public domain. They are and should be the subject of public discourse. Constituted by a political process, these organisations are subject to judgement in that process. Their work should be informed by that process since their role, pattern of working and activities depend on public consent. If, in their management, the necessities of discourse, the source of their authority and the condition of consent are ignored, then they are managed without regard to the purposes and conditions of the public domain and that is ineffective management, since it is management unrelated to the nature of the organisation being managed.

This does not mean that the impact of the political process on management in such organisations is and should be the same as in central government or in local authorities which are directly under political control. Management has to take account of the differences between organisations within the public domain, but the absence of direct political control in an organisation does not remove the relevance of the political process to management or mean that their constitution by the organising principles can be ignored.

Exploring the Tensions

Management should support and express the political process. That is not easily achieved. There are tensions that have to be faced, but they are not tensions that derive from an opposition between management and the political process, but tensions that are inherent in the public domain.

There is a tension in the duality between the requirements of discourse and the necessities of collective choice. Argument, debate, pressure and protest can be seen as delay in achieving necessary action. That should not be regarded as a tension between the political process and management, for that would be to assume that the political process was not directed at action and that management action had its own justification. The political process provides the basis for collective choice as authoritative decision-making leading to action. Management is concerned not with action for its own sake, but with achieving the purposes of the organisation which in the public domain are determined by political processes. The tensions are not between political processes and management, but within the public domain. They are the tensions between discourse and choice and between choice and consent.

The perceived tension between the political process and management is often assumed to be equivalent to the actual tension in relations between politicians and officials in central government and in local authorities reflected in the quotations earlier in this chapter. In this relationship two worlds meet: the lay person and the expert; the temporary politician faces the permanent official. In the relationship different cultures, backgrounds and ways of working meet. Inevitably there are difficulties. Difficulties in a relationship are, however, not the same as necessary opposition and if one does not assume necessary opposition then ways can be sought to overcome difficulties.

Those ways will not be found, if it is assumed, as is too often done, that politicians have no role in relation to management and that officials have no role in relation to the political process. Such an assumption reflects what Metcalfe and Richards have described as an 'impoverished concept' based on 'inadequate conceptualisation of management' (Metcalfe and Richards, 1987, p. 17) whose main elements in the Civil Service were as follows:

Management is an executive function, i.e. it presupposes the clear definition of objectives, policies and, if possible, corresponding performance measures

– Management is an intra-organisation process, i.e. it is what goes on within organisations: it is concerned with how work is done within organisations, with internal routines and procedures

– Management control is hierarchical: co-ordination and control are achieved through well defined hierarchies of responsibility and authority. Ideally these are structured into distinct cost or responsibility centres

– There are broad principles of management which apply with only minor adaptation to all organisations. Many of these principles are already known from private business practice. (ibid.)

To argue that these constitute an impoverished concept of management is not to argue that these elements are wrong but rather that they do not comprehend the full nature of management: 'they limit the role of public managers to the programmed implementation of pre-determined policies. They disregard the problems of adapting policies and organisations to environmental change' (ibid.)

Heymann has argued that management and the political processes are necessarily interdependent:

The manager who is prepared to seek new directions for her organisation and new meanings for government activity in the area of concern, who envisages her task as creating form out of, rather than simply accepting, and negotiating with, the powers and constraints surrounding her and her organisation is inevitably the agent of democratic forces. Forbidden to appeal directly to voters by Federal Law she can do no more than offer that opportunity to elected officials, showing them what constituencies may want and broader publics may come to believe. The manager can bring energy and insight to a political process that is stagnant or confused. But in doing so the manager is no more, at best, than a partner of elected powers and a servant of those who choose them. In the end, legitimacy belongs entirely to elected officials; far sighted yet realistic vision, often to those charged with managing the ongoing activities of government. Bringing these attributes together ... hope of representative democracy, is the responsibility of both. (Heymann, 1987, p. 189)

Some of the difficulties of the relationship between politicians and officials are echoed in the relationship between members of appointed boards and officials. These difficulties may give rise to less tension because lay appointed members of a board lack the legitimacy of the elected member and can therefore have difficulty in establishing a role. The inherent tension is then resolved by the domination of the officials.

> By comparison with company boards and local councillors, health authorities appear to be in an even weaker position to set objectives and monitor them. For all the restrictions on them, Council members in the majority party have policies which are open to some monitoring and which give a clear direction to policy. But health authority members are appointed, not elected. They come and go, often with no clear idea of their precise role and usually receive little advice or education on what they are supposed to do. Rather, in the classic style of the British amateur, many of them are expected to pick things up as they go along. Indeed, even authority members who have a detailed knowledge of the service often find the role of a member to be a frustrating one. It is almost impossible for them to get direct access to all the information they might need on an issue of direct interest. Instead they are always in the hands of their officers who can reveal more or less of a story according to their own objectives. (West, 1988, p. 112)

The relative weakness of the appointed member may be increased rather than lessened by the new constitution of district health authorities where they sit alongside officers of the authority who are themselves full members of the board.

The danger is that the weakness of the appointed member of the health authority and their lack of a relationship to the political process will encourage the belief that health authorities can divorce themselves from the political process, except in so far as they are subject to accountability through hierarchical control to the Secretary of State. In the same way Next Steps agencies can come to see their relationship to the political process as restricted to the terms of the framework agreement.

The Meanings for Management within the Political Process

If management is to support and express the political process, then the language of management and the conceptual framework from which it is derived must gain meaning from the political process. Management has to find:

- a language of search
- a language of interests
- a language of difference
- a language of balancing
- a language of the vote.

Management in its language can easily assume a commonality of purpose that belies the differing interests of those within the public domain. The public interest can be sought. It cannot be assumed it has been finally found. The political process is concerned with who gains and who loses. Yet management may assume in its language a unity of purpose that ignores that reality. The political process looks outward to an environment of differing interests both conflicting and cooperating, which can too easily go unrecognised in a closed statement of objectives that assumes rather than seeks consensus through debate and discussion or bargaining and negotiation.

In the political process opposing views are expressed, different interests advocated and different values sought:

> Perhaps the foremost obstacle to public sector OD [Organisational Development] ... is the probable incompatibility of the ideal organisation underlying most OD efforts. Political systems seem distributive in thrust ... For example, they often fixate on win – lose games, as in distributing a finite amount of resources among competing groups. (Golembiewski, 1985, p. 31)

> OD ideology stresses the *integrative* character of the ideal type of organisation, in contrast, which is more consistent with prevailing attitudes about well-functioning organisations in the private sector. (ibid.)

The meanings of management in the public domain must not assume integration, where the starting point is difference. Differences are brought into the organisation through political processes, as a visit to Parliament or any council meeting shows. Differences are resolved at least in part through processes of discussion and debate in which shared values can be found and in which a balance can be sought between differing interests. That balance may reflect existing power structures, but no interest can ever be totally excluded from the arena of public discourse in a democratic regime.

The language of objectives misconstrues the political process if it suggests that objectives are separate and absolute, rather than interrelated and balanced. Management can then assume the simplicity of separate objectives, hiding the potential conflict between them. Policies for economic development in a local authority do not necessarily fit with policies for conservation, yet both may be objectives set by the authority. In practice balance has to be sought. A language of management has to be found that encompasses balancing.

Yet decisions have to be made and decisions cannot always be reached in discussion or in negotiation, but are made through the vote. The vote legitimates as well as authorises. Voting may be used in many organisations, but it is not the basic norm of behaviour on which action rests. Although votes in councils or in Parliament may appear to be a time-demanding ritual, they are the expression of legitimate authority. The votes at elections on which both Parliament and councils rest provide the basis of that legitimate authority. Discourse may narrow differences or highlight them. Agreement cannot, however, be assumed. The vote is the language of decision-making in disagreement.

The language of management should not permit an escape from the political process but should draw meaning from that process.

The Necessities of Understanding

If management in the public domain gains its defining purpose from the political process, then understanding of that process is a requirement for management. Understanding requires more than knowledge, although knowledge is necessary to understanding, for, in ignorance, misjudgements are made. Understanding must also encompass the organising principle sustained by the political processes. Understanding is necessary to realise the full potential of the contribution of politics.

> This means that the civil servant in addition to her professional training also has to have political skill in order to know when the politician can aim at a 'real' good and when he has to select agenda management as his goal. It is up to the politically skilled civil servant to make intelligent judgments and thereby at the stage when relevant options are identified and compared,

perform the clever trick of combining rationality and accommodation. (Gustaffson and Richardson, n.d. p. 57)

In each sector of the public domain failures in understanding
and attitude can limit the capacity of management. In health
authorities as in other organisations with appointed bodies,
politics can be seen as irrelevant. It will be accepted that health
authorities are subject to ministerial direction, but the political
nature of their task will not be so readily understood. Perrin
argued that unit general managers should be part of the district
management team, leading to 'a lively and constructive interaction with the health authority' in which:

it should more easily be brought home to them that they are in
post to run a complex service with multiple objectives and a
local community to serve and satisfy. Otherwise there is a risk
that unit general managers may become too focussed on
satisfying just the interests and priorities of the staff of their
own units, and too reliant on narrow performance criteria
relating to cost reduction or on avoiding conflict with internal
pressure groups such as clinicians. (Perrin, 1988, p. 61)

That danger has been increased rather than lessened by the
reorganisation of the health services since unit general managers
will focus on achieving the contractual arrangements with the
district health authority.

In local authorities there can be a reluctance amongst some
senior officers to accept the rationale of political control or to
realise that pressure and protest not merely impact on but are
necessary to local government. The dominant professional
culture implicitly if not explicitly denies political processes.
Underlying that culture is the belief that decisions should be
based on expertise rather than that decisions in the public
domain are based on public consent expressed through political
processes, which can be informed by and achieved through
expertise, but should not be determined by it. It has been argued
in relation to the civil service that the:

British political system has increasingly come to require its
senior officials – those supposed political eunuchs of the state –
to exercise an acute political awareness ... Officials must be

expected to read in advance the mind of their political master and be aware of all the complexities of the parliamentary and political pressures bearing upon him. Yet these very same officials may in the space of twenty-four hours after a general election be expected to service with equal loyalty and dedication their former chief's political enemies. Political nous is, therefore, an important element of the make-up of a successful mandarin. (Greenway, 1988, p. 21)

In central government, however, the dominance of the ministerial model can exclude understanding of the political processes beyond Parliament. Limited experience limits understanding. Even civil servants who advise ministers on school closures will probably never have been to a protest meeting about such a closure unless it be for their own children. They have not had to face the immediacy of protest as an education officer has to do at meeting after meeting.

The necessities of understanding the political process in all public organisations can best be met by widening training and experience. In the civil service it is normal for those likely to hold senior office to serve for a period in a minister's private office. In local authorities management development lays increasing stress on political awareness and understanding. Career experience that crosses more than one type of organisation can deepen understanding of the political process. Listening to and learning from political protest can be part of management development for all who work in the public domain, whether in that work they experience it directly or indirectly. But in the end understanding must encompass the rationale of the political process in the public domain: 'Career officials ... should concern themselves far more strongly with the nature of public administration as profession and with questions about the proper role of government. Without thinking and talking much more about the rationale of what they are doing they will never do it better' (Self, 1987, p. 44).

The Requirements of Management in the Public Domain

Management in the public domain depends upon the organising principle of public discourse leading to collective choice based on public consent. That organising principle depends upon the effectiveness of political processes in their impact on organisations in the public domain. On this basis directions can be set for management, both strengthening the arena of public discourse and enhancing collective choice.

Strengthening Access to the Arena of Public Discourse

Management should seek to strengthen both access to the arena of public discourse and the discourse within it. Public discourse has many settings. It is structured into the workings of Parliament and of local councils, in which voice can be given to public concerns and from which the public can learn of decisions made and arguments put forward. The meetings of appointed bodies are not structured for public discourse, so have to find other ways by which public discourse can be enhanced. In neither type of organisation is public discourse limited to the requirements of the institutional setting. The media leads to discourse, as do the activities of pressure and protest groups. Individuals can raise demands or press complaints; public discourse requires voices that speak directly and are heard in the public domain. Management should enhance the arena of public discourse so that voices often unheard can be heard clearly. For the arena of public discourse can be more than the arena in which issues are tested. It should be the arena in which ideas and initiatives can be given expression and citizenship realised. The arena is the setting for pressure and protest but also for the active involvement of citizens in forming policy.

Pressure and protest require a management response both in informing the arena of public discourse and in judging what is said and what is left unsaid. Management requires interpretative skills that can read pressure and protest and a readiness to test that reading in discourse.

Management has to find processes through which pressure and protest can be listened to, understood and responded to. Management education and training rarely deals with the management of protest, preparing those who have to attend a public meeting both to respond, and most difficult of all, to listen, while remembering that there are voices that will remain unheard.

Public discourse for active citizenship involves more than the handling of pressure and protest. It implies the seeking of discussion and, where appropriate, decision through public participation. Communication has to extend beyond organisational boundaries if the arena of public discourse is to be developed. Effective public discourse requires access to the information, opinions and arguments that lie within organisations, because discourse must be informed if it is itself to inform. This implies an organisational openness for which there are few examples outside the public domain and indeed too few inside it. It means that organisational discourse should as far as possible become public discourse.

Thus while the Local Government (Access to Information) Act 1984 opens up the local authority in form, it may not open it up in reality. Certain doors are opened, but to give the public rights to information is very far from opening up organisational discourse subject only to respect for privacy. Central government does not even go that far and institutional changes replacing elected bodies by appointed ones may restrict access rather than enhance it. The publication of specified pieces of information as performance indicators is no substitute for the opening up of organisational discourse to and for the public. The development of public discourse for active citizenship requires a review of structures and procedures which have built barriers where there should be discourse.

Judging the Balance

Collective choice does not necessarily flow directly from discourse. In discourse issues will be raised that cannot be resolved and interests expressed which cannot be reconciled. Collective choice can then involve judging the balance between different interests and different values. Costs may have to be balanced against benefits, gainers against losers or short-term against longer-term considerations.

Political processes reflect the requirements of judging the balance in collective choice; they involve persuasion, bargaining and negotiation between different interests. Majone points out that models of policy-making that emphasise conflict of interests neglect the reality that conflict leads to persuasion. If policy-making is grounded in conflict it still uses argument. Reasons are put forward, ideas defended. Democratic theory 'emphasizes something [other] theories have neglected – the extraordinary power of persuasion and the centrality of two-way discussion to democracy' (Majone, 1989, p. 2). In the end political processes lead to a political judgement on the balance to be struck.

Management processes should support those political processes. Judgement can be informed by management if the processes by which it is arrived at are appreciated. The danger is that those processes will not be helped by management based on an oversimplified private sector model. Thus attempts can be made to set political processes within a framework of objectives to which decisions can be related. That is to treat the objectives as reflecting absolute values to be pursued directly as it is to assume that particular activities relate only to particular objectives. If these assumptions were correct, calculation would replace political judgement and data collection would replace discourse.

In the budgets of local authorities or in the public expenditure decisions of central government, objectives are balanced. Even if a priority is given, let us say, to law and order and health, it does not mean that expenditure on other objectives will be stopped, but that the balance of expenditure will be changed – possibly marginally – in favour of expenditure on those objectives. Budgeting, if it is about objectives, is about their relative, not their absolute, importance. This is clearly the case in local government and central government which are constituted as multi-purpose institutions, but it is also the case in what are apparently single-purpose institutions, such as district health authorities, who have to weigh expenditure on the acute sector against the care of the mentally ill.

Nor can it be assumed that activities relate to single objectives. Activities may meet one objective but create problems for another objective. In decisions on a motorway line, different objectives have to be balanced. The line which best meets transportation needs may create environmental problems and use good agricultural land. Different objectives and different interests have to be balanced, and while cost – benefit analyses may appear to reduce decision to calculation, in the end a political judgement has to be made – often in the heat of pressure and protest.

If management is to assist that political judgement as an expression of collective choice it must work with the grain of the political process rather than against it. The political process has its own rationality which reflects the requirements of balance in political judgement. Ambiguities in statements of objectives reflect the political danger of treating objectives as absolute. Discussing policy through individual cases can be testing out where balance lies. Processes of bargaining and negotiation aid conflict resolution. Delay may be a means of retaining flexibility. It is too easy to wish away the political process, but to do so is to neglect the political judgement that is involved in collective choice.

The challenge for public management will be to support the development of a more elaborate political process of participative and representative democracy that can enable the political judgement required for the learning society. This will require institutional renewal of the public domain.

Summary

The rationale of action in the public domain rests upon the organising principle of public discourse leading to collective choice based on public consent. The organising principle is expressed through political processes. Management in the public domain should therefore be structured to support those political processes, informing discourse, realising consent and enabling collective choice.

The perceived tension between political processes and management processes can be resolved by a perspective on management grounded in understanding of the conditions of the public domain. To realise that perspective, management has to find a language of interests, difference and balancing to encompass the political process and to enable public discourse. Collective choice involves political judgement which management can constrain if they do not work with the grain of political processes.

There remains a dilemma in the tension between public discourse and forms of collective choice that seek to restrict it, and in doing so destroy the basis on which that choice must rest in a strengthened public domain for the learning society. That dilemma can only be resolved if it is accepted that collective choice based on consent depends upon undistorted public discourse.

5

Renewing Democracy

Institutional Conditions

If the purposes of the learning society are to be realised then the
institutional order of the public domain will need to be reconstituted to support the purposes of active citizenship and the
government of public choice, enabling members of a society to
deliberate together, serve public needs equitably, and take responsibility with others. Institutions are constituted to create and
sustain the values and purposes of society. We distinguish between
the *necessary characteristics* of any institution, those which define
the nature of institutions as such, and the *constitutive conditions* of
a particular institutional order, those which provide the necessary
requirements to sustain the development of its defining purposes.

Institutions are the way a society seeks to order those spheres of
living that are potentially, for individuals as well as the community,
the most volatile, emotive, turbulent and painful: for example, the
pursuit of power, the ownership of property and wealth, the expression of religious beliefs, the satisfaction of sexuality, the shaping of
life chances through education. Thus the spheres through which
people, separately and together, define their identity and place are
those in which a society will wish to institutionalise its cardinal
values. Institutions strive for order by providing *frameworks of rules
and procedures* that establish what is expected but also the sanctions
which define the boundaries to acceptable action. Institutions typically seek to internalise in their members, through *routines and
rituals*, appropriate beliefs and behaviour: for example, the sacra-
ments for the congregation, the rituals of election, the school

111

assembly. The routines of institutions, as Durkheim (1964) grasped, encourage members to understand their necessary cohesion, one to another, while internalising those values and beliefs which express their 'conscience collective'. Thus institutions are most effective when their *formal structures, statuses and authority* remain implicit because their beliefs have become widely shared over time.

The power of institutions, therefore, resides less in their ability to regulate and more in their capacity to generate and recreate the '*provinces of meaning*' which interpret and make sense of their worlds. Gouldner's 'domain assumptions' or Goffman's 'frames' shape the orientation of an institution's members, establishing what is known, how it is to be interpreted and valued. It is the shared background of mutual understanding that constitutes 'the agreement between members that enables the orderly production of roles and rules' (Brown, 1978). Institutions lie at the centre of any society's creation of a moral and political order constituting its values and purposes.

This significance of institutions is being rediscovered, as March and Olsen (1989) argue, because they make a connection between the organising of practices in society and the deeper moral and political ideas which inform them. The context of change is causing a resurgence of concern for institutions and their capacity to embody moral ideas.

> our efforts proceed from a more general concern with interpreting political institutions as fundamental features of politics and with understanding the ways in which they contribute to stability and change in political life ...
>
> Political institutions define the framework within which politics takes place. (March and Olsen, 1989, pp. 16, 18)

The regeneration of society, we argue, requires the recreation of an institutional order that is appropriate to the constituted purposes of the public domain. Such a framework will provide the conditions for citizenship in the learning society.

The public domain is that institutional sphere which seeks to strengthen the processes of creating cohesion within diversity by emphasising the value of activities undertaken in common. In times of stability such activities might involve the provision of goods and services to those in need. In times of political change and challenge the 'activity' facing the public domain will be not merely to provide goods but to create the very language and provinces of meaning which establish what is held in common and what is not, to enable agreement about those common purposes and rules which are the precondition for the community to exist as a community at all.

The public domain provides the condition for those goods that are necessary to support the individual as much as the welfare of all. Liberty and justice are goods which depend upon civic virtues expressed in institutional arrangements. The central value which the public domain accords to citizenship derives from a realisation that if the quality of personal life and its unfolding depend upon the vitality of the public domain, then our society can only renew itself by encouraging its members to revive their practice of contributing to public life. Only when citizens take part in the life of the whole can they develop understanding of the needs of the whole, which are at the same time the condition for sustaining their own rights and identities. Citizens thus need to recover the civic virtues of service to others and of public discourse.

Virtues require the renewing or recreation of institutions necessary to sustain a public domain, the meaning and practices of which have atrophied over time. The public domain has become a diminished and hollowed shell bereft of the processes and practices that provide it with meaning and purpose. The challenge for the time is to regenerate an institutional order to renew and reconstitute the public domain in the conditions of the present. Only through such an order can a learning society develop.

Constitutive System: Democracy and Government

The distinctive challenge facing institutional reform of the public domain is the daunting task of supporting and enabling the necessary duality of publicness: enabling citizens to express their contributions to the common life of the community and out of that plurality to enable a process of government and collective choice to emerge in the general interest. The organising principles of the public domain need to be drawn together to constitute a system of participatory democracy for discourse to support and reinforce the processes of representative government for collective choice.

Participation and Representation

The constitutive conditions for active citizenship and public choice in government are a necessary balance in the institutions of participatory and representative government. The public constitutes Parliament and the council of a local authority by electing representatives who will act in the polity on their behalf. These representatives are held to account by the public at each election. The active political role of members of the public is constituted as a periodic citizenship and so is the formal accountability to the public through the electoral process. The rationale of representative government is grounded, first, in practicability: it is not feasible to involve all citizens in decision-making all of the time. A process of organised representation of the public views is arguably the only means of taking collective decisions in a large society. Second, it is based on decision-making and action: representation ensures that collective decisions are actually taken. Third, it enables clarity of accountability: representation ensures, in the last resort, clear responsibility and answerability for actions on behalf of the public.

The issue has to be raised as to whether representative democracy alone is an adequate basis for our society. It allows the views of the electorate to be expressed only occasionally and in the most general terms. The election and direct involvement of a small number of representatives does not give an adequate opportunity for the participation and expression of public views which can strengthen democracy during a period of social change. If citizenship is to be taken seriously then more appropriate constitutive conditions will have to be developed to ensure it can be achieved. As Bogdanor (1986) has argued, government can be made more visible and exciting: 'This can be done by giving the electorate a more direct influence upon the policies adopted in the locality. Consideration should therefore be given to reviving those institutions of direct democracy which provide for greater popular participation' (p. 33).

A number of institutional developments are considered below.

Extending the consultative process.   It is necessary for government to reach out to its public and enable citizens to make their opinions and needs known. Too often consultations by government preclude discourse. Government seeks views for itself, not in interaction.

New forms of consultation are required to enable discussion between those concerned with proposals: even opponents may find resolution in discussion. More imaginative strategies need to be devised to ensure that the disadvantaged and less powerful are provided with an opportunity to have their views considered, by using new public inquiry techniques, workshops and seminars or local opinion polls, that seek out views and voices often unheard.

Encompassing public protest, pressure and discussion. An active politics of community strengthens government. The voices of pressure and protest are part of the discourse by which government learns. Hearing, listening and responding to the perspectives of the public are critical to the government of the learning society. Leaflets, petitions, marches or delegations can enable the public to express a view – the problem is to ensure it is taken into account. If it is taken into account then pressure and protest can lead into discussion and the possibility of resolution.

Active participation in the polity. Citizenship involves more than a process of being consulted or even protesting. It seeks, as Pateman has argued, an active participation in decision-making and taking responsibilities within the government of the community. Real involvement in the public domain requires a capacity to engage in and influence the emerging political discourse and our emphasis is on discourse as participation. But participation can be extended to accountable control of the implementation of decisions, as well as the delivery of services reducing thereby the burden on representative democracy. Strategies to develop such public participation, which will inevitably be focused at local level where access is within the scope of the many, could include: coopting community representatives on to the committees of public bodies; 'user control' which enables users – such as a tenants' association – to control the delivery of a service; and the constituting of community councils to enable direct participatory democracy to operate.

We argue that if citizenship is to be established in the public domain then the institutions of participatory democracy must be strengthened. Yet a balance has to be maintained if the duality of publicness is to be protected. This requires constitutive conditions which integrate the strengths of both representation and participation. The latter enables the plurality of interests to be voiced and discussed. The former enables the possibility of public choice and action in the public interest to be achieved. Representation and participation need not be seen as opposed in the institutions of the learning society. The quality of representation grows with the quality of participation, ensuring as it does that representation is informed by an active citizenry.

Subsidiarity and Partnership

Any reformed institutional order of government for the learning society needs to recover and further develop democracy through the progressive decentralisation of decision-making. The principle of subsidiarity is that responsibilities for action should be placed as close as possible to the citizen. The accelerating centralisation of power within the neo-liberal state has stifled the active public it has, purportedly, sought to empower because it denied the public any role except that of customer and national voter. When powers are distributed and devolved to levels which are appropriate to discourse on the assigned responsibilities, then the agreed tasks are likely to be accomplished more effectively.

Realising the values and purposes of the public domain will require a more complex institutional order than has existed hitherto. Neither the 'duo-polis' (central and local government) of the social democratic state nor the monopolising unitary state of neo-liberalism can alone provide the conditions for active citizenship in the public domain. The commitment to centralised regulation from Whitehall erodes space locally for democratic participation, while even the earlier commitment to local government as an instrument for service delivery was not designed to involve the public. A reformed polity needs to develop interdependent democratic forums at three levels: a national parliament, the local council, and forums within the community. Only a further extension of democratic organisation can institutionalise the active participation of citizenship.

The principle of subsidiarity would reserve for higher levels of authority, including Europe, only those functions which cannot be performed more effectively at a more immediate or local level and a primary test of effectiveness should be openness to discourse. The burden of power distribution towards decentralisation then requires an emphasis on partnership and mutual answerability.

The centralisation of the recent legislation should give way to the understanding once more that public services need to acknowledge plural centres of power – European, national, local, and the communal – that must collaborate in learning and in action. The new partnerships are based on a presumption of cooperation that derives from a common mode of working in shared membership of the public domain. The necessity of cooperation rests upon the recognition that learning at any level is limited by distance or scope. A learning society requires many levels.

Enabling Government

Organisations in the public domain are constituted to take collective choices based upon the consent of the public. Traditionally the emphasis has been upon the due processes which surround the exercise of public authority. Laws are enacted by the exercise of authority and provide authority. Both in their enactment and their enforcement specified processes have to be observed so as to ensure this legitimate exercise of authority.

If the public domain is now to espouse and enable a new 'province of meaning' – of active citizenship rather than control of passive citizens – then the role of the public domain will need to be strengthened by giving greater recognition to the distinctive roles of government. Government in its many levels and in its many forms has differing roles in society. They can be conceptualised as:

- a sustaining role
- a maintenance role
- a responsive role
- a developmental role

The sustaining role. Government sustains the framework of law and order within which society exists and develops. Parliament legislates, legitimating social institutions whether of property, family or companies, prohibiting and sanctioning actions. The framework of law and order is maintained by the police and through inspectorates and other regulatory agencies. In the sustaining role, government resolves or provides the means to resolve disputes between individuals and/or organisations within the framework of civil law.

The local authority seeks to impose a framework of 'planning order' upon the physical development of its area. The local authority, or the Secretary of State upon appeal, uses development control powers to determine conflicts of interest, as when local residents resist commercial or industrial development. In the sustaining role, a concept of order is maintained by government and sustained through actions and decisions by many different organisations.

The maintenance role. Government has a maintenance role in society. Present-day society depends upon that role, since the activities of government are written into its functioning. A physical and social infrastructure built by organisations in the public domain underlies social action. A network of highways is provided and maintained. Water and sewers are provided in the public domain, even where the organisations involved are private organisations, for they are required to meet specified public standards. The health of society is sought by government. The social fabric is built through public processes of education and depends upon a network of social provision. Government acts upon the economy even when the instruments used are limited in their range. On each of those issues there can be and is argument about the extent and nature of government action required for the maintenance role. It is, however, argument about the extent and nature of the maintenance role, not about the need for it, for civil society cannot be envisaged without the maintenance role of government.

The sustaining and maintenance roles express societal continuity. They are not directed at change in the pattern of society, but at ordering and maintaining the present pattern. The responsive and developmental roles are, however, concerned with change and therefore critical to the development of a learning society. Ordering and sustaining represent the static public domain while the responsive and developmental roles represent the dynamic public domain. The distinction is not necessarily between activities, because the same activity can be used in different roles; town and country planning can and does play each role. The distinction is about the purposes at which the activity is directed.

Although both the responsive and the developmental roles are concerned with change in society, there is a basic distinction between the two roles. The responsive role follows upon societal change. The developmental role seeks societal change: it moulds change, rather than reacting to it.

The responsive role.   This can be seen as a natural development of the ordering and maintenance role. In order to fulfil those roles in a changing society, government has itself to respond to change. Ordering and maintenance cannot remain unchanged in a changing society. If changing technology builds demands for new knowledge and skills, then the process of education itself has to change to provide that knowledge and skills, as it can also change to use the educational opportunities created by that technology. As AIDS emerges as a threat within society, then both health and social services have to respond. As new environmental hazards grow, then demands grow for a response from government. When old industries decline, then government can intervene to protect them or to assist in dealing with the problems created. An activity may be structured to provide for automatic adjustment. As unemployment grows, so does the amount paid in benefit – but that in turn may lead to other changes because of its impact on budgetary provision. In the responsive role, government is not concerned to bring about change but to react to it.

The responsive role is linked to the sustaining and maintenance roles. The recognised responsibilities of government are already wide. What is required by most changes in society is not a change in those responsibilities but in the way they are carried out. As Hogwood and Peters have pointed out: 'In reality, "new" policies are rarely written on a *tabula rasa*, but rather on a well-occupied or even crowded tablet of existing laws, organizations and clients. Thus most policy-making is actually policy succession: the replacement of an existing, policy, program or organization by another' (Hogwood and Peters, 1983, p. 1), because the activities of government are pervasive in society. What is then required to meet changes is not new activities by government, but modification and change in existing activities. The 'dynamics of the evolution of government policy will require that governments devote an increasing proportion of their time and energy to concerns arising from existing policies' (ibid., p. 2). Much of that concern, although not necessarily all, will be in the responsive role, adjusting existing policies to meet societal change.

The developmental role.   Government has a developmental role as well as a responsive role. In the public domain values are pursued and collective choices are made. These values can require and those choices can be directed at change in society. The developmental role of government expresses the purposes and values of the public domain. If equity is sought through collective action and injustice is recognised in society, then more than a responsive role is required from government.

Government can itself be the means of achieving change in society. Physical well-being, social health, a positive environment and economic strength may be sought by collective action beyond the scope of any previous action. The existing form of the economy, the environmental condition or stresses in society do not have to be accepted. In the developmental role government gives expression to aspiration for a different society: it builds therefore on the involvement of an active citizenry. This may be sought through change in existing policies or in new policies extending the activities of government.

In practice the responsive role cannot always be clearly separated from the developmental. Change in society suggests the need for a response from government, but in that response government may adopt a developmental role. The emerging of new environmental hazards may lead to a redrafting of existing governmental regulations to restore previous environmental standards, but could lead to a fundamental change in the role of government in relation to the environment. The responsive role is about changing the means of achieving collective choice. The developmental role is about making collective choices. The issue for responsive change is what to do to achieve established purposes, but the issue for developmental change is what those purposes should be.

In many activities choices are involved on the balance between continuity and change and between responding and development. Those choices are decisions on the scope for societal development and gain importance in a learning society. But what is clearly required for societal development is that organisations in the public domain have the capacity for all four roles, and that the capacity for change in the responsive and development roles is strong, for in them the learning society is given expression.

Empowering the Citizen

If the purposes of the learning society are to be realised a programme of institutional reform will be needed to transform the public domain. Only the reality of institutions can achieve the challenge of diffusing power and responsibility enabling citizens to participate in the polity, to express their opinions, influence policy-making and contribute actively to the development of the communities in which they live. The challenge is to empower citizens to participate actively within the government of the community. This may form a broadly shared agenda, yet there are differences about the institutional forms required.

From the early 1980s there has been a belief that the public can be empowered as consumers sustained by the institution of the market. The realisation has grown over time that the market frustrates rather than enables the choices of most consumers because they lack the resources to impose their choices in competition with others. The market, however, contains a more fundamental flaw in that its very organising principle, 'exit', denies the possibility of different groups 'voicing' their interests in a process designed to enable resolution of difference. The market denies the principles that are central to the public domain as we have articulated them. A different institutional frame is needed in which groups are enabled to express their purposes, so as to develop a shared understanding for the learning society. The forum rather than the market is the institutional form upon which the new public domain will need to build to support the participation of citizens in the government of their community.

We seek to illustrate the kind of institutional developments designed to create forums, which enable the plurality of groups and interests in the community to participate as citizens in order to reach agreement about policy and action. The forums range from those with a particular purpose to those with a general responsibility. We draw upon experience in a number of countries to show a wide range of public involvement. This will lead, in the final section, to a discussion of the conditions for strengthening the processes of community governance for the learning society.

Issue Forums

The citizen's rights to know, to be informed, to be listened to and to be involved need to be given institutional expression. The reformed public domain requires settings in which the citizen can be actively involved in the decision process. User control can be developed in the running of public institutions, from leisure centres to health centres. The jury principle is an example of active involvement which can be used to examine issues in the public domain. Panels of citizens can be constituted as sounding-boards to bring together a balanced cross-section of citizens. Public inquiries and consultations could become settings for discussion.

Citizen panels.   These could become a valuable forum to enable a diverse range of views within the community, especially those from different ethnic minority groups, to be expressed and taken into account in decision-making. In Holland, a local authority has formed a panel of citizens, balanced to represent the composition of the population, which meets monthly to discuss the work of the authority. Its composition changes over time, with a tenth retiring each month. There have been developments in America and Canada in new forms of consultation that seek to find 'consensual approaches to resolving public disputes' (Susskind and Cruikshank, 1987) by bringing together the parties involved for discussion with or without facilitators.

Inquiries can be widened to extend public disourse. 'An example of democratic interaction' is the process followed by the Bergen Inquiry in Canada which evaluated the proposed natural gas pipeline from Prudhoe Bay through the Mackenzie Valley. All parties to the inquiry were required to submit a list of all pertinent documents in their possession and to share this information on request. Funding was provided to native groups, environmental groups, municipalities and small businesses to improve their ability to participate on an equal footing with the company laying the pipelines. Community hearings were held throughout the affected area in which all participants could speak their own languages. As a result of the process a range of views was heard that broadened the usual definition of costs and benefits (Adams *et al.*, 1990, p. 234).

The jury used as an expression of citizenship is limited in the United Kingdom to its use in the courts, but it is used in other European countries. In Germany it is used as a principle in government:

EXHIBIT 5.1

Consensual approaches to environmental issues

Susskund and Cruikshank in *Breaking the Impasse* (1987) set out a wide range of examples of 'Consensual Approaches to Resolving Public Disputes'. These represent disputes between public organisations and environmental groups and community groups. The aim is to replace situations in which one side to a dispute achieves its aim or one side blocks the proposal by solutions acceptable to all. Different forms are discussed (unassisted negotiation, facilitation, mediation and non-binding arbitration). An example of facilitation relates to a proposal for a large-scale transportation project extending a rapid transit line out to a circumferential highway around a metropolitan area, which threatened environmentally sensitive wetlands separating two towns. This was called Riverend for the purpose of the case study. It was an area designated as a site for migratory birds and other forms of wildlife. In fact, piecemeal developments of highways and railway lines and housing and industrial development had already injured the area. Environmentalists saw the transportation proposal as a huge step in the wrong direction. They also considered that the proposal, by destroying the wetlands, would create dangers of floods. There was also general opposition from local residents to further deterioration of the environment. Opposition grew, but advocates of the proposal became even more committed to it.

In the end the issue was resolved through discussions aided by a facilitator. These discussions lasted over fourteen months, with meetings in the evening every two weeks. Participants included engineers, landscape architects and environmental scientists, with professional credentials as great as the agency personnel selected by the state government to assist the groups. Neighbourhood representatives also took part. The facilitator was asked 'to chair all the meetings, to regulate the pace and topics of conversation and to assume whatever other responsibilities for managing the process be deemed necessary' (Susskund and Cruikshank, 1987, p. 153).

He created a climate in which joint problem solving was possible. Significantly, he did not offer proposals. He did not meet privately with the parties before the meeting. He did not carry confidential messages back and forth among the factions at the bargaining table. He did not help the parties produce a written agreement or invent mechanisms binding each other to their commitments. [He] basically 'managed' the group discussions – and, by the time those discussions concluded, all parties felt they had achieved a fairer, more stable, more efficient and wider agreement than would otherwise have emerged. (ibid., p. 157)

In this case the facilitator spent little or no time meeting with the parties. Instead he devoted most of his energies to making the meeting work. He was able to clarify the sources and nature of the disagreements, and to make sure everyone understood what was being said (ibid., p. 161).

Brainstorming, role-playing, collective image-building were amongst the approaches used. In the end a solution was reached through a focus on the environmental opportunities created by the transit proposal with a scheme for a linear park along the transportation corridor.

The *issue raised* is the potential of public discourse – when it actually takes place.

A more radical innovation in representation has been the creation of the 'planning cell' as an instrument for many small planning tasks in a community. A sample of the inhabitants is drawn and exempted from normal work for the necessary planning period (0–24 months or so), during which they had full access to the local administration (staff, technical support, data). Experience has shown a convincing and often surprising quality in the results, for example in the designing of the central square around Cologne Cathedral. (Grunow, 1991, p. 1)

In these and other ways institutions are seeking to widen and deepen public discourse not necessarily for all, but for many and for more. The emphasis is upon discussion in which views and interests are tested in interaction, rather than on the separate submission of views for an authority to judge, upon discourse rather than the collection of evidence. These are merely examples of the variety of ways and forms that can be taken by public discourse. They recognise, however imperfectly, some of the requirements of the learning society. They recognise that 'the enlightenment of actors can only take place within a domain of practical discourse over the efficacy of the situation' (White, 1990, p. 145).

The multi-cultural forum.   A multi-cultural society has a responsibility to develop amongst its members understanding and respect for its many cultures and faiths. Education legislation has constituted important forums (Standing Advisory Councils on Religious Education (SACRE)) that are designed to realise this objective on behalf of young people. The role of religious education in promoting a tolerant multi-cultural society has been recognised in the 1988 Education Reform Act (ERA) which requires the local education authority (LEA) and schools to secure a curriculum which: '(a) promotes the spiritual, moral, cultural, mental and physical development of pupils at the school and of society; and (b) prepares such pupils for the opportunities, responsibilities and experiences of adult life' (Section 1). The acknowledgement of the role of education in a plural society was asserted more explicitly in

---

EXHIBIT 5.2

A citizen panels

The Agriculture/Water Quality Panel was set up in 1984 on the recommendation of state officials by the Center for New Democratic Processes at the University of Dakota to examine the impacts of agriculture on water quality in Minnesota. The panel was claimed to be 'the first official use of a *randomly* selected group of citizens to study a social or political issue' (Crosby *et al.*, 1986, p. 173). It was not in fact pure random selection, but selection from those attending information meetings, balanced by attitude and by the area of the state.

The panel had 60 members (who were paid a daily fee) divided into regional panels which met for four full days of hearings of which the first was devoted to staff presentations, while the second and third hearings were devoted to testimony. On the fourth day members 'were asked to respond as a group with recommendations about the significance of the issue, the need for action, spending provisions, funding sources, and specific actions to be taken by appropriate authorities' (ibid., p. 175). Each regional panel then selected three members for the state panel. The state panel met for two three-day sessions. The first three days covered presentations by the agencies involved and the formulation of an agenda for the final three-day session, which was devoted to panel deliberations and the preparation of a plan to address the impact of agriculture on water supply. The panel decided to use 'frameworks' prepared by the staff, but like the regional panels found it a difficult process.

The state-wide panel's plan was issued as part of a project report given to the sponsors and other appropriate organisations, key members of the legislature, and the media. A sub-committee of panelists was invited to testify before two legislative committees. Staff were asked to make presentations before the governing boards of each sponsor and the state's Environmental Quality Board and were asked to speak to a number of farmers and environmental organisations about both the issue and the process. The report stimulated one sponsoring agency to set up a special committee of its board to deal with non-point source pollution. It was also served as a stimulus to a major piece of legislation dealing with the 'set-aside' of marginal lands. (ibid., p. 175)

The *issue raised* is the form that can be taken by public discourse. The jury principle applied to policy issues expresses citizenship in action.

---

a subsequent circular: 'The Government believes that all those concerned with religious education should seek to ensure that it promotes respect, understanding and tolerance for those who adhere to different faiths' (Circular 3/89, p. 5).

SACRE can be criticised for unequally representing the constituent interests and thus, potentially, biasing the outcomes. For our purposes here, the significance is the ambition to develop institutional means that can support the values of a plural society and enable them to be realised. Only institutional arrangements which allowed the diversity of interests to participate in a discourse about RE in schools could enable shared understandings and agreement to emerge. These arrangements focused upon councils and conferences which sought to constitute discourse and agreement. The politics of belief should resolve in consensus, choice and action.

In one SACRE the process of reaching agreement about the curriculum was by no means straightforward:

> the whole process was really valuable even though it was like walking on glass. Reaching agreement was a difficult process of painstakingly attending meetings night after night; every 't' has been crossed and 'i' dotted; there was negotiation, there was compromise; we were very lucky in our multi-faith committee, they were very supportive, they understood each other, they respected each other, there was a lot of give and take whereas in other LEAs ... we heard of people storming out of meetings and it was pretty hairy, but we were very lucky, we did not get any of that.

There were differences and 'sticking points' often focusing upon language and interpretation. Agreement between the interest groups depended upon their approach to the process of negotiation.

> It says something about the quality of the people who served in the Statutory Conference, they were hard working, intelligent and what they had at heart was the education in religious understanding of every pupil in the LEA and they always kept that to the forefront, and they were very positive and very supportive; so sometimes when things got sticky they would take a step back even from their own faith standpoint... There are a lot of factions and divisions and groups within the LEA and although they come under the umbrella title Christian or the umbrella title Islam within that there are differences. Largely

we were able to produce that document because of the attitude of the people that served: they were very positive, very moderate, and did not take up polarised positions, but I can imagine that if other people had represented factions, sects and groups it would have been much more difficult, would we have got an agreement at all.

The members while representing their communities had to grasp the dual nature of their responsibilities: to the task for the whole community as well as to their own tradition; when they acted as representatives with discretion in negotiation, rather than as delegates with detailed instructions, then compromise could emerge. The Chair of the Statutory Conference could conclude: 'Our Statutory Conference has been very fortunate in its members. We have come from many different faiths and traditions, but by meeting together and discussing each other's ideas we have achieved this document.'

Community Councils

Institutional reform to empower the citizen will need arenas which provide an opportunity for the community to be involved in a decision-making *process*. We discuss here two local authorities which have experimented with community councils. One northern local authority, Middlesbrough (Shepherd, 1987), in the context of unemployment and deteriorating infrastructure of public housing, communications and public health, sought to review how it could enhance the democratic process in order to involve the public in the process of regeneration and to ensure services were more responsive and accountable to the changing needs of the community. New forms of participation could enable communities to translate their concerns into action – that 'something should be done about such-and-such'. The unit might vary – an estate, a ward – but what was important was 'a sense of local identity where issues reflected common concern and communication could be relatively easily achieved within the area'. Motivation was perceived to be of critical importance: the idea of participation would only succeed 'if people genuinely believed that the exercise was worthwhile, that there was a real opportunity to have a say in local issues and to influence decisions'.

Eleven community councils were originally established with their own budgets with the prime objective being to extend the influence of the local community over the decisions made by the local council and other agencies which affect the lives of people in the area. The community council had a right to be consulted and its views taken into consideration. The community council was composed of all the residents and representatives of any voluntary organisations in the area were invited to attend the meetings which usually took place on a monthly or six-weekly cycle. The meetings to begin with were chaired by a local ward councillor, but in time local residents should undertake this role. Local authority officers would be expected to report on services to the councils and a 'lead officer' would be appointed to provide support for the work and deliberations of the councils. Each was provided with a small budget, which lent some authority to the work of the community council and enabled it to support local initiatives.

Mounting social and economic problems were the catalyst for a London borough, Islington (duParq, 1987), to begin to consider more democratic forms of local government:

> there was a need to counter feelings of alienation in the community and to tackle issues of political credibility associated with the measurable decline in service quality. There were ... feelings of powerlessness in the face of an apparently uncaring bureaucracy, the structures of which were geared to the convenience and economy of the service providers rather than the needs of the consumers. (p. 25)

The first priority was to open neighbourhood offices from 1985 and locate all the principal services in them. Devolution of power to local forums would follow. The aim was to improve accessibility of services, to coordinate their delivery, and to devolve power to the local community to control the delivery of those services. In setting up the offices, consideration was given to their geographical location, their accessibility for people with disabilities as well as those with minority languages, and the need especially for a new style of openness, and service orientation amongst staff who would increasingly represent in their number the ethnic composition of the borough. The changes had their beneficial impact on services. Professionals from different services began to communicate and work together while tackling intransigent local problems. The new approach had the effect of increasing demand and the expectations of local people. Although frustration persisted relations with the public began to improve. But better service provision was only part of the agenda of change. The commitment to decentralisation 'contained a promise of local democracy and transfer of decision-making on a range of issues to neighbourhood offices':

Setting up and staffing 24 neighbourhood offices was an enormous undertaking but politically it was the easy part. Much more difficult has been the democratising process, giving power back to the community and enabling local people to set the service priorities and become genuinely involved in the resource allocation process. (p. 26)

Six neighbourhood forums were constituted with advisory powers in the first instance. They advise the officers how to spend budget allocations for environmental improvements and a small revenue community budget. They sought to exert influence on policy choices and the capital programme.

Interest from the community in the forums is real but as yet limited in extent. For some sections of the community – notably the disabled, minority ethnic groups, the elderly, the young and many women – neighbourhood forums offer the first real chance of influencing the way council services are delivered. (p. 28)

Caution and suspicion remained about the integrity of the council's commitment to democratic change and conflicts emerged between the new forums and the interests of particular sections of the community, such as tenants' associations. Similarly, conflicts of interest and power emerged between the centre and the periphery of the authority about whether senior elected representatives and chief officers were really committed to giving up power: 'the test is whether individual local officers had room to make their own mistakes'. Doubts arose, moreover, about whether people really wanted power, and whether staff had the capacities or skills to support a new style of local government. Nevertheless, the experience and achievements indicated cause to continue to develop the initiative: there was evidence that local people were 'identifying with their neighbourhood and their offices in a way which was unthinkable under the old system ... The debate is continuing on how best to democratise the process and share power with the community'. That is the key challenge for the future.

Conclusion: Towards Community Governance

If the public domain is to revitalise citizenship for the learning society then institutional reform has to renew the institutional conditions for public life within communities, leading to a new style of governing for the learning society, linking the discourse of democracy and the government of collective choice. The conditions and lines of development are as follows:

1. An infrastructure of community forums – both of place and of interest – can provide the foundation to strengthen the constitutive principles of the public domain: enabling and expressing public discourse leading to collective choice based upon public consent. The examples given from different countries are intended to suggest the variety that is possible rather than to provide blueprints to be slavishly followed. The building of community forums must in its diversity reflect the diversity of the learning society.

2. Local government must be reconstituted as the community governing itself. It will have the responsibility for the development of community forums representing the diversity of communities within. As the expression of representative democracy it will set the framework for the development of participation through community forums and the means of discourse for reconciling difference and, if necessary, determining collective choice.

    The upshot of such reform would be an institutional framework of community governance – with a capacity for integrating participative democracy and representative government – that can repair the vacuum of a polity the public legitimacy of which has withered.

3. Local government, as the expression of the community governing itself, provides the systemic conditions for renew-

ing the public domain. By establishing a framework of institutions, it enables the participation of citizens to be tied into the contribution of elected representatives in the forming of collective choice. In this way political capacity is enhanced, drawing together diversity of perspectives and values into a common process of discourse and decision, that enhances the possibility of choice acquiring the authority of consent. Community governance thus provides the conditions for reconstruction, for what is demanded is a high capacity for learning both of the nature of the problems faced and about the approaches to adopt. The institutional arrangements of community governance enable citizens to participate and thus generate a more informed and responsive system of elected representation. It transforms representative democracy from a periodic event to a continuous process of representation. The interdependent complex of institutions provide the capacity for effective action monitored and evaluated by the public.

4. The role of central government should reflect the development of community government. The key role of the centre is to enhance the quality of the learning society and to draw upon the learning generated. Again based on representative government it can set the framework for community government, seek to reconcile difference through discourse and determine through collective choice that which is beyond the capacity of community government. In that role it expresses the principle of subsidiarity in action. Such changes would confront directly the dangers of an overloaded and isolated centre which necessarily is limited in its learning.

5. The fifth line of development would be to build a new sense of public accountability, which requires both clarifying the lines of accountability by grounding institutions in processes of election where now appointment is the norm and spreading accountability by the development of community forums.

6. A sixth condition for developing institutions for a learning society would be through constitutional protection of the organising principle of the public domain and in particular public discourse supported by freedom of information. Such protection could be given by a bill of rights.

These conditions and developments can start from existing institutions but should enable new ways of working within them to permit that learning. It is not our task to suggest how these conditions should be expressed in institutional detail or how those institutions should develop. That has to be learnt. It will be our aim to show how those institutions can be managed to achieve the organising principles of the public domain: public discourse leading to collective action based on public consent. That process of management can enable the institutional development of the learning society.

6

Interdependence and Cooperation

A public organisation is set within a network of organisations in the public domain. Although each organisation has its own tasks, all the organisations share the purposes and values of the public domain, are governed by its organising principle, subject to its distinctive conditions, and have to carry out its tasks. Because of that shared framework there should be a presumption of cooperation between those organisations. The presumption of cooperation can be realised by the development of system management in structuring and reviewing the organisational network and by the development of inter- organisational management within that network. This chapter explores those requirements and their implications.

The Network of Organisation

The organisational geography of the public domain is complex and changing. It is one indication of the complexity that even organisations which are formally unitary can be regarded as collections of separate organisations. Thus there is unity in the machinery of central government, represented by the role of the Cabinet, expressed in constitutional doctrine by the principle of collective responsibility. Yet it is more realistic to see central government as a collection of separate departments, each with their own political head, their own purposes and their own culture. As Rhodes has said:

133

The centre has been described as a diverse federation, with departments playing a variety of roles, including the lead, service, guardian and rival roles. The centrifugal forces in the centre are restrained by the Treasury ... and the Cabinet and its committees. But the alliance of bureaucratic and ministerial interests is a formidable obstacle to central co-ordination, creating weakness at the centre of British government. (Rhodes, 1988, p. 142)

Local authorities show many of the same characteristics. Professional cultures reinforce the separatism of departments, each responsible to their own committees, limiting the ability of the corporate organisation to provide purposive direction to the authority.

Yet despite the centrifugal forces, both central government and local authorities have the formal capacity of a unitary organisation. They face management problems in securing strategic direction and coordination in action, but those are problems that lie within the organisation. Many management problems in the public domain cannot be resolved within one organisation.

Clearly both in the UK and elsewhere an important feature of public administration is the attempt to co-ordinate and negotiate interests, especially across administrative units. (Gray and Jenkins, 1985, p. 35)

Organisational boundaries cannot and do not set limits to public concern. The environmental issue, which many voices have raised in the arena of discourse, requires choice and action not by one organisation but by many.

Management in the public domain is necessarily management in an inter-organisational context. The departments of central government carry out many of their responsibilities through other organisations, rather than directly. The Department of Health carries out its responsibilities for the National Health Service through regional and district health authorities, health service trusts and family health service authorities. Indirect management or management through other organisations is dominant in much of central government. Indeed it is likely to grow as the Government creates executive agencies to take over responsibilities for specific tasks.

The organisational geography has become increasingly complex. In 1974 the powers of the county borough in England and Wales were divided not merely between county and district, but between health authorities and water authorities. Training and Enterprise Councils play a critical role. In specific areas Urban Development Corporations and other agencies have taken over responsibilities from local authorities. Murray Stewart has commented that there has been a 'proliferation of semi-autonomous and/or centrally accountable institutions' within inner-city policy (Stewart, 1987, p. 143).

Recent developments have added to the organisations in the public domain. Opting out in the health service does not mean that hospital trusts have opted out of the public domain, but only that they have opted out of direct control by health authorities. The process of opting out has not lessened the scope of the public domain, but has added to its differentiation. The development of management by contracts in the relationship of health authorities to hospitals or other health units as of local authorities to their direct services organisations, of devolved management in schools, and of grant-maintained schools has created a new series of autonomous and semi-autonomous units within that domain.

The development of contracting out in central government and in the health services and the legislative requirement on local authorities to put out specified activities to compulsory competitive tendering, as well as developments that were taking place under the initiative of particular local authorities, has meant that private sector organisations have been given the task of undertaking certain activities (for example refuse collection or office cleaning) in the public domain. The services and activities involved are not removed from the public domain but remain the responsibility of a public organisation as purchaser or client. It is misleading to describe the development as 'privatisation'; it has even been suggested that it would be more appropriate to describe these developments as 'publicisation' as private sector organisations move into the public domain.

The organisational geography of the public domain is becoming more complex with increasing differentiation and different forms of relationship between organisations. Differentiation is a necessary element in any system of government, but as differentiation grows, so does the need for integrative mechanisms, if fragmentation is to be avoided and the shared purposes and values of the public domain realised.

The Necessities of Inter-Organisational Working

Each public organisation has its tasks, but those tasks will often necessarily involve other organisations:

● Health inspections in schools are carried out by doctors from the health service
● Local authorities act as agents for water authorities in the maintenance of sewers and drains
● The Training and Enterprise Council works with and through colleges of further education in the provision of training

These are defined tasks in which joint action is required. Joint working is established at the operational level through the tasks to be performed. The tasks of different organisations in the public domain do not always sit easily together. An organisation 'can create turbulence for another by its reaction to the uncertainties that both of them face' (Evans, 1987, p. 48). There can be problems created by procedures, which, while designed to serve the purposes of organisation A, restrict or influence the response of organisation B, leading to an 'emphasis or defensive reaction by a particular organisation rather than on the needs of the whole system' or to a 'legacy of institutional rigidity' (ibid., p. 49).

Performance of the tasks of organisations in the public domain can assist or can make more difficult the tasks of other organisations, because in implementation and in interaction those tasks are interrelated. The public domain is, however, wider than the boundaries set by the tasks of the different organisations within it. It is the setting for the arena of public discourse. In that arena issues are raised. Those issues do not necessarily fall within the boundaries of any one organisation or set of organisations. Both in learning about an issue and determining how an issue should be resolved, many organisations are, or can be, involved.

Consider the variety of public organisations which are, or could be, involved in such issues as: the care of the elderly; environmental pollution; drug abuse; youth unemployment. In each of these issues different departments of central government are involved. In all these issues local authorities are involved. Health authorities are involved in at least the first three issues. The police are involved in all these issues with the possible exception of environmental pollution. Training and Enterprise Councils are involved with youth unemployment, as water companies are in environmental pollution. In each issue and for each organisation, the potential involvement is not necessarily limited to present tasks. The extent and nature of that involvement can be determined and changed in the public domain.

If within the public domain societal issues are to be raised and explored and strategies and policies derived for guidance and for action, then these have to be managed within an inter-organisational network. Management in that inter-organisational network involves the management of issues as well as the management of tasks.

A Presumption of Competition or of Cooperation

Management in the public domain should not assume organisational autonomy. Public organisations should be seen as part of that domain, sharing its purposes and values and subject to its conditions. The presumption of competition based on private sector models should therefore be replaced by a presumption of cooperation, in which organisations in the public domain work together to achieve the shared purposes and values of that domain, subject to its organising principle.

The presumption of cooperation does not exclude the possibility of competition. Different departments and different organisations compete for resources. Different organisations may compete for responsibilities as health authorities and local authorities have competed in the arena of public discourse for responsibilities for community care. It may be a normal feature of bureaucratic life that those who work in particular organisations will seek the interests of that organisation or of the part of the organisation in which they work. None of this invalidates the presumption of cooperation underlying the public domain as a whole. The point made is not that there is no competition in the public domain, but that public organisations are not constituted to compete.

EXHIBIT 6.1

Planned markets in Scandinavian health services

In Scandinavia models of planned markets have been developed. In Stockholm an experiment was undertaken in which expectant mothers selected maternity units. In the first half of 1990, 19 percent of expectant mothers asked to be transferred under this scheme.

Viewed overall, this experiment succeeded in enabling patients to choose the facility at which they would receive care, based on location, reputation and general information about the practice style in each facility. Several maternity units found it to be in their own best interest to adopt a more interactive delivery approach. In as much as operating revenues for all seven Stockholm maternity units became linked to performance, issues of internal efficiency and responsiveness to patients became an important element in how maternity units were managed. (Saltman and Van Otter, 1992, p. 52)

Overall patient numbers remained much the same in five of the seven facilities. One 'highly respected facility' (Karolinska Hospital) increased numbers, but one hospital lost numbers and eventually had to close a delivery ward, which was, however, recognised as reflecting public choice. 'The success of this experiment in turn has led to the development of the Stockholm model which ... will combine expanded patient choice of hospital site and provider with primary care based controls over hospital reimbursement' (ibid.).

Similar developments elsewhere in Sweden and in Finland are described by Saltman and Van Otter. They draw a distinction between a 'public competition' model and the 'mixed market' model of the United Kingdom. The 'public competition' model as it has emerged first in the Stockholm experiments but now more fully in Malmohus and Bohuslan, seeks to generate a public market restricted to publicly capitalised, politically accountable provider units. The central agent of change is the patient, who, with his or her choice of physician and treatment site, brings along both institutional budgets and personnel bonuses (ibid., pp. 83–4).

The *issue raised* is the different form that can be taken by the use of competition in the public domain, when governed by the conditions of the public domain.

Competition is not part of the rationale of the public domain, as it is of the private sector economy.

Whereas competition is sought for the market-place, cooperation can be sought in the public domain. Whereas in the private sector, two competing organisations reaching an agreement on policy could be seen as restraint of trade, such an agreement between

public agencies should be welcomed. A model of perfect cooperation underlies the rationale of inter-governmental relations in the
public domain as a model of perfect competition underlies the
private sector – although both may be equally unrealistic.

The presumption of cooperation underlying the public domain
implies that no particular organisation can be regarded as in principle autonomous, setting its particular purposes before the purposes of the public domain. The variety of relationships between
organisations should be such as to produce an overall pattern of
relationships that supports those wider purposes. Cooperation is
in principle, if not always in practice, the dominant mode because
of the nature of the public domain.

There is a variety of relationships between organisations in the
public domain, because many modes of action are possible. Unlike
the market sector which is defined by its mode of action, the
public domain is defined by its purposes and values achieved
through its organising principles and hence modes of action are
judged by their contribution to those purposes and values and
their consistency with those principles. This permits a variety of
modes leading to different relationships within the overall presumption of cooperation. Those relationships can even include an
extension of competitive relations. The Government has recently
introduced legislation to permit greater parental choice between
schools, arguing that greater competition will improve the quality
of education. This is, however, a means to ends defined within the
public domain, and the development of competition between
schools is associated with the introduction of the National
Curriculum, limiting the scope of competition. The particular
structure of competition has been determined by requirements set
in the public domain. In effect, competitive relations are being
developed in a part of the public domain, but the role of that part
is still governed by overall requirements set in the domain, and
between the parts, the presumption of cooperation still remains.
The health service and the education service are still expected to
cooperate in carrying out tasks set in that domain.

The variety of relationships includes:

• competitive relations, as when more than one agency is made
  responsible for a task, and the scale of operation depends
  upon their capacity to attract clients

- trading relations, as when one agency sells another its services
- supervisory relations, as when one agency is given responsibility over another agency
- coercive relations, as when one agency can lay down rules that another agency has to obey
- planning relations, as when one agency operates according to a plan laid down by another agency
- consultative relations, as when agencies discuss with each other shared problems
- joint working relations, as when agencies agree to work together on a shared task
- financial relations, as when one agency provides grants for another agency

While particular relations may not realise it, the combination of organisations and the relationship between them should realise the presumption of cooperation.

The presumption of cooperation in inter-organisational working can be contrasted with the reality of conflict in the arena of public discourse. There is contrast between the model of the private sector which assumes organisational harmony (however unrealistic such an assumption) and competitive relations between organisations and the model of the public domain argued for here, which assumes conflict in the organisation and yet of cooperation between organisations. The tension between the competition of voices in the arena of discourse and the presumption of cooperation is a dilemma to be managed in the public domain.

The Need for System Management

The presumption of cooperation can be realised through system management to design, maintain and control the structure of organisations and the variety of relationships between them.

The primary task of system management falls upon central government. It calls for skill in organisational design and analysis, in developing the organisational framework within the public domain and for organisational understanding in its maintenance and guidance. Yet system management has been given but little recognition in central government. Major institutional change in, for example, the health services or in local government may be planned by civil servants who have not previously undertaken any major responsibility in organisational design. It is almost as if a group of individuals were given the task of designing a cathedral without any architectural training.

Organisational design structures, by effect, if not always by intentions, the pattern of inter-organisational relations. The 1974 reorganisation of community services created health authorities on a new basis, taking over the responsibilities of local authorities for community health. The arguments in favour of the integrated government of health prevailed over the arguments in favour of the integrated government of community services. There was an arguable case to be made for that change, as there was against it, but although that change resolved certain issues within the health service – or at least made them issues for management within health authorities – it inevitably created problems for relations between health authorities and local authorities – not least in the provision of community care. These problems have been the subject of almost continual appraisal and reappraisal as governments have sought to overcome the divisions built into the original design of the structures.

Whether or not the particular division made in 1974 between the health and other community services was justified, organisational divides in one form or another are inevitable. Effective system management would ensure that organisational structures and relationships encouraged cooperation across such divides. Where organisational divides are necessary, structures can still be designed to encourage or to discourage cooperation. Due to a failure in organisational understanding, the structural division between health and social services was reinforced by organisational design. Divisions were built into the structures by:

- the difference in governance between the *elected* local authority and the *appointed* health authority
- the difference between the finance of health authorities totally dependent on grants and of local authorities with their own taxation powers
- the difference between the capital finance of health authorities through grants and of local authorities through loans

- differences in the management structures with no equivalent in health authorities, when first created, to the chief executive in local authorities
- differences in the hierarchical relationship between health authorities and central government and the relative autonomy of local authorities

The result has been different organisational patterns of working, different organisational assumptions and even different organisational languages, which reinforced rather than lessened the structural divide. That divide was further reinforced by the decision to place all doctors with health authorities and all social workers with local authorities, so that professional boundaries reinforced organisational boundaries. A profession has a capacity to communicate across organisational boundaries, but that capacity was not used to aid inter-authority cooperation.

There was a failure in organisational design. Only in one respect – the coterminous boundaries between health and local authorities – did organisational design support the presumption of cooperation; and even that was later abandoned. Generally, the organisational design, far from realising the presumption of cooperation, set barriers which have not easily been overcome. As a result progress in cooperation

> has been slow. Collaboration is no easy task given the existence of authorities with quite different organisational structures, administrative and political cultures, sources of finance, planning cycles and relationships with central government. (Webb and Wistow, 1986, p. 150)

The fault was in organisational design and in a lack of system management. It was not that the need for cooperation was not recognised. A requirement was laid on health and local authorities by the National Health Service Act, 1973, Section 22(1), to cooperate to 'secure and advance the welfare of the people of England and Wales', but the measures designed to secure this were afterthoughts added on to structures designed, probably unwittingly, to make cooperation difficult. Local authorities and health authorities were required to set up statutory joint consultative committees bridging the divide. This was itself an error in design, imposing a mechanical solution on an organic problem. The committees were not owned by either health or local authorities and were generally unable to find a meaningful role. The introduction of joint finance for projects of benefit both to health and local authorities in 1976 gave the committees a limited role. But joint finance represented only a limited part of health service finance. The main systems for distributing central government grant – RAWP (Resource Allocation Working Party) for health authorities and RSG (rate support grant) for local authorities – gave no recognition to the need for cooperation and remained separate in organisation and design. In focusing the attention of joint committees on joint finance, the emphasis was on limited cooperation over peripheral resources.

The result of the failures both in organisational design in particular and in system management in general was seen in community care for the elderly, for the mentally handicapped and the mentally ill, involving as it did not merely health authorities and local authorities but also social security.

EXHIBIT 6.2

A failure in system management

In 1986 the Audit Commission prepared a report on *Making a Reality of Community Care*. It argued that: 'While the Government's policies require a shift from hospital-based (health services) to locally-based (local authority and health) services, the mechanisms for achieving a parallel shift in funds are inadequate' (Audit Commission, 1986, p. 2). It pointed out that the grant system penalised local authorities 'for building the very community services government policy favoured' (ibid.) and that perversely: 'Supplementary Benefit polices fund private residential care more readily than community-based care of which there is relatively little in the private sector' (ibid., p. 3). They went on to argue that while 'central government attempts to achieve equitable distribution of public funds across the country, through the use of complex formulae both with the NHS and local government, the effects can be largely offset by Supplementary Benefit payment for board and lodging'. (ibid.).

The Commission argued that

Responsibility for introducing and operating community-based services is fragmented between a number of different agencies with different priorities, styles, structures and budgets who must 'request' cooperation from each other. For community care to operate, these agencies must work together. But there are many reasons why they do not, including the lack of positive incentives, bureaucratic barriers, perceived threats to jobs and professional standing, and the time required for interminable meetings. (ibid.)

The report of the Audit Commission was followed by the Department of Health commissioning a report on *Community Care: Agenda for Action* (Griffiths Report, 1988b). Sir Roy Griffiths saw the problem not as one of organisational restructuring but as a requirement for system management:

At the other extreme the urging to be radical has generally implied that I should tear up the present organisational structures and start afresh. I have decided to be even more radical. Nothing could be more radical in the public sector than to spell out responsibility, insist on performance and accountability and evidence that action is being taken; and even more radical, to match policy with appropriate resources and agreed time scales. (Griffiths, 1988b, p. 10)

Legislation followed in the form of the National Health Service and Community Care Act 1990, introducing reforms which mainly became operational in 1993. The main effects were that local authorities were given a lead role in assessing individual needs, arranging services to meet those needs and commissioning them in what is seen as a mixed economy of care. The care element of social security income support for nursing and residential home care is transferred to local authorities for new claimants. The adequacy of these arrangements – both financial and otherwise – remains to be tested.

The *issue raised* by the Audit Commission was a clear failure in system management, in failing to realise the presumption of cooperation. The measures taken have been an exercise in system management, whose success or failure remains to be seen.

System management should be a key task of central government. Central government not merely has a responsibility for the structure of institutions in the public domain, but works with and through other organisations more often than it acts directly. That requires organisational understanding and an awareness of the special requirements of system working. An investigation of relations between central government and local authorities concluded. 'Central government's knowledge about what is happening can best be described as patchy. This is true both in general and in relation to specific attempts by central government to influence the provision of services' (Central Policy Review Staff, 1977, p. 33). It is a reflection of a wider problem. Metcalfe and Richards have concluded:

Since the unit of public management is often a network of organisations jointly involved in the delivery of services, com-

petence in designing and negotiating effective working relationships between organisations are vitally important. Skills in
'fighting departmental corners' fall well short of what is
needed, though they are what is expected in the culture of
Whitehall.

Public management problems at the level of organisational
and inter-organisational design have been neglected. Whitehall
devotes few resources to machinery of government questions.
Even the label 'machinery of government' has a period charm
about it. Mechanistic metaphors have been superseded in
organisational analysis ... At this level, policy and management
issues concerning the development of objectives and performance standards for multi-organisational units should be
handled together. (Metcalfe and Richards, 1987, p. 18)

Solesbury approached inner-city policies from a system management perspective: 'The starting point must be a recognition of the
multi-agency nature of inner city policy' (Solesbury, 1986, p. 393).
That involves the recognition of two 'basic operational constraints; the capacity of the individual component agencies and
the strength of the systems that bind them' (ibid.). He argues that
'the reality is the old bureaucratic grind of notification, consultation, negotiation between agencies which strictly owe each other
nothing' (ibid., p. 366) but sees potential in leverage and joint
ventures. Leverage involves resources which are provided to a programme on condition that resources are obtained from other
sources, as with urban development grants. Joint ventures are distinguished from other forms of joint action because 'the partners
enter a contractual relationship whereby mutual obligations are
clearly and bindingly defined' (ibid., 1986, p. 397). This is an
example of system management seeking to overcome constraints
on cooperation within the public domain.

The emerging fragmented structure of government increases
the need for system management. As the number of organisations
grows through the creation of executive agencies, the removal of
functions from local government and the introduction of contracting out, it is possible to envisage a public domain inhabited
by separate organisations conducting their relationship with each
other through contractual or quasi-contractual relations. While
such an organisational differentiation of the domain has strengths

in focusing management attention on clear tasks, there is a danger of system failure in the lack of integrative mechanisms. One has to ask of such a patterning whether it has the capacity for development beyond the capacity of the separate units. Has it the capacity for the learning required for the responsive and developmental roles, or will learning be retained in the units? Will the values of the public domain be realised? System management becomes more, not less, important in the new patterning. Challis and his colleagues have argued that:

> the key features of successful co-ordination and collaboration are
>
> a strong value predisposition toward systems-wide thinking and other regarding behaviour ...
>
> uninterrupted and possibly prolonged opportunities for interaction across boundaries in order to permit learning about divergent paradigms, practices, constraints and competence – as a basis for the development of trust and soundly-based system perspectives
>
> external catalysts to such learning – including powerful representation of the clients interests and needs, as well as resource pressure which nonetheless permits opportunities for the pursuit of 'positive' sum co-ordination
>
> the consistent exercise of political and administrative authority in support of system-wide thinking, political analysis and co-operative action
>
> the provision of other incentives including resources incentives to bargaining and collaborative behaviour ... (Challis *et al.*, 1988, p. 274)

Through such means and through organisational design, system management can realise the presumption of cooperation.

The Requirements of System Management and of Inter-Organisational Management

Management in public organisations is set in an inter-organisational network, itself potentially determined by system management, but more likely in practice to be indeterminate because of its absence.

Within those organisations, actions are subject to management control – at least in principle if not always in reality. In an inter-organisational network, actions are no longer under the control of any one organisation – in principle as well as in practice. System management should set the conditions within which both influence and action develop to realise the presumption of cooperation, but the realisation of that presumption also requires a capacity for effective inter-organisational management within organisations.

The Necessity of Understanding

In both system and inter-organisational management, understanding is necessary both of the range and potential of the network of organisations and of the organisations within it. Without understanding, system management will be ineffective in realising the presumption of cooperation and inter-organisational management will remain underdeveloped.

Within the network, patterns of relationships will have developed between organisations, but the potential of the network may not be fully realised by present practice. Thus relations between health authorities and local authorities have tended to be based on the work of social services. The contribution of the range of local authorities' services to the health of the community can be neglected. The focus of the inter-organisational link between health authorities and local authorities on social services limits the development of the potential network.

Past experience reinforces itself in the present. The organisations which work with each other become accepted as the organisations which should work with each other. System management should be concerned with extending the range of inter-organisational relations and inter-organisational management with developing those relations. Plotting the organisations potentially concerned with an issue is an instrument for both system management and inter-organisational management. An inter-organisational audit can identify both the organisations actively concerned with an issue and those that could or should be concerned. It is a first step in realising the potential of the network.

Organisational understanding should extend beyond knowledge of structure to appreciation of culture and ways of working, for those will be major determinants of inter-organisational relations. Those who would work with and through other organisations should understand their languages, for words can mislead if they have different meanings in different organisations. Organisations have different seasons when budgets are settled or plans laid, and approaches by one organisation can be disregarded by others if put forward at the wrong seasons. Values can be confronted unnecessarily if their significance is not appreciated. Organisational assumptions about ways of working may not be shared, leading to unnecessary conflict. Proposals or communication grounded in the understanding of one organisation can assume a different meaning in another organisation.

The rigidities of past experience provide the greatest barriers to organisational understanding. Where experience is limited by careers or training confined within organisational boundaries, the need for understanding may not even be appreciated. Management can build understanding through personnel policies encouraging cross-organisational career patterns, training and development.

Working for Cooperation

Inter-organisational working does not just happen. System management must try to realise the conditions which encourage cooperation and eliminate barriers. That depends upon organisational design and review. The aim should be to secure that organisational working throughout the public domain sustains the organising principle since that links together the shared purposes, conditions and tasks on which the presumption of cooperation rests.

Organisational barriers to inter-organisational working can distort the arena of discourse, since they restrict the flow of information. They can limit the effectiveness of choice by establishing boundaries to the scope of action. We have described how barriers were built into the relationships between health authorities and local authorities. System management should seek mechanisms for overcoming those barriers by, for example, moving towards coterminosity, relating the processes by which grants are distributed, and encouraging career development and joint training between authorities.

System management sets the conditions for the realisation of the presumption of cooperation. Its realisation depends upon the development of inter-organisational management. Inter-organisational management can take many forms depending on the nature of the relationship. The management of contracts differs from the management of partnerships and both differ from the management of influence, but all differ from the management of direct action.

Yet most organisations in the public domain are structured for direct action. They operate through hierarchies of control, structured on the assumption that decisions are implemented directly. Their procedures reflect this assumption and staff are trained to accept that assumption, even when experience belies it. The assumption affects the relationship between central government and other agencies such as health authorities, where circulars are issued with an attention to detail as if they were directly under the control of the Department of Health or at least the NHS Management Board, although organisational reality, never mind inter-organisational reality, teaches otherwise.

Each form of inter-organisational management has its own requirements. The need is to distinguish the nature of inter-organisational management and to develop appropriate structures, processes and staffing. This need has been recognised for contracting, with the development of the client or purchaser role, processes of contract management and monitoring and review, although the emphasis is perhaps placed too strongly on control through contracts, rather than on building relationships of trust between client and contractor, which may be nearer to realising the presumption of cooperation. Kanter's analysis of the skills required in managing partnerships is relevant to the public domain.

> Thus authority gives way to influence, and command to negotiation. Success at resolving issues within a partnership and at leading discussion towards the outcome a representative seeks is dependent on both his relationships within the alliance and his personal communication skills, as well as on his understanding of how best to manage group decision-making. (Kanter, 1989, p. 156)

The management of mutual influence is of even more importance in the managing of networks, which lack the formal structure of the partnership. It has its own requirements which differ from the management of direct action. The subtlety of suggestion replaces the apparent certainty of decision. Areas of influence replace points of decision. The management of influence does not follow predetermined paths but rather follows openings or opportunities for it depends on interaction. Yet there must be a sense of direction or in merely following openings the organisation may be misled.

Conclusion

Public organisations are set in a complex network of organisations. Inter-organisational working is therefore a condition of working in the public domain. Although from time to time organisations will compete, the shared purposes and conditions of that domain mean that a presumption of cooperation is necessary to the realisation of the domain's full potential. This depends upon system management of the structuring of organisations and their relationships and upon the development of inter-organisational management. Both system management and inter-organisational management require organisational understanding and an appreciation of the special conditions of inter-organisational working, in which the management of mutual influence is of more importance than the management of direct action.

PART III

THE CHANGING TASKS OF PUBLIC MANAGEMENT

7

Beyond Codes and Contracts

Public management is designed to serve the purposes of collective choice. In public organisations activities are carried out to maintain and sustain ways of life, but also to enable change in society through response and development. Through these activities, values are realised in the public domain. Public management in a learning society is concerned with the overall effect of activities and the realisation of the values of the public domain.

The form in which management has served public purpose has varied radically with the nature of the polity in the postwar period. In the period of social democracy, a conception of public management reflected a belief that the power of professional expertise, reinforced by the rules of fairness administered by welfare bureaucracies, could deliver the good society. The neo-liberal polity challenged those purposes, attacked the means, and substituted contract management as best suited to deliver alternative purposes of public choice and accountability. Neither the codes of professionalism, the inflexible rules of welfarism nor the contracts of the New Right are, we argue, appropriate to the management tasks of delivering the learning society.

The Codes of Public Management under Social Democracy

In the social democratic polity, it was assumed that organisational guidance required only organisational control to ensure collective

153

choice was achieved. The assumption was that once that choice was made it would be accepted – the need for the continuing process of judgement inherent in the learning society was not realised. The model of organisational guidance was therefore a model of organisational control. There were two approaches to organisational control. The first relied on direct hierarchical control, while the second relied on professional practice – or control by expertise.

Direct Hierarchical Control

Direct hierarchical control meant that, wherever possible, public management was achieved through rules to be applied specifying in detail how, for example, houses should be allocated or benefits paid. Where that was not possible, direct control drew decisions up the hierarchy, so that in local authorities and in health authorities detailed decisions were made by the governing bodies. The result was seen in detailed agendas. In government departments detailed decisions required ministerial approval. The model of direct control was justified as a means of ensuring that collective choice governs decisions on action to be taken and where this cannot be achieved by rules, by as many decisions as possible being made through the governing body as the instrument of collective choice.

The requirements of public accountability appear to justify direct control. Thus on public purchasing it has been argued:

> In setting levels of delegation two factors have to be borne in mind. For maximum efficiency the work should be delegated to the most junior level that do the work effectively. But consideration of accountability will tend to reduce the level of delegation in order to ensure that decisions which have financial or operational repercussions are taken at a sufficiently high level. Getting the balance right is a matter of judgment. (Cabinet Office, 1984, p. 2)

This is a restricted approach to accountability, focusing on formal processes rather than on a relationship of stewardship. The model of direct control frustrates more often than it secures the achievement of effective performance. It focuses on the requirement of collective choice, but control over detailed decision does not necessarily achieve the political purposes underlying that choice. In the detail, purpose can be lost. Individual decisions made on their merits can have consequences that frustrate intentions.

Direct control can prevent the realisation of the full potential of the organisation – not least for learning from the public. Management responsibility is weakened by reference upward – 'the committee has decided' is a denial of that responsibility. Too often in the public sector, management has been restricted in its capacity to manage resources. Virement between budget heads has been restricted, forcing issues up the hierarchy.

Attempts to secure direct control are frustrated by the necessity of discretion. Detailed control can never eliminate discretion – particularly in services and functions carried out far away, both organisationally and geographically, from those who make decisions at the centre of the organisation. Discretion, if it is accepted and guided, can aid effective performance. The requirements of collective choice do not mean that each and every decision has to be predetermined. Collective choice can be expressed in requirements which leave room both for management responsibility and responsiveness in action. Effective public management can use discretion, but in detailed control, discretion can be seen as frustrating achievement.

The issues become greatest in central government. The very scale means that detailed control by ministers is impossible. Yet the doctrine of ministerial responsibility remains in form if not in reality. The effect has been to make civil servants proxy ministers, who apply a concept of 'the ministers' views', even when those views have not been spelt out. Decisions are drawn up the hierarchy even if they do not reach ministers, lest they overwhelm them. The result is that, as an investigation of central government's property services pointed out in a passage that has wider application than its immediate focus:

a disproportionate amount of time and expense is incurred in operating the current systems of control, and a more effective approach could be adopted without any significant decrease in the levels of control. Indeed if accompanied by more appropriate management information we believe a more effective control would be achieved. (Department of the Environment, 1983, p. 113)

Detailed control can be ineffective public management even on the assumptions of the social democratic polity. Its focus on what is done rather than on what is achieved means that it is based on an inadequate model of organisational guidance for a learning society.

Professional Control

In certain activities reliance has been placed not on bureaucratic principles of control through hierarchy or the application of rules, but on professional authority. Decisions are made by professional judgement. There is a world of difference in the control exercised over a doctor in an operating theatre and that exercised over a clerical officer in a social security office. Doctors in their treatment of patients, social workers in their relations with clients and librarians in their choice of books make professional judgements. Clerical officers in social security offices apply or are supposed to apply the rules.

Reliance on professional judgement alone does not fully meet the requirements of the public domain. It neither ensures the achievement of collective choice nor provides the basis of public discourse. Professional accountability can be argued to eliminate the need for public accountability, but although it may do so in practice, it cannot do so in principle.

In the social democratic polity reliance was placed on professional expertise, but limits have to be set to that reliance in a learning society. Professional judgement is in the public domain and it is subject to the requirement that those who act in that domain are subject to public discourse and public accountability. The Butler-Sloss inquiry into the Cleveland child abuse cases was not limited by the boundaries of professional judgement.

Reliance on professional judgement does not exclude the need for effective public management. Professional judgement can extend its area of concern beyond the limits of professional skill and knowledge as when ministerial attempts to change priorities in the health service between acute care and care for the elderly and the mentally handicapped were frustrated by professional status. Professional accountability may prevent public accountability rather than secure it. Reliance on professional discourse alone limits public discourse.

Building the Conditions for Effective Public Management

Effective public management requires a framework for organisational guidance that is neither the frustration of direct control as it happens nor reliance on professional control alone. Within organisations there is a capacity for self-management on which their working depends. Organisations have a way of life beyond the requirements of formal rules or the commands of the hierarchy. Effective public management in the public domain must use that quality in order to achieve public purposes. This requires not direct control but setting the terms within which organisational capacity can develop.

> Improvement of bureaucratic accountability then does not only imply remedying deficits of specific controls by means of improving the overseer's resources and power in order to achieve a better oversight, as the 'comptrol' (i.e. direct control) almost exclusively suggests, but also designing institutions and organisational systems and networks that strengthen immanent mutual control and self-control. (Wirth, 1986, p. 610)

A new model of organisational guidance is required for effective public management that is based on specifying requirements – leaving space for action – and on accountability and review. The organisation is not controlling events as they happen, but in anticipation and in retrospection.

Collective choice can be reconciled with realising organisational potential both for the effective management of resources and for responsiveness in action, by stating requirements but not by over-stating requirements. There is, however, no simple division restricting collective choice to the general and leaving the detail to day-to-day management or to front-line staff. What is required can and should be specified in detail, if that is what is necessitated by collective choice, as it will be in laying down rules for social security payments, or in setting standards for certain inspection services.

Equally, in controlling professional decisions, the aim should not be to eliminate professional judgement, but to ensure that professional judgement meets the requirement of collective choice. Professional judgement can be allowed full scope for development within the limits set by that choice. In developing a process of effective organisational guidance based upon a cycle of

- setting requirements for the organisation
- creating conditions in which management action can be taken to meet the requirements
- reviewing performance to establish both whether requirements have been met and whether requirements should be changed

regard must be had to the purposes and conditions of the public domain and to the realities of political and organisational behaviour. Effective organisational guidance is not developed to deny collective choice, but to ensure it, and to ensure the testing of that choice in public discourse.

Public Management as Contracted Responsibilities

Within the public sector generally there are attempts to build effective public management on these principles of organisational guidance. We shall, however, argue that many of these approaches do not meet the purposes and conditions of the public domain and that they ignore the realities of political and organisational behaviour, because they have been developed for the neo-liberal polity. They have been drawn from the private sector model rather than based on the public domain. They have released management capacity to achieve collective choice, but have neglected the need for continuing judgement on that achievement to be tested in discourse.

The Audit Commission has said:

Local authorities are relatively large organisations; objectives may be set centrally, but they are put into practice by committees, individual departments and their front-line managers or increasingly, by external contractors under council supervision. These departments, individuals, or contractors will only do what the council wishes to be done, if both sides know and agree what is expected of them, in other words, if their responsibilities are clearly spelled out. This too is an old principle of good management which will be more critical in the future. The only way properly to harness politics and management is for members as a whole to assign very clear management responsibilities to officers, to set a framework of accountability and then to let them get on with it. (The Audit Commission, 1988a, p. 7)

The Griffiths Report on management in the National Health Service (Department of Health, 1983) made similar recommendations. It argued that each unit should develop management budgets, involving clinicians and relating workload and service objectives to finance and manpower. Similar developments were promoted in central government by the Financial Management Initiative.

These developments require public organisations to

identify key services, outputs and indicators of performance; define management responsibilities in terms of service delivery; analyse and present costs and outputs in terms of service to be delivered, as well as vehicles for the delivery of those services; develop resources and output budgets for services and organisational units and monitor inputs and outputs; develop mechanisms for setting priorities at the highest level on the use of resources (G. Yates, 1987, p. 169)

Management should be set targets to be achieved within specified resources, should be given the maximum management freedom to achieve those targets and should be held accountable for their achievement. This however depends on certain conditions:

Targets must be:

Feasible within a given set of constraints
Agreed through discussion and negotiation with management imposed ...
Explicit in the sense that a move away from the target should be unambiguous in what it tells about performance

and if managers are to be held accountable variances must be:

Attributable to a specific individual who by his actions can control an activity
Subject to corrective action through a management protocol which specifies the range/scale of management interventions open to departmental managements, for example overtime control, staffing/grade mix, purchasing policies

---

EXHIBIT 7.1

The Financial Management Initiative

In central government the Financial Management Initiative was launched in 1982

to promote in each department an organisation and a system in which managers at all levels have

  (a) a clear view of their objectives; and means to assess, and wherever possible measure, outputs or performance in relation to those objectives;
  (b) well-defined responsibility for making the best use of their resources including a scrutiny of output and value for money; and
  (c) the information (particularly about costs), the training and the access to expert advice which they need to exercise their responsibilities effectively. (Cmnd 9058, 1983, p. 1)

Gray and Jenkins point out that 'Accountable management represents the guiding ideology of the FMI' (Gray and Jenkins, 1991, p. 47) and that was operationalised through three developments:

● Top management systems which 'are intended to provide senior departmental officials and their ministers with information on the scope and scale of departmental operations and their use of departmental resources' in order to inform choice about programme development (ibid., p. 47)
● Decentralised budgetary control which is designed 'to assist departmental managers focus on their operational and *financial* responsibilities by providing a hierarchy of cost centres' (ibid.)
● Performance appraisal based on 'a range of indicators of both operational achievements and their costs' (ibid.)

The introduction of FMI was overseen and guided by the Financial Management Unit, later succeeded by the Joint Management Unit whose responsibilities were eventually taken over by the Treasury.

The *issue raised* is the limit to accountable management as it has developed in the Civil Service. Gray and Jenkins have concluded: 'it is still very much about financial management; while manpower planning was loosely incorporated into the running cost regime in 1988, there remains only a weak integration with human resource management in general, quite apart from broader concerns with planning and control. The argument in central departments is now less about strategic objectives, priorities and effectiveness than about expenditure justification' (ibid., p. 56)

Differentiated between changes in the volume of activity ... and changes in productivity/efficiency of a management cost centre. (Nichol, 1986, p. 94)

Accountable management requires clear targets, achievement of which is within the responsibility of managers. Once separate management units are identified with clear responsibilities it is possible to separate them from direct control as with Next Steps agencies and opted-out schools and hospitals.

Public organisations can also contract with other organisations for the provision of the service – with private contractors, with voluntary organisations, with another public agency or with a joint organisation which they may partly control. Accountability is secured through the contract. In principle the public organisation remains responsible for the service. It has the same need to state its requirements and to keep performance under review. Indeed, lacking the direct controls of bureaucracy, what has been argued to be desirable in other forms of accountable management, becomes a necessity in contract management. It is only if what the organisation requires is specified in the contract that it will happen.

Accountable management, whether achieved by devolved management or by a contract, ensures that managers have clearly understood tasks and targets to achieve, and are given responsibility for the resources required to achieve those tasks. They are held accountable for their performance. The political requirements set the conditions, but within those requirements space is provided both for management responsibility and for management responsiveness.

This approach appears to meet our principles for organisational guidance, yet in some of the forms in which have been developed it has proved hard to introduce. Richards has asked the question, 'Why has the civil service found it so hard to decentralise?' (Richards, 1988, p. 15). The model of accountable management that is being used

is essentially a model sprung from production management, extensively used in the management of mass production processes in Western economies, although now being questioned even there. (ibid., p. 11)

She concludes that there are problems in applying the model to services, where the key transactions are between front-line staff and their customers and quality depends on the nature of that contact. She argues further that management in the public domain is driven not by 'individual choice in the market place' but by 'collective choices, made through the political system' (ibid., pp. 13–14). The problem is not necessarily with the attempt to build systems of effective control, to encourage decentralisation or even to develop accountable management, but that the approaches pay little regard to the special requirements both of public service and of management in the public domain.

The basic problem is that the model of organisational guidance on which they are based is still a model of organisational control, concerned only with the achievement of collective choice and neglecting the need for a continuing process by which the results are judged and tested in public discourse. It assumes a static polity, not the dynamic polity required for a learning society. Accountability is not a continuing relationship of stewardship, but the reporting of defined tasks achieved. The forms of accountable management suggest that the task of the manager can be reduced to the requirements set out in the key tasks and that targets can be set in relation to those tasks that enable effective performance to be measured. This approach meets three problems:

(a)   There is an assumption that the tasks of management can be predetermined. Little space is allowed for learning. It would not be done by expressing 'learning' as a key task or measuring the number of new ideas! The point is that accountable management assumes the predictability of continuity while management in the public domain faces the unpredictability of change.

(b)   Actions taken in the public domain are likely to be the subject of public criticism, which necessarily involves the political process. The manager in the public domain can never be insulated from the political process. One cannot allow a definition of key tasks to build isolation from the arena of public discourse.

(c)   There can be no final measures of performance in the public domain because the areas of concern are not bounded. An activity which is felt to have a simple output may be found to have side effects, which can become the subject of concern in the public domain. Nor can the judgement of performance be predetermined. Judgement is formed in the public domain by public discourse.

The points made do not remove the need for effective control but a model of organisational guidance based on that alone is inadequate. What is wrong with accountable management as described is not the attempt to encourage management responsiveness and management responsibility, or to secure statements of requirements, but the belief that these are sufficient to encompass the totality of the management task in the public domain. Performance management cannot be confined to the requirements laid down. The mechanics of accountable management should be a part, but only a part of performance management.

Accountable management can only develop to meet the purposes and conditions of the public domain if it is set in an organisational culture supportive of that domain. If managers are to be given greater responsibility, it is important that they appreciate not merely the tasks but the manner in which they are to be carried out. The role of collective choice, the importance of the political process, the imperatives of public accountability, the need for public discourse and the requirement for public learning have all to be reflected in the values expressed in management action in the public domain, for it is through these processes that performance has to be tested and its meaning established.

In any case the allocation of responsibility in democratically accountable organisations is likely to be confused by the perennial uncertainty as to which specific issues and events will in practice be politically significant ... Accountable management in general and the Financial Management Initiative in particular with its emphasis on clear allocation of responsibilities or on unambiguous information about activities, cost and outcomes, is in principle at odds with all this. (Flynn *et al.*, 1988, p. 187).

Managers given devolved responsibility have to accept the requirements of the political process and the necessity of public discourse. A manager should not assume that because she has delegated authority, there is no need to seek political or other guidance. A manager in the private sector has to be close to the market. A manager in the public domain has to be close to public discourse and that requires understanding of the political process.

> A trading organisation, which lives or dies by the success it has in meeting its customers wishes has a great incentive to ensure that decisions are taken in the full light of what those wishes may be, and the people who know that tend to be close to the interface with the customer. Management in the market sector is driven by the imperative of individual choice in the market place. Management in the public domain is driven by a different imperative ... The primary purpose is to service collective choices made through the political system. (Richards, 1988, pp. 13–14)

The argument is not that accountable management should not be introduced; but that it should not ignore the reality of the political process or the importance of public discourse, any more than its equivalent in the private sector can ignore the reality of the market. The tests of effective performance management include political sensitivity and recognition of the need to test political reaction to the unexpected and to the emerging patterns of public discourse.

The Special Case of Contracting

Any system of accountable management in the public domain has to be related to the political process and open to public discourse. The problems identified in accountable management also place limits on the extent to which contracting out is compatible with the purposes, values and conditions of the public domain. Where a task can be defined, targets specified and quality identified; the task is relatively stable and unaffected by other developments; the task is largely outside the issues raised in public discourse; the task only makes limited contribution to organisational learning – then contracting out can develop within the purposes and conditions of the public domain, but otherwise learning can be restricted, the capacity for adaptation can be lost and public discourse confined.

It is too readily assumed that in the private sector markets dominate hierarchies even within organisations, and that the development of contracts in the public sector follows best private sector practice. Leaving aside the relevance of that practice in the public sector, it ignores the analysis by Williamson (1975, 1983) who argues that firms are unlikely to contract out activities where there is high uncertainty, high transaction costs or the possibility of opportunistic behaviour. But whether or not they contract out work, public organisations cannot surrender responsibility for collective action, whatever organisation carries it out on their behalf.

The impression given by advocates of privatization in all its forms is that it offers an either/or choice, not just alternatives, but substitutes for public management. Reality is more complicated. Public and private management are often complementary. Even if government sheds blocks of work and direct production responsibilities, it retains high-level public management responsibilities for defining the framework within which business methods are used. (Metcalfe and Richards, 1987, p. 176)

The introduction of compulsory competitive tendering in local authorities can illustrate the issues involved. Even when the contract is won in-house, management by contract replaces management by hierarchy. It has led to the client–contractor split (paralleling the purchaser–provider split in the health service). 'Competition has led to a clear distinction between client and contractor roles in the authority, both at committee and departmental level' (Walsh, 1991, p. 4).

The development of management by contract has extended beyond the services subject to competitive tendering, particularly in relation to central services, where service-level agreements (or a form of internal contract) have been introduced to govern relationships with other departments. The development has been seen in its initial stages as 'offering significant gains to the authority, in requiring examination of services and the way that they are managed' (Walsh, 1991, p. 6). That is the result for particular services. Rather different issues arise for the system as a whole.

The development tends to turn multi-purpose organisations into a series of autonomous or semi-autonomous units which conduct their relationship with each other through contracts. Issues arise about the capacity for public learning where learning is bounded by a contract, for public discourse where accountability is to a contract and about adaptability where tasks are specified in a contract.

> In a word the contract makes the wrong assumptions about the world – for example that it is unchanging and made up of disparate elements – and then further limits the search for productivity gains by focussing exclusively on the specific production quotas and so on required for contract compliance. (Latimore, 1980, p. 122)

Contracting focuses attention on the contract. The continuing requirements of the public domain cannot be contained in a contract.

Conclusion: Developing Public Management for Learning

If public management is to overcome the limitations of management by contract, it must encompass the learning processes of public organisations. Learning cannot and should not be confined to key tasks or to specified requirements for that is to imply that nothing has been learnt beyond what was already known.

Space for learning is required beyond the mechanics of management by contract. That space has to be protected in the structuring of public organisations whether at the level of the individual manager, of a service, of an organisation or of system management. Understanding is sought of what has been done and what has been achieved not merely to record success or failure but to learn of change and the need for change. Such analysis in the public domain extends beyond organisations because achievement has in the end to be judged in the arena of public discourse.

If public management is to realise the purposes and conditions of the public domain it must develop beyond the codes of the social democratic period and the contracts of neo-liberalism and develop forms appropriate to the learning society. The new public management must develop its tasks in a way that is informed by the challenge of renewing the public domain. This requires a capacity for change. The remaining chapters are preoccupied with establishing the new management of the public domain:

- *public learning*: Chapter 8 will analyse the organising of learning
- judging *public choice*: Chapter 9 will focus upon the contribution of strategic management
- enabling *public accountability*: Chapter 10 will focus on reviewing performance and accounting to the public
- empowering a *public culture*: Chapter 11 will focus upon staff and organisational development

8

Public Learning

A learning society requires public learning as the necessary condition for its growth and development. The public domain provides the setting for public learning in the arena of public discourse; the requirement of management is to develop the strength of that arena for public learning and to ensure that the learning is realised and used. These requirements will only be met if public organisations themselves are learning organisations.

Theory of Learning and Organisational Learning

Learning is a process of discovery about why things are as they are and how they might become. Such understanding grows from processes of reflection that reveal the connection between things which had previously been unrecognised or opaque. Discovery is most likely to occur through experience, when people immerse themselves in the practice of activities so that their meaning becomes transparent. Once the working of a particular system has been revealed, it then becomes amenable to change, and it is the experience of change that provides the catalyst to learning. For Dewey (1950) this theory of learning expressed a whole philosophy of being in the world: through active experience we come to understand the world and thus to change it. Knowledge only lives and has meaning through action. This 'action learning' perspective has been applied to modern organisations by Revans (1982) and Handy (1989) for whom 'a theory of learning is also a theory of changing'. Learning implies understanding that will lead into

168

action, and also implies that ongoing practice will be transformed as a result.

The significance of these learning processes for organisations as well as for individuals and the conditions which enable learning have become a distinctive tradition of study. The nature of the learning organisation has been explored in different sectors: in health (Harrow and Willcocks, 1990, 1992; Attwood and Beer, 1988); in planning (Friedmann, 1987); in education (Holly and Southworth, 1989); and in business (Pedler, Burgoyne and Boydell, 1991; Lessem, 1993). A distinctive framework for analysing the learning organisation has become influential in this literature.

Loops of Learning

In 1978, Argyris and Schon (see Argyris, 1993) introduced an important distinction between levels of complexity in processes of learning: single- and double-loop learning. In single-loop learning a simple change is made to an activity which is not working effectively. For example, within an incremental budgeting system overspend could be corrected by reducing the level of increment to each service. Double-loop learning questions the underlying assumptions which inform the activities, in this case perhaps reviewing the principles on which budgets are constructed.

> Single-loop learning is like a thermostat that learns when it is too hot or too cold and turns the heat on or off. The thermostat can perform this task because it can receive information (the temperature of the room) and take corrective action. Double-loop learning occurs when error is detected and corrected in ways that involve modification of an organisation's underlying norms, policies and objectives. (p. 34)

Certain problems cannot be resolved without reflecting back on the very principles which inform practices and which are usually taken for granted. Argyris and Schon believe that whereas most organisations do quite well at the simpler learning they have great difficulties in the more complex double-loop learning. This is because many organisations are predisposed to inhibit processes of reflection which bring into question fundamental objectives and beliefs.

What are the Conditions for Learning

Different kinds of learning, Argyris and Schon argue, require different conditions. Simple problems can be resolved by forms of inquiry which enable new information to come to the surface, or connections to be made within an activity which had not hitherto been appreciated but the recognition of their interdependence is essential for effective action to proceed. In these inquiries certain processes are vital for their success: the value placed upon questioning to elucidate information, clarity of ideas, testing ideas against the evidence, and building up patterns or trends of activity. It is helpful to perceive these learning processes as a cycle (see Handy, 1988; Revans, 1982; Kolb, 1973, 1984):

Learning starts with curiosity about a particular problem or puzzle which issues in questions to be answered. These we describe as triggers for learning. The inquiry stimulated by such triggers leads us to form ideas or conjectures or 'theories' about what causes the problem and then to test these ideas. Deliberation on the experience can illuminate the underlying processes and produce learning which changes the way we arrange an activity. It might even change the way we think about the activity or lead us to new activities.

FIGURE 8.1
The learning cycle

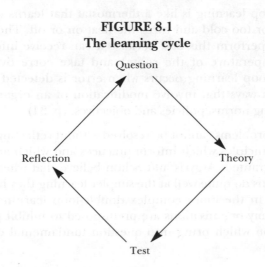

The source of some problems, however, lies in the differences of perspective or belief which individuals or groups within an organisation may have and which may prevent them reaching agreement about what counts as evidence or a relevant question. Understanding falls down because of the failure of communication: individuals cannot understand each other because they do not grasp the meaning and significance of the other concepts. The solution depends upon the willingness of groups to listen to opposing interpretations and reach agreement about a new framework of values and assumptions. For many organisations, however, the reality of conflicting perspectives may not be recognised or be actively suppressed. Organisations may need to develop skills in conflict management. The task is to create the conditions for double-loop learning:

> the consequence of learning should be an emphasis on double-loop learning, by means of which individuals confront the basic assumptions behind the present views of others and invite confrontation of their own basic assumptions, and by which underlying hypotheses are tested publicly and are made disconfirmable, not self-sealing
>
> ... an enhancement of the conditions for *organisational* double-loop learning, where assumptions and norms central to organisational theory-in-use are surfaced ... publicly confronted, tested and restructured. (Argyris and Schon, 1978, p. 139)

In the right conditions, people can react in different ways, so that they are more amenable to the difficult processes of questioning their own beliefs and becoming more receptive to the value of others' beliefs: if double-loop learning is to occur, people would

- feel less defensive
- feel free to take risks
- search for inconsistencies in their own speech and encourage others to confront their own
- be able to state their views in ways that are disconfirmable
- believe that public testing would not be harmful.

The conditions that are most appropriate for supporting double-loop learning are those which reinforce open discussion

in search of agreement. Such a context mirrors within the organisation Habermas's (1981) conditions for communicative rationality: in which speakers in public strive to make claims which are
true, correct and sincere. When committed to these principles
speakers are oriented to correct mistaken perceptions and to syn-
thesise perspectives when rationally possible:

> the correction of ... errors requires the conditions of the good
> dialectic, which begins with the development of a map that pro-
> vides a different perspective on the problem (e.g. a different
> set of governing values or norms). The opposition of ideas and
> persons then makes it possible to invent responses that approx-
> imate the organisation's espoused theory.(Argyris and Schon,
> 1978, p. 143)

The struggles between groups present dilemmas for organisations but also opportunities when they can lead into double-loop
learning, because it can enable an organisation to unify around
shared purposes. But the dialectic which prepares for any such
synthesis of perspectives may not be an easy process:

> [The good dialectic] is not a matter of smoothness of opera-
> tion or elimination of error. On the contrary, its goodness is
> inherent in the ways in which error is continually interpreted
> and corrected, incompatibility and incongruity are continually
> engaged, and conflict is continually confronted and resolved ...
> the dialectical process focuses attention on incompatibility of
> norms and objectives which are not resolvable by a search for
> the most effective means. For norms set the criteria by which
> effectiveness may be judged. (ibid., p. 146)

Learning to Learn

The most effective process of learning forms a third stage of complexity: learning how to learn. Organisations experiencing change
need a general predisposition to learn if they are to succeed.
Bateson (1973) has called this 'deutero-learning' in which individuals become creative at learning about how they have been
learning: they reflect on and analyse their previous styles of learning or failing to learn. They clarify what enabled or blocked their
learning so that they can take remedial action and develop new

strategies for learning. In organisations, Argyris and Schon propose, the new strategies become encoded in mental maps that reshape organisational practice.

> learning continually questions the status quo, the theories in use people have to learn how to learn, discover how to discover, invent, generalise, learn how to establish a good dialectic. (Argyris and Schon, 1978, p. 144)

The learning organisation becomes self-aware about the cycles of learning and the conditions for learning. It becomes proficient at asking questions, developing ideas, testing them and reflecting on practice.

Awareness of the cycles of learning encourages participants to explore continually the conditions of learning, why it is that individuals and groups are open to new ideas, new ways of thinking which keep them at the front end of change. Learning pushes back the boundaries of inquiry about the conditions which support and constrain change, laying bare the deep structures of social action. The individual explores the constraints and opportunities of the organisational context in which she works; while the organisation similarly questions the limits of the wider society in which it is located. Learning continually extends the cycle of learning.

In this way the learning process explores the structures of action: the values which underly the perspectives, the forms of interaction and the nature and distribution of power that drives action. Learning about these systems of action within organisations is best nurtured within 'action learning sets' that enable the participants, through collaborative working and reflection, to open out to and accommodate the value in each perspective and to develop the predisposition to change practice. The capacity for learning is the capacity for dialectic in changing practice.

What has been written about organisational learning has special relevance to organisations in the public domain as the site of public learning, a necessary condition for the development of the learning society. The organising principles of that domain are principles for learning, which must involve double-loop learning, that can challenge existing organisations and activities. That will be achieved by open public discourse which is not bounded by existing activities. The process of discourse in the public domain is the basis for learning to learn. Public learning in this sense depends upon the institutional framework fulfilling the conditions set out in Chapter 4 and upon the organisations within that framework sustaining public learning.

Public Learning

We distinguished in Chapter 5 between the continuity roles of maintenance and sustaining and the change roles of responsiveness and development. Each set of roles has its own requirements for organisational learning in the public domain. The maintenance and sustaining roles are focused on continuing activities. They are concerned with change to improve the efficiency or effectiveness of those activities but not the nature of the activities. The learning required is single-loop learning. It is about:

- whether the activities were carried out
- whether the activities were carried out efficiently
- whether resources were used as planned
- whether the activities had the planned effect

Learning is expressed through change in working methods, in resource allocation or in operational management.

The responsive and developmental roles require double-loop learning for they are concerned with change in the activities themselves. Learning is about:

- whether the activities should be carried out
- whether the nature of the activities should be changed
- whether new activities should be introduced

The learning society requires the enhancement of double-loop learning to support the responsive and developmental roles, as a necessary condition of societal development.

Learning of the need for response and development does not come automatically in the working of an organisation. The learning for response is of societal change. Some of this can be learning from present activities in the public domain – if those activities have ceased to have their expected impact, it may be because change in society has made their present form ineffective. But the learning required for responsive change cannot be limited to that which comes from present activities. Government needs an understanding of societal change beyond the present pattern of activities. The learning required is about

- problems and issues which render present policies ineffective
- aspirations which cannot be met by present policies
- emerging problems and issues which are not being adequately met within present society
- changing knowledge which can lead to the possibility of more effective action by government
- the capacity of organisations inside and outside the public domain to meet the problems and issues faced and to realise the aspirations held

The learning required for responsive change is relevant to development. Problems unmet can stimulate not merely response but also development. The difference lies in the use made of such learning. Development is not predetermined by existing policies and the use made of the learning is not constrained by existing categories formed by those policies.

> If government is to learn to solve new public problems, it must also learn to create the systems for doing so and to discard the structure and mechanism grown up around old problems. (Schon, 1971, p. 116)

Development requires, therefore, a deeper understanding and a wider learning achieved in the arena of public discourse.

The danger within organisations in the public domain is that learning is restricted to single-loop learning because it is governed by present practice and therefore cannot meet the requirements of learning for change in response and for development.

The Organisational Conditions for Public Learning

Organisational learning for change requires triggers to stimulate new thinking and to break up past ways of thinking. Triggers can be sought in the environment, but there are limitations:

> Organizations cannot afford to scan their environments, con-
> tinually searching for conditions that require actions. They
> search intermittently, they rely on attention-directing standard
> operating procedures, and they question these procedures only
> when problems begin to mount. (Hedberg, 1981, pp. 13–16)

Nor are triggers for learning enough, unlearning has also to take
place: 'To learn, unlearn and relearn is the organizational walk:
development comes to an end when one of these legs is missing'
(Hedberg, ibid.).

Any organisation has a tendency to set barriers to learning that
can lead to triggers for learning being ignored or resisted. While
most would recognise that organisations need to change in a
changing environment, they cannot and should not seek to
respond to each and every change. Stability is necessary for the
performance of activities. Organisational interests in the form of
staff committed to existing activities reinforce stability and set
their own barriers to learning.

> Organisations are characterised in part by the division of labour
> and by specialisation. The environment is frequently changing,
> complex and uncertain. Personnel have their own goal and
> values and differ from one another in terms of their abilities. To
> manage this situation, organisations are bounded by rules, rou-
> tines and procedures which necessarily make them inflexible,
> undemonstrative and slow to change. (Jackson, 1982, p. 253)

The triggers to learning in the public domain differ from those
in the private sector. The triggers for the private sector are to be
found in the market. The market sends its messages from a changing environment and those messages will normally have an impact
on the organisation, although there are enough examples of firms
that have not responded to signs of market change. The dilemma
of the private firm is that the messages the market sends will be
about the present state of the market – they do not tell directly of
the future, although the future can often be read in present
changes by those prepared to do so. The private firm needs to read
the future as well as the present, for the future requires present
action. A firm that waits for market decline may face market failure.
Market influences provide a countervailing force to the barriers to learning for the private firm. A marketing department

crosses the boundary between an organisation and its environment. Within the overall organisation it represents the external world of customers although it too can become enclosed in its own boundaries and be unable to see beyond present services or products.

If the market provides the triggers for learning in the private sector, then the triggers for the public domain have to be found in the arena of public discourse and the political processes that lead into and from that arena. In the arena of public discourse learning comes from listening to the voices that express issues, concerns and aspirations. The political processes that carry that learning operate through 'voice' as opposed to the option of 'exit' in the market. Voice is expressed in many ways. Demands are made, problems are raised, aspirations are stated, ideas are tested and claims are asserted by individuals and organisations. Interest groups pose issues in pressure and protest. Political parties gather differing voices into programmes and policies and contend in debate and discussion. Voice can be a trigger for learning and, if strong enough, can overcome the barriers to learning through political processes.

Policy units in government developed as a trigger for learning:

> Policy planning units were to be thinking organisations, generally active and sensitive to new issues. Policy units were seen as a means to improve the capacity of government bureaucracies to comprehend and respond to public needs and changes in those needs. The Fulton Report argued that the Civil Service must show initiative in working out what are the needs of the future and how they might be met ... For Seebohm research represented 'important insurance against complacency and stagnation'. (Prince, 1983, p. 28)

Yet such units have often failed to overcome the barriers to organisational learning. The views of such units have failed to command organisational attention or even where given, attention has not been translated into action. Such failure has often been because the units have relied upon triggers for learning based not upon the conditions of the public domain and its organising principles, but on analytical techniques unrelated to those conditions. The data and analysis produced by such units is a necessary part of organisational learning, but data and analysis require triggers of attention to secure their use and use is necessary to organisational learning. Such triggers are to be found in the arena of public discourse and through political processes.

Political processes can be assisted in developing organisational learning where policy planning units are close to the political processes. Then data and analysis can both inform the processes but also respond to them, for organisational learning in the public domain requires both the softer data of opinion and aspiration and the harder data of quantitative analysis. Such units grow in impact if linked to political processes and lose in impact if they are separated from them as the history of the Central Policy Review Staff shows.

It is through political processes that the voices of the ethnic minorities have begun to be heard in government. Councillors from the ethnic minorities have now been elected to local authorities, transforming the balance of interest and concern. It is through political processes in their widest sense of voice raised that other public sector organisations are slowly learning of the demands and needs of a multi-ethnic society – if too slowly, for the arenas of discourse and political processes can, like a market, have their own imperfections. So far there are only a few Members of Parliament from the ethnic minorities.

Certain groups may gain access more easily or be heard more readily. The information available may be distorted. Some signals from the political process, like the signals from the market, tend to tell more of the present than of the future, although, unlike the market, some voices at least will speak for the future, for it is a mistake to assume that the political process is necessarily and invariably dominated by the short term. The politics of issues can reflect views that are about the future as much as the present. The future can be argued for in the arena of discourse, as it has been powerfully argued for by environmental groups. Such groups assert the rights of the future against the present in the aspiration to sustainable development.

If the barriers to organisational learning in the public domain are to be overcome, it will be achieved through strengthening and widening access to the arena of public discourse and the political processes that relate to it. The more open the arena of public discourse is to those who seek access to it and the more open public organisations are in informing it, the more likely is organisational learning in and from the arena, but it still depends upon the strength of political processes. The development of community forums extends discourse, but political processes have to be strengthened to build that discourse into the organisations of government. The appointment of political advisers in central government, the institution of select committees in the House of Commons or advocacy of open government are all means of strengthening political processes for organisational learning. That does not ensure organisational learning, but the stronger the political processes, the more likely they are to command attention within the working of the organisation.

Certain organisations in the public domain such as appointed boards are institutionally separated from the political process. They neither operate in the market nor are directly subject to the political process. They are however subject to political control. Thus health authorities are subject to the control of the Department of Health, and are subject to demands, pressure and protest in the arena of public discourse. Community Health Councils were set up as a formal means for channelling public views into a semi-consultative process. The development of health committees in local authorities should be welcomed by health authorities as opening up their learning processes. The danger is that health authorities isolate themselves from the political process and cut themselves off from the arena of public discourse on which organisational learning in the public domain should be based. As district health authorities develop their role as purchasers of health services on behalf of the public the arena of public discourse becomes yet more important. Some health authorities are developing local purchasing (Ham, 1992) as a response to that need.

Organisational learning is important for organisations in the public domain as it is important for any organisation, but the special feature of such organisations is that they build public learning as a necessary condition of societal development. That is achieved through the arena of public discourse and political processes. Effective organisational learning in the public domain therefore requires not merely what would be required in any organisation, but the development of that arena, the effectiveness of those political processes and an organisational capacity to learn from them.

EXHIBIT 8.1

The development of local purchasing

As purchasers of services district health authorities have the responsibility for assessing health needs, but in carrying out that responsibility they have to be sensitive to local communities. Yet in order to increase their purchasing power DHAs have joined in consortia or been amalgamated. Locality purchasing seeks to combine

the advantages of purchasing for a bigger population with enhanced sensitivity to small communities. The interest shown in locality purchasing also reflects a growing recognition that health authorities, to be effective purchasers, need to give practical expression to their oft-quoted role as 'champions of the people'. This means being active in seeking people's views and promoting an informed debate about health issues in the context of localities with which people identify. (Ham, 1992, p. 1)

In Dorset there have been attempts to involve the community. A steering group has been formed for each small community containing a wide range of community representatives drawn from public bodies, voluntary organisations, the churches and local representatives. It supports the work of co-ordinators whose key tasks are:

To form friendly relationships with people
To listen to what people have to say
To facilitate discussion
To ensure that any personal information remains confidential
To obtain information during discussion, where appropriate
To value the time people have spent giving their views

In essence, then, it involves listening to what local people have identified as the main health issues and working collaboratively to improve the health of the community through practical action. (ibid., p. 13).

The *issue raised* by locality purchasing is how to extend learning beyond organisational boundaries. The Dorset example highlights the role of public discourse.

The Management of Learning

Organisational learning does not just happen. Nor if it happens is it actually used. Organisational learning has its own requirements and its own special requirements in the public domain: for management this means:

- an appreciation of learning
- the balance of learning
- the strength of learning from the political process and from the arena of public discourse
- reconciling the hard and the soft data of learning
- using the learning
- building public learning

An Appreciation of Learning

The management of learning must start from an understanding of existing processes of organisational learning and of the biases in them. Any organisation learns; the issue is how it learns. If learning is structured around existing tasks and existing processes, then learning will tend to reinforce present practices, rather than to open up possibilities. In other words, the learning process is single-loop learning which supports the maintenance and sustaining roles rather than double-loop learning for the responsive and development roles. The bias towards present practices needs to be balanced by learning processes that open up the organisation to societal and environmental change beyond the scope of present activities and present policies.

Even in relation to present activities, there may be bias in the learning processes. If a service discriminates implicitly even if not explicitly, then the learning processes built around the operation of the service will reflect that discrimination. If the deprived and the inarticulate have difficulty getting access then their demands are likely to be unheard and their needs unmet.

The organisation may be structured to learn in particular ways. Organisations in which professionalism is dominant will learn most easily of needs and problems that can be met by professionals, and of knowledge that builds upon existing professional knowledge. The danger for organisations in the public domain is that if they are not structured to learn from the arena of public discourse or if that arena is distorted they are limited in their capacity to meet the purposes and values of the public domain. These are pathological conditions for organisational learning in the public domain, against which management grounded in the nature of that domain has to guard.

The Balance of Learning

An appreciation of learning processes should lead to action to correct biases in the learning processes. This will not normally mean the elimination of existing learning processes, but the opening up of new channels of learning. If the learning processes are biased against certain groups then the effective management of learning requires organisational action to open up channels of access for such groups bringing in voices and ideas, problems and aspirations otherwise unheard. How such a bias is redressed is a political issue, for organisational learning in the public domain both reflects and supports power structures. The management of learning requires that the political issue is raised.

Health authorities which can easily be isolated from the political processes should consider how they can learn from those processes. Pressures and protest should have a special significance for them, as should the views of local authorities expressing local voice in the arena of public discourse. Local authority departments dominated by professional processes of learning should consider how other channels for learning can be developed.

EXHIBIT 8.2

Searching out voices not always heard

The London Borough of Hammersmith and Fulham carried out a survey of public attitudes, as has been carried out in an increasing number of local authorities. However, before the survey was carried out panel discussions were arranged to ensure the questions raised reflected key issues felt by local people. Special panels were formed to consider the needs of groups whose views would not have been heard in general discussion because even if they had been present, their views could easily have been overlooked. Panel discussions with specific groups were arranged with, for example:

- elderly women in sheltered accommodation
- male and female members of an Afro-Caribbean social centre
- members of an Asian women's group
- members of an organisation for the unemployed
- members of two centres for people with disabilities

The *issue raised* is the need for learning to extend to those whose voices are not always easily heard.

Central government departments which work through other agencies and organisations should consider how they can learn of the reality faced by such organisations and of their way of working.

The Strength of Learning from the Political Process and the Arena of Public Discourse

The effectiveness of organisational learning in the public domain depends upon the vitality of the arena of public discourse and the strength of the political processes. The rich source of learning through political processes is often untapped by existing organisations. The complaints or demands that come from elected representatives are rarely seen as part of organisational learning, but more as a series of inconvenient letters to be replied to or points to be answered, yet they provide a map of public concerns for those who have the capacity to read it. As community forums develop so must the capacity to learn from them.

A protest campaign has many lessons for those who have the ability to listen to the complex issues raised as well as respond to them. It can be so readily assumed that the closure of a hospital or the building of a road will raise protest that the voices of protest are not attended to. Yet public meetings can be used to turn protest towards discussion by forming groups to explore issues. The process of debate, discussion and argument is a means of learning that can challenge past assumptions for those who are ready to be challenged.

Interpreting and Reconciling the Hard and the Soft of Learning

Translating from political processes into organisational practice requires the capacity to use and work with the soft data of opinions, views and suggestions as well as the hard data of analysis. Perceptions of problems and issues in the political processes have to be matched with the quantitative analysis required for organisational action. Data requires interpretation. The hard data of examination results provides limited meaning without interpretation.

Learning can use both soft and hard data. Learning processes that are restricted to one or the other limit organisational capacity for learning. One danger is that concern for the hard data of analysis drives out the soft data which may be necessary to understand the analysis. Another danger is that action on the soft data of opinion is unrelated to the hard data of analysis. But the greatest danger is the development of two separate processes – each based on its own type of data, without the capacity to translate between them.

Using the Learning

Learning accumulated may remain unused. Learning unused is not organisational learning because it has not affected organisational practices. Learning that derives from the working of the organisation will be readily used by the organisation in the maintenance and sustaining roles, but such learning is likely to derive from and support existing practices. The problem arises as new channels of learning are opened up that challenge existing practices or open up future possibilities in the responsive and development roles. Such learning may have little impact unless it can gain leverage on existing ways of working.

Research and intelligence units in local government have produced analyses that remain unused and possibly unread. The government statistical services produce material, but the production of material does not ensure its use. Policy planning units can, as we have seen, be isolated in their work from the organisations they seek to influence.

Organisational learning, if it is to be used not to support existing organisational practices but to change them, needs leverage on present ways of working. Triggers for change must not merely be found but be paid attention to. In the public domain, that requires effective political processes that can lead to the changes required. The management of learning must not merely provide channels for learning from the political process, but must support that process as an instrument for organisational change.

Building Public Learning

The management of learning is directed at organisational learning. In building an organisational capacity for learning, management is also building a capacity for public learning. Learning draws upon the arena of public discourse, but also informs that

---

EXHIBIT 8.3

Attitudes to policing

A survey for the Operational Policing Review, 1990, commissioned by the Association of Chief Police Officers, the Police Superintendents' Association and the Police Federation, found that amongst the public:

- 70% of people thought there were too few police on the beat in the neighbourhood;
- 2% thought there were too many police around;
- a quarter said they had never even seen one on foot patrol;
- many thought they should concentrate on preventing crime. (Shearer, 1991, p. 14)

But amongst the police:

- 69% thought that the distribution of foot and car patrols was about right;
- a third thought that advising the public on crime prevention was important;
- 56% thought it was important to get to know local people;
- 93% thought it was very important to detect and arrest offenders. (ibid.)

Shearer concludes that what 'people want of the police is that they prevent crime, police the community and make themselves visible by walking the beat. The police on the other hand, give priority to attending to emergencies, making arrests and solving serious crimes' (ibid.).

The *issue raised* is in so far as there is a difference of view about how the police should respond, the answer may lie in public discourse for learning – the public from the police and the police from the public.

---

arena. Learning informs, but also develops in community forums as an arena of public discourse. The vitality of the arena has to be a responsibility of management in the public arena. When government issues Green Papers or White Papers they act to inform that arena, but the informing is occasional and can be distorted rather than a continuing process. Learning, to be public learning, has to be drawn into the arena of public discourse.

The management of learning should build a continuing cycle of learning in which management both draws upon and informs the arena of public discourse.

Conclusion

Our argument has been that a learning society depends upon the depth and quality of public learning which must be mediated by management in the public domain. Organisations in the public domain, like any organisations, can become dominated by the necessities of present activities. In such organisations single-loop learning prevails, reinforcing present activities and restricting learning to the boundaries of those activities. Management in the public domain, if it is to sustain a learning society, cannot be limited to those boundaries. Its triggers to learning have to be found in the conditions and organising principles of the public domain – through the arena of public discourse and the political processes that link the organisation to that arena. That learning to be used must inform the processes of public choice to which we now turn.

9

Judging Public Choice

The Necessity of Judgement

The task of public management is to support the processes of the polity, enriched by participation as well as representation, thus enabling discourse about the purpose and shape of public policy. Public choices which endeavour to reconcile and embody the variety of expressed needs are likely to acquire legitimacy because the public invests its authority in them. Determining which choices express the public will is inescapably a matter of forming judgement about purpose in the context of a complex of interests. Judgement grounded in practical reason is the indispensable task that lies at the centre of public management. Management in the private sector can use quantitative calculation to determine decisions about market efficiency. In the public domain, however, while judgement can be informed and tested, it cannot be reduced to calculation. The quality of judgement can be supported by the distinctive tasks of strategic management which, by grounding analysis in public discourse, can lead to informed choices for policy and community development.

Judgement is the condition of action in the public domain. Because that domain is unbounded, judgements have to be made to determine the scope of action. Because any voice has access, judgements have to be made on the response. In that domain, objectives do not predetermine action, because in a plural community objectives can compete and conflict. Values and interests in society have to be balanced. In the public domain the public interest is sought, but can never be finally determined – a judgement has to be based on public discourse.

Judgement in the public domain is necessarily a public judgement made through political processes – it is with the nature of political judgement that we are concerned. The role of public discourse is to involve the public in developing an understanding of and influencing those judgements that are to shape public policy. The processes of debate and discussion explore the basis of judgement and test it out. Voices raised in discourse record reaction and impact.

The nature of management in the public domain is conditioned by the task of enabling political judgement. Its role is to support and express that judgement and for that, understanding of the nature of judgement is required. A faculty is required which avoids the illusion of determining objective, 'scientific', decision-making, while at the same time avoiding the immanent possibility of arbitrary subjectivism. Judgement, argues Beiner (1983), offers the precious, indispensable, faculty which requires individuals, through deliberation, to reach detached reasons for decisions and action. The issues that we face in everyday public life are then made amenable to reflective reason, public discourse, dialogue and common deliberation. The faculty restores public life to the responsible participation of the citizen against the encroaching domination of technocratic 'expertise':

> if the faculty of judging is a general aptitude that is shared by all citizens, and if the exercise of this faculty is a sufficient qualification for active participation in political life, we have a basis for reclaiming the privilege of responsibility that has been prized from us on grounds of specialised competence ... Politics removed from the sphere of common judgement is a perversion of the political and as such cannot help but manifest itself in political crisis. (Beiner, 1983, p. 3)

The world of the political involves everyone and is everyone's responsibility. An expert can advise but not appropriate that responsibility. It requires of citizens a recognition of that responsibility and a willingness to learn about and to exercise the faculty of intersubjective deliberation. Judgement gains importance in a learning society as learning grows with judgement.

The vehicle for supporting the learning process in public organisations so as to lead to wise judgements about the public good is strategic management.

The Contribution of Strategic Management

Strategic management mediates an organisation and its changing environment, enabling it to clarify and judge the significant changes of purpose and priority in policy that will determine the future development of the organisation. Strategy provides the capacity for managing change. The guiding sense of direction emerges from processes of enquiry which explore the fundamental questions any organisation must answer: what is our essential function? Who is our public? How are we to serve them? What implications are there for the way we are organised? The analyses can provide a vision of organisational purpose and the shape of priorities for planning over time.

The development of strategic management is thus about generating the capacity for strategic change, enabling the organisation to respond positively to the challenge presented to it by social, economic and political transformations in its environment. Its fundamental analyses identify how the organisation will need to change if it is to continue to flourish. Strategic management recognises the strength that lies in the rituals of organisational working to inhibit the capacity to respond to change. The distinctive purpose of strategic management is to protect the capacity of an organisation to adapt to change and to redirect day-by-day routines in the light of strategic choices. If strategic management is to achieve a different perspective from that of operational management this perspective will:

- recognise choice in the continuity of existing activities
- look beyond the short term of immediate action to the longer-term horizon of choice
- focus not on the services provided but on the arena of public discourse and on the societal changes reflected in that arena
- accept the primacy of the political processes over the operational requirements of public action

- be aware of the uncertainties of present impact and future issues rather than the certainty of continuing activities
- be selective in focus rather than encompassing the comprehensiveness of operational activities
- be concerned with the network of organisations in the public domain rather than be limited to the capacity of separate organisations

A strategic management perspective will need to be protected in the working of organisations, lest the dominance of operational management allows neither organisational time or space for its development. That protection can be provided by processes of strategic management, not as ends in themselves but as a means of achieving organisational change where and when it is required.

EXHIBIT 9.1

Strategic issues in the health service

Pettigrew, Ferlie and McKee (1992) identify as examples of strategic change in the health service:

- The introduction of general management into the NHS as an institutional reform by the Department of Health and Social Security.
- Rationalisation and redevelopment in the acute sector as a response to financial retrenchment in Inner London Health Authorities.
- The response of Inner London Health Authorities to a major new health care issue of the 1980s – HIV/AIDS.
- The problems faced by two North Western Health Authorities in closing large Victorian institutions, while at the same time providing new non-institutional arrangements for the mentally ill.
- Changes undertaken by two district health authorities in provision for the mentally handicapped as a response to the planned closure of a long-stay institution.
- The creation of a district general hospital to meet the requirement of a new town.

The *issue raised* for this chapter is what makes these themes strategic. Each theme involves a change in the organisation of health services to bring about changes in the way of working, to overcome perceived organisational weakness, or to respond to a changed environment or to emerging ideas.

The Relevance of Private Sector Experience

The concept of strategy is found in many organisations – both in the public domain and in the private sector. At a conceptual level it is possible to delineate strategy in generalised terms that apply to all organisations. Formulating strategy involves mediating environment and organisation. As Mintzberg (1983) argues: 'Strategy formulation ... involves the interpretation of the environment and the development of consistent pattern in streams of organisational decisions (strategies) to deal with it'(pp. 13–14). Johnson and Scholes add that

> Strategic decisions are concerned with the scope of an organisation's activities; the matching of an organisation's activities to its environment; the matching of the activities of an organisation to its resource capacity; the allocation and reallocation of major resources in an organisation; the values, expectations and goals of these influencing strategy; the direction an organisation will move in the long term; implications for change in the organisations. (Johnson and Scholes, 1984, p. 9)

The problem is, however, to give meaning in practice to these concepts and then regard must be had to the distinctive purposes, conditions and tasks of the public domain. Strategic management in the private sector focuses on a firm's product/market mix, identifying the need for change to enhance its competitive stance. That is not a helpful model in the public domain. Public organisations do not face market choices in that sense. They may well be required to provide services because of market failure. They do not respond to market signals but to voices raised in the arena of public discourse. Nor do they normally face choices about the geographical areas in which they will operate. Hampshire County Council cannot decide that it would be better to operate in Lancashire. In addition,public organisations are not, nor should they be, judged by their competitive stance, but rather by their co-operative behaviour.

In the past, the main emphasis in strategic management in public organisations has been placed on strategic planning using approaches developed from the private sector. Bryson has examined a range of such approaches. He concludes

that corporate strategic planning is not a single concept, procedure or tool. In fact it embraces a range of approaches that vary
in their applicability to the public and nonprofit sectors and in
the conditions that govern their successful use. The approaches
also vary in the extent to which they encompass broad policy and
direction setting, internal and external assessments, attention to
key stakeholders, the identification of key issues, development of
strategies to deal with each issue, decision making, action and
continuous monitoring of results ... A strategic planning process
applicable to public and nonprofit organisations and communities will need to allow for the full range of strategic planning
activities, from policy and direction setting through monitoring
of results. Such a process will contrast, therefore, with the private
sector approaches, which tend to emphasise different parts of
such a complete procedure. A further contrast would be that private sector approaches are focussed only on organisations, not
on functions that cross governmental or organisational boundaries, not on communities or large entities. (Bryson, 1988, p. 43)

Grounding Strategic Management in the Public Domain

Strategic change has been a key feature of recent reforms to the
polity in the period of neo-liberalism:

● the reform of the education system, changing the balance of
   influence and interest between school, local authority and
   national government
● the recognition in some authorities that the traditional committee structure of local authorities cannot contain the new
   politics
● change in recruitment policies to ensure equal opportunities
   become part of accepted working in public organisations
● the appointment of general managers in health authorities
   intended to bring about changes in the balance of power and
   influence in the working of the authority
● the creation of executive agencies by central government
● the search for improvement in public services through the
   introduction of the Citizen's Charter
● the development of contracting-out for public services, and
   the separation of client and contractor roles

- the reorganisation of the health service involving the introduction of the internal market

Such strategic change reflects the capacity of the political process to challenge and break through the forces for continuity in the public domain. We would argue, however, that the process of strategic change has neglected the organising principle of the public domain and has therefore introduced change that frequently has lacked the authority of public consent. Strategic management in the public domain has to be grounded in a more enriched political process which involves the public in debate, bargaining and balancing as conflicting interests are weighed and judged. Strategic management which learns through public discourse of the differing and even conflicting values will lead to more authoritative judgements of public purpose. The development of strategic management is about generating the capacity for responding to and supporting the needs of the learning society.

Strategic management in the public domain should not, for example, seek a fixed set of objectives which can be assumed to guide all action. To do so would be to impose certainty upon the judgements that have continually to be reached in the political processes of the public domain. Rather 'a planned bargaining approach' may be required which 'seeks to combine the top – down formal approach to co-ordination with the bottom – up spontaneous interaction approach' (Challis *et al.*, 1986, p. 274). Such an approach sets the framework for the continuing processes through which particular issues are perceived, resolved and acted upon.

The Phases of Strategic Management

To develop strategic management requires processes that can protect it in the working of public organisations. They can be expressed in a number of cyclical phases:

(i)   learning from the public:
- opening the agenda to the public
- looking outward to expressed problems and needs in the communities

- developing strategies of access for, and listening to, the public
(ii)   interpretive analysis:
- reviewing the environment, organisation and policy
- exposing the options for strategic change
(iii)   strategic judgement and collective choice:
- prioritising policy development and resource allocation
- clarifying the vision and key directions for change
(iv)   planning and the prioritising of resources:
- drawing up medium-term guidelines setting priorities for financial plans beyond the immediate year
(v)   evaluation:
- in reviewing services to establish the appropriateness of existing policies and practice and to sharpen the focus of priorities

Strategic management is a continuous process, searching to clarify the judgements that are to provide a recognised sense of purpose for all in the public domain. Each of the phases of strategic management is necessarily governed by the organising principle of the public domain. This means that the environment with which strategic analysis is concerned is not the environment of the market but the environment of discourse. In the public domain choice is made through political processes. Strategic organisational development should encompass the public to whom those who act in that domain remain accountable. It is with the public that we begin the cycle.

Learning from the Public: Opening Access to Agenda-Setting

The policy agenda in the public domain can never be finalised. Issues can arrive on the policy agenda at any time and from any source. Any issue can become part of public discourse and be transferred from the arena of discourse to the policy agenda. Issues are formed by the interaction of changing experience, values and knowledge. The movement of environmental issues on to the policy agenda of government has been a process in which both small changes and significant events have played their part. Over time, problems have grown in their scale and in their visibility, as, for example, acid rain has taken its toll. Particular events –

Chernobyl; the epidemic that laid waste the seals – have resonated in public discourse.

Changing knowledge can help an issue on to the public agenda. Acid rain can more easily obtain leverage on the public agenda when it is linked to identifiable causes. Problems without known causes do not easily lead to effective policy. But knowledge can also lead to new and early perceptions of policy issues. Knowledge of the growing gap in the ozone layer meant that the issue came on to the policy agenda before its effects become fully felt, although its movement on to the agenda was assisted by the growing saliency of environmental problems generally. A new method of environmental control may even find its own problem. Solutions are argued to find problems in 'garbage can' processes (Cohen, March and Olsen, 1972). Values change through new problems and knowledge, but revised values also lead to reinterpretation of experience. The greater value placed on environmental issues reflects both perceived problems and greater knowledge, but itself leads to new problems being perceived and new knowledge being sought.

Changing experience, values and knowledge bring issues into the arena of public discourse. That does not by itself immediately ensure access to the agenda of policy-making. Access is variable and varying. When the intensity of public discourse on an issue reaches a certain point, it will become part of the agenda of policy, but the intensity required will vary from issue to issue, dependent on the interests involved and their ease of access.

Issues can come on to the agenda in a variety of ways. They can come because of general public or media pressure or because of the pressure of certain interests. A political party may ensure an issue is on the agenda through its programme. An issue may arise because existing policies are creating problems for the working of the organisation or because of formal procedures for policy review either internal to the organisation or external to it, as with Select Committees of the House of Commons, the National Audit Office, the Audit Commission or service inspectorates.

Public management focuses on the adequacy of access for the public, and is concerned with eliminating barriers to the public, especially the voices of minority and disadvantaged groups, which have been excluded from contributing to public dialogue on policy. Barriers can be because:

EXHIBIT 9.2

Food policy issues on the agenda

In 1988 and 1989 a series of issues about food became the subject of political controversy and media attention. Salmonella in eggs, the prevalence of listeria and BSE disease in cattle became issues in the arena of public discourse. The issue of salmonella in eggs had been appreciated in the relevant policy network but that network 'was almost completely dominated by the agricultural community. For most of the post-war period the food industry did not see its interests as conflicting with agriculture' (Smith, 1991, p. 238).

The food policy community realised that a link between eggs and *salmonella* existed and it was a problem that could develop in Britain. Yet policy makers in DoH and MAFF chose to keep the information out of the public domain. It appears that although there was no conscious decision to mislead the public, the attitude of the policy community was that the public should only be informed of the issue once there was hard evidence. (ibid., pp. 241–2)

The reason that salmonella became a political issue was due to changes in the policy network widening the arena of discourse.

Not only have the food manufacturers and the Department of Health become increasingly active but new groups have become involved. The food retailers have enhanced their influence and political interests, the BMA have become more concerned with issues of diet, scientists and nutritionists, consumer groups and more radical groups like the London Food Commission have all become involved in food policy.(ibid., p. 245)

The *issue raised* is how food policy became a subject of political controversy. In effect restricted discourse became public discourse because new voices were heard.

- too high a threshold exists before public concern is heard within public organisations
- there is highly differentiated access for different groups of the public to the arena of public discourse and to government
- areas of organisational concern are defined too narrowly to permit access for certain issues
- traditional forms of public administration may not respond rapidly enough to change in political control, bringing new issues on to the agenda
- processes of policy review within the organisation can become routinised, so that existing policy and practices are not challenged effectively

Public management is concerned with the conditions for access to public discourse:

Pertinent information may enter the decision process or it may be screened out, depending on how it relates to the existing pattern of belief. (Stinbrunen, 1974, p. 35)

Inevitably much of the work of public organisations is structured around existing procedures and practices and is based on the assumptions of those procedures and practices. The main external contact of most public organisation, especially in central government, is with interest groups that are involved in those procedures and practices. Access is often defined by procedures which limit acknowledged concern to such groups and which exclude the unacknowledged publics. Routine patterns of working build and reinforce barriers.

The system is not completely closed. A traumatic event or disaster, such as the Brixton riots or the Hillsborough football disaster, demand a government response as they lead to intensity of public discourse. When protest on an issue reaches a certain intensity, it can break through. A political party in government can impose issues on the agenda on which it is determined and for which it is well-prepared. Financial pressures can give an edge to policy review procedures. But these possibilities do not remove the tendency to define present issues by past practice. New and emerging issues may not even be perceived, yet alone understood, by organisations structured to deal with other issues. They will only be dealt with when pressure overwhelms.

Countervailing forces can be built by policy management into organisations to extend the perspective beyond that of present practice so that review of policy does not have to depend upon crisis or pressure. A local authority is structured on functional principles into service committees and departments. Issues tend to be defined by that structure and those that do not fall within departmental boundaries will not be seen by the authority, never mind be dealt with. Some local authorities have created a structure of area committees and area offices, not to replace service committees and departments (although Tower Hamlets has done

---

EXHIBIT 9.3

The fat-intake issue or a conflict of interest

It has been widely accepted that a reduction in fats eaten, and in particular saturated fats, would improve the health of the nation. Yet at the same time government policies have encouraged farmers to produce products with a high saturated fat content.

For many years farmers have faced a government-controlled grading and pricing system for meat which meant that any farmer selling lean animals would face a price penalty ... Dairy farmers receive a premium for high fat milk. Until the late 1980s the government-controlled Milk Marketing Board ensured that all the pintas delivered to our door steps were full fat milk, thereby ensuring that our fat intake was almost 15 per cent higher than it need have been. The Board's concern was not our health. They wanted us to drink the fat and ruin our health rather than have it skimmed off and thrown on the already embarrassingly large mountain of surplus butter. (Robbins, 1991, p. 44)

The *issue raised* is how one ensures that in policy more than immediate organisational needs are taken into account. The answer has to be found in the public domain and in the potential of the arena of public discourse.

---

that) but to complement them. While the main working of the authority remains structured on functional lines, the areal structure provides an alternative source of access to the policy agenda. An area committee is part of the authority and although it may have little power to act, it can extend discourse and command attention. The areal structure provides a countervailing force to the functional perspective in the working of the authority.

An organisation whose dominant culture overemphasises certain activities will not find it easy to take fully on to the agenda issues that suggest alternative priorities. Organisations which focus on treatment do not always readily accept that greater priority be given to prevention. Such is the recurring dilemma in the government of health services, which will only be resolved by building and protecting countervailing forces through extending public discourse.

Public management can build procedures to ease access to agenda-setting because they enable, extend and learn from public discourse. Reports on issues can be required to cover perspectives previously neglected, as some public authorities have required reports to cover the equal opportunities implications of any proposals. Consultation procedures can be reviewed to identify bias and barriers to access and to stimulate ideas on how the publics involved can be extended. Public management can develop scanning procedures, encompassing voices little heard or, if heard, little listened to.

Political processes link the arena of public discourse to the agenda of collective choice and political parties are one means of bringing issues on to the agenda. Procedures are required that recognise, for example, party manifestos as part of that process. Procedures for manifesto review are required not merely in central government or even in local authorities, but in other public organisations, for they too are governed, if indirectly, through political processes.

Interpretive Analysis

Public organisations need to learn from discourse with the public about key issues facing communities and their pressing needs. When analysing change, management needs the capacity to:

- identify the important event among the apparently routine series of events
- hear the highly valued in the arena of public discourse
- see the incompatible between problems raised in the arena and organisational capacity
- recognise the politically significant in environmental change
- see opportunities for organisational cooperation through new relationships within the public domain
- listen to messages in the arena of public discourse that challenge organisational practice
- use and translate between different organisational languages and between them and the languages of public discourse
- accept the uncertainties of change

The management task is to develop an interpretive analysis of the strategic issues that emerge from the review of policy and practice:

with its stress on purposive agency and transformation of self-identity through practical activity, the interpretive approach would provide policy analysis with an impetus to investigate the effect that a given (or contemplated) policy had (or would have) on such things as the vitality of civic life in a particular area, opportunities for participation, the creation and preservation of neighbourhood organisation incentives for the establishment of co-operative projects of mutual aid, the encouragement of voluntary social service provision and finally the delegation of authority and the distribution of decision-making power within the programme implemented by the policy. Similarly, given its stress on both the functional and normative importance of stable social practices and cultural traditions (i.e. they provide a sense of meaning and belonging, the experience of which is an intrinsic human good) the interpretive approach would raise the question of a policy's effect on community and would take the mitigation of alienation and anomie to be fundamentally legitimate and important policy considerations. (Jennings, 1987, p. 148)

This interpretive approach shows the many value issues that can be raised by a policy proposal which can rarely be encompassed in a single statement of objectives. There is a need for policy analysis that can provide the basis for

● understanding of the problem area
● deriving the alternative options for action that will provide the basis for judging public choice

Understanding the problem area: Interpretive analysis is more likely to start with a perceived problem than a perceived objective. A problem gives leverage to a policy review. Policies are not made or remade in the abstract, but in the reality of problems raised in public discourse. Improving access from public discourse to the policy agenda can strengthen policy review, by deepening awareness of problems.

Understanding the policy area in which the problem is located can give an appreciation of the scope for public choice in the reality of conflicting interests and values. Understanding is assisted by analysis setting out past policies, and relevant statistics projecting trends, and assessing costs, but more is required than such analysis. What is sought is political understanding for collective choice. Political understanding separates out the significant from the insignificant, establishes linkages between interests and explores possible balances between conflicting interests and values. Interpretive understanding of the issue area requires exploration of:

- the assumptions normally made and the extent to which these are confirmed, for each policy area is approached through assumptions about the nature of problems and the likely solutions
- the apparent constraints upon action and the strength of those constraints
- patterns of behaviour – social, economic, political – dominant in the policy area
- interests at stake in the policy area and what is valued by those interests
- lines of conflict that mark out the policy area
- the direction of change and the likelihood that change will meet obstacles
- public perceptions of the policy area, including differing interpretations of the problem, as found in the arena of public discourse

The aim is to explore the geography of the policy area. The test in the end is that the exploration should inform public discourse, and gain understanding through that discourse.

Deriving options. The range of options for policy development is at the heart of interpretive analysis and yet too often models of analysis focus not on how options are derived, but on how to choose between them. In any policy report, alternative proposals are likely to be put forward, but the contribution of analysis should be to extend the range of options beyond those that would otherwise be considered, since options are constrained by the assumptions built into organisations and by their dominant mode of working.

Thus the assumption of self-sufficiency has shaped much past action in the public domain. It has been assumed that if government is given responsibility for a function, that function has to be exercised directly, and that all the staff involved in the activity have to be employed directly. That assumption has been challenged by the development of competitive tendering. The possibility of government by contract has been opened up and other possibilities can be found, once the assumption of self-sufficiency is challenged. In the same way individual choice has too often been assumed to lie outside the scope of public service provision. Choice has been seen as the prerogative of the market. It has been assumed that public provision required uniformity of provision or that where different needs were identified as requiring different services, it was for the organisation to determine either by the application of rules as in social security provision or by professional judgement as in medical treatment.

In some areas, particular modes of public action have dominated. In environmental protection regulation has been the dominant mode. It is then difficult to see the potential of other modes in organisations that are structured around environmental regulation. The principle that the polluter pays has not been readily accepted in such organisations. Constraints are imposed by past practices in the organisation rather than by external pressures.

Deriving public choices can be assisted by analysis that challenges assumptions and questions constraints, breaking out of the limits of organisational thinking. Options do not spring immediately out of a challenge to assumptions, but a challenge to assumptions is a necessary stage in opening up policy space. There are approaches to creativity within organisations such as brain-storming, scenario-building, and multi-disciplinary groups that can help the search for options, both in breaking out of the limits on thinking, but also in generating new options. In the public domain, it is not necessary or desirable to restrict analysis within the organisation – rather it should develop beyond the organisation in the arena of public discourse, where new approaches can be argued for, challenging organisational assumptions. The political process is itself a means of challenging existing assumptions. Political priority given to equal opportunities challenges the assumptions of existing policies and practices.

Public discourse and political processes extend the range of policy options, because they are not confined by past organisational patterns of working and of thought. Analysis is inadequate if it is separated from these challenges. That requires, however, the capacity to listen to and respond to what is said by those unfamiliar with organisational constraints. It is too easy to dismiss as naive and unrealistic ideas from public discourse which can provide a basis for new options if worked on. Analysis should also work with the uncertainties of political discourse: 'Like dialectic, policy analysis usually starts with plausible premises, with contestable and shifting viewpoints not with indisputable principles or hard facts' (Majone, 1989, p. 6). Or again: 'Policy analysis, like dialectic, contributes to public deliberation, through criticism, advocacy and education' (ibid., p. 7).

Ideas stimulated by discourse or by the political process have to be crafted in options for strategic change. The design of options is relatively unexplored because of the dominance of analytical technique. While certain policy problems with defined parameters can be 'solved' by analytical techniques (for example, the location of premises, given a set of assumptions about the values to be attached to travelling times), this is because the problem has been defined as limited – often by removing it from public discourse and politics into the realm of technique. Policy design should be seen as a craft:

> Like surgery the making of policy, and the giving of policy advice are exercises of skills, and we do not judge skillful performance by the amount of information shared in the former or by the amount of formal planning. Rather we judge it by criteria like good timing and attention to details; by the capacity to recognise the limits of the possible, to use limitations creatively and to learn from one's mistakes; by the ability not only to show people what should be done but to persuade people to do what they know should be done. (Majone, 1989, p. 20)

Policy design as a craft needs to be developed as a means of interrelating problem understanding, public discourse, political requirements and policy instruments. 'In policy analysis as in traditional crafts, successful performance depends crucially on an intimate knowledge of materials and tools, and on a highly personal relationship between the agent and his task' (ibid., p. 45). A knowledge is required of the range of instruments or tools and the variation within them.

Hood has analysed government administration as a set of tools: 'What government does to us – its subjects or citizens – is to try to shape our lives by applying a set of administrative tools, in many different combinations and contexts to suit a variety of purposes' (Hood, 1983, p. 2). He distinguishes between 'effectors' as tools for impact and 'detectors' as tools for learning. Effectors are divided into

- Advice, Information, Persuasion
- Treasure and Cheque-book Government
- Tokens of Authority
- Organisation, Direct Action, Treatment

and within each category Hood sets out different tools with their differing implications. The point is that government can act in many different ways. It can subsidise, tax, inspect, license, prohibit, and provide services directly or indirectly. It can attach different conditions to these or other policy instruments, or combine them in different ways. Interpretive design draws upon different instruments in crafting options for strategy and policy development. This process should be developed through the arena of public discourse, which informs and tests designs.

Strategic Judgement and Public Choice

Listening and learning through interpretive analysis need to inform judgement about strategic choice:

> Moreover, some of the big decisions about policies, service priorities and resource use should be a matter of public choice – not professional or management prerogatives – in a public system. Managers therefore find themselves trying to inform public choices and to hold together many different views of what the NHS should be about. (Maxwell, 1987, p. 142)

Public choice can be *informed* by evaluative analyses but these should not determine choice. There are methods of evaluation that can appear to do so, predicting the impact of alternative proposals and measuring that impact against prescribed objectives. Cost–benefit analyses prepared for the Department of Transport on road schemes are an example. Such evaluations are not an exercise in collective choice. The collective choice has already been assumed in setting the specification for the evaluation, limiting consideration to that specification.

Choice should not be bounded by stated objectives. Effects out-side those objectives, whether intended or unintended, have to be weighed in the balance of collective choice. The exploration of policy in discourse cannot be bounded by the presumptions of these

---

EXHIBIT 9.4

The location of magistrates' courts

The number and location of magistrates' courts were reviewed in several areas in the 1980s. Work was, for example, undertaken on behalf of a Working Party of the Hampshire Magistrates' Courts Committee by Raine and Scott. At first sight, the issue could be seen as involving quantitative analysis 'such as court case-loads, crime rates, population estimates, staffing and expenditure levels' (Raine and Scott, 1982, p. 2) and the report analysed all these issues.

Raine and Scott, however, argue that other issues are involved which must in the end rest upon judgement:

> The discussion so far in this report has focussed upon the present circum-stances of the Hampshire Magistrates' Courts and upon an evaluation of those aspects which might influence the volume of future workload. However, while this in itself provides a vital basis from which to plan for the future, the choice of a strategy additionally calls for consideration of the desirable style and character of the magistrates' courts service, some-thing which is inevitably as much a matter of philosophy and judgement as of fact. In particular, two key issues require such a judgement. The first is the question of *how local* the magistrates' courts' organisation should be, while the second concerns the *standards of facilities* which are considered acceptable. The former of these obviously relates to the *number* of courts and their *location* within the county, while the second impinges upon the perception of where the main *accommodation shortcomings* and *priorities for future investment* lie. (ibid., p. 46)

They considered various options to equalise workload by transferring cases or by reviewing boundaries in accordance with the quantitative analysis.

> The problem with either of these possibilities is that they would almost cer-tainly imply some loss of the value of local knowledge arguments, and therefore potential change in the nature of magistrates' justice. However, a third option, which ... would avoid such a disadvantage would be to trans-fer not just the cases, but also the local bench of magistrates to hear them in another court house. (ibid., p. 57)

The *issue raised* is the inevitability of judgement in the making of public policy in this as in other fields.

advocating the policy. Because choice does not follow automatically as if it were a calculation, a judgement has to be made. Evaluation should aid that judgement and not attempt to foreclose it.

Political judgement will weigh the interests affected. The gainers and the losers from a policy can easily be hidden in forms of policy evaluation that assume a unitary society, in which all benefit from a proposal. Political judgement will test the assumptions on which a policy rests, for they will show its robustness in changing circumstances; will search out flexibility, not closing options in unawareness; will weigh risk; will explore the problem of carrying the policy into practice, for without the possibility of effective implementation, only the costs of the policy will be realised and few of its benefits.

Political judgement involves balancing these factors, but also balancing objectives and interests. It is because judgement involves balancing differing objectives that evaluation directed at testing proposals against particular objectives is of limited use to support political judgement. In the development of energy policy at national level, economic factors have to be balanced against environmental factors and short-term consideration against long-term consideration. Policy judgement can be assisted in a search for balance but balance can never be finally determined. In the end a judgement has to be made, but judgement can be informed – or ill-informed. Judgement can be informed by answers to such questions as:

- How reliable are the assumptions on which the proposal is based?
- Who gains and who loses from the proposals?
- Which interests support and which oppose the proposal?
- How robust is the policy in the event of change in the environment?
- What is the scope for flexibility in response to change?
- What constraints have to be overcome for the policy to succeed?
- How difficult will the policy be to implement?
- Which objectives will be aided and which harmed by the proposal?

In answering, or at least exploring, these issues political judgement can be informed as well as by the data on the cost and likely effects that routine evaluation will produce.

Judgement can be informed by public discourse, testing out proposals. When policy proposals are discussed, politicians and the public will often explore those policies through discussing particular cases. That can be regarded as a retreat from real policy discussion by those committed to processes of decision-making based on the assumption that decisions follow statements of objectives. Discussing cases can, however, be seen as a means of testing proposals, understanding the factors involved and searching for balance, in other words a means of reaching judgement. The natural flow of policy discussion is to move from generalities to particulars. Far from being resisted, policy management should encourage that flow as a means of forming judgement. What is required is to complete the process. Policy proposals are tested through particular cases in order to determine how they should be changed. After moving from generalities to particulars, one should move back to consider the implications for generalities.

Choice and the Prioritising and Planning of Resources

In the public domain the management of resources is inseparable from the foregoing discussion of forming judgements about public purpose based upon the processes of public discourse leading to collective choice. Choice has to be made both on the overall resources to be devoted to public purposes, which is the decision on taxation and on borrowing, and on the allocation of these resources. That is the starting point for resource management – collective choice based on public discourse. Resources allocated have to be managed. Resources are likely to fall short both of perceived need and actual demand. Resources, therefore, have to be rationed. The task for management is then the management of prioritising. Resource management in the public domain has these two interlocking elements:

- collective choice on the resources to be made available, which can take account of both perceived need and actual demand
- the management of the prioritising process which relates needs and demands to resources available and which in practice can support or distort collective choice

Collective choice and the budgetary process. The starting point for the management of resources is the budgetary process in which decisions are made on the level of expenditure, the level of revenue to be raised and on the allocation of that expenditure. In all its forms and variations the budgetary process is underlain by an act of collective choice. There is a fundamental distinction between the role of the budget in the public domain and the role of the budget in the market domain.

> it is a fundamental difference between private and public sector organisations that the public organisation is related to its sources of finance by a budget, while the finances of the private organisation are moderated by market forces. Therefore a great deal of attention is paid to budgeting in the public sector, while performance in the market place provides the equivalent focus for the private sector organisation. (Jönsson, 1984, p. 129)

In effect the budget in the market is a forecast which may or may not be achieved and which can and will be modified as market conditions change. The budget in the public domain is an exercise in choice and the expectation is therefore that the budget will be kept to.

> Although private sector organisations have annual budgets that function in much the same way, they have more of the flavour of a forecast than a formal decision. When you deal with a market you do not have an exclusive right to decide about revenue; the customers will have their say too. However, in the public sector the budget is built on the exclusive right to tax citizens, which, in turn, makes it necessary to make visible the decisions on both the tax rate and the appropriation of funds. (ibid.)

In the public domain the budget is an exercise of collective choice made through a political process. It is the role of management to support and express that choice. Effective management of the budgetary process should clarify the choices to be made and show the consequences of those choices. The management processes should not predetermine the budgetary choice. That choice is a collective choice which should be made through a political process and explored and tested in the arena of public discourse. Pressure for expenditure or protest about taxation levels are part of the process of public discourse. 'In politics the budgetary process, while responding to the requirements of administrative life, is also a battle field for conflicting priorities and alternative policies' (Natchez and Bupp, 1973, p. 955). Public discourse can be seen as a demand process, and resource management has to be concerned with the effectiveness of that process:

The efficiency of the demand articulation process is, therefore, central to any discussion of public sector efficiency. Does the system generate ill-conceived demands, is the political process representative of the interests of the electorate, is the process of representation more heavily weighted towards some interests than others and do bureaucrats influence the valuation of alternative policy? (Jackson, 1982, p. 187)

Thus it is possible to raise the question of whether resource allocation within health authorities is dominated by the medical profession. Ham (1986), basing his argument on a research study of decision-making in health authorities, has stated that the 'power of medical professions was manifested not so much through formal bids for development considered by the health authority as through the continued process of medical innovation which itself pre-empted resources for development' (p. 127). He went on to argue that his study showed that:

Although the configuration of interest involved in policy making and the individuals, groups or organisations who held power varied between issues, the overall picture which emerges is of DHAs faced with pressure from below in the form of demands from consultant medical staff. Chairmen and chief officers played the major role in mediating these pressures and in articulating their own ideas in the policy process. (ibid., p. 128).

Structures of resource allocation are necessarily structures of power and influence. That does not mean that those structures should not be the subject of critical appraisal. The changes in the health service brought about by the Conservative Government from 1987 to 1992 were based on and aimed to alter the structure of power and influence by the introduction of an internal market and of contracts. Effective resource management in the public domain has to be judged by the purposes and conditions of that domain and that requires the effectiveness of the basic mode of operation, and the issue is whether the changes, far from supporting that mode, weakened the process of public discourse on which that mode depends.

The requirements of budgetary choice.   There are two different but interrelated choices in the budgetary process. The first is a choice in the level of expenditure with implications for the level of revenue to be raised. The second is the choice in the allocation of that expenditure to the different activities of the authority. The relationship between these two decisions varies between the type of authority. In central government both choices have to be made, but central government may aim for a surplus or a deficit on current account, so it by no means follows that the level of expenditure will balance the level of taxation. The choice in level of expenditure will be determined by macroeconomic considerations, as well as by political judgements on service requirements and the level of taxation. In local authorities, both choices had to be made, but the expenditure decision was more closely related to the decision on the level of taxation and increasingly of fees and charges. In health authorities the main choice is not in the level of expenditure, but in its allocation between different activities. The level of expenditure is predetermined by central government, as indeed is now the level in local authorities through the capping regime.

The budgetary choice is a choice of balance. The need for public expenditure has to be balanced against the costs of taxation and of private goods foresworn. The level of expenditure has to be allocated between functions and within different functions. This is for multi-purpose organisations clearly a multi-valued choice, but even for health authorities there are value choices between, for example, acute care and care for the mentally ill, or between prevention and treatment. Value choices are not merely about how to achieve certain ends, but about the ends themselves. They are rarely clear choices, asserting the absolute primacy of one value as opposed to another. In the public domain, and above all in the budgetary decisions, values are balanced.

Balancing is an act of judgement, not of calculation. The budgetary process necessarily involves bargaining and negotiation, and it is through that bargaining that balancing is achieved and judgements made. The nature of that bargaining and the outcome of the pressures can, however, be affected by the way the budgetary process is structured, as judgement can be affected by the way information is arranged. Resource management in the public domain should ensure the structuring of the process of resource allocation and the arranging of information, so that they enable the organising principles, eliminating distortion in the arena of discourse and presenting the choices to be faced.

Movements for budgetary reform. Movements for budgetary reform have been based on a critique of existing budgetary processes. Broadly these critiques are that key choices are not clearly presented and relevant information not arrayed, leading to distortion in the arena of discourse. It has been argued that:

- budgetary formats are designed more for financial control than for choice
- budgets focus on a one-year period, whereas many of the items included have implications over a longer time period
- the budgetary process tends to focus on marginal changes rather than on base expenditure
- the budgetary format focuses choice on activities and departments rather than the purposes at which expenditure is directed
- the budgetary format focuses on input, rather than on what is achieved by the expenditure

These criticisms led to proposals for change in resource allocation processes. The main reform movements were the introduction of Planning, Programming, and Budgetary Systems and the introduction of Zero-Based Budgeting. Planning, Programming and Budgetary Systems combine statements of objectives, the related presentation of expenditure, output and performance data, and regular programmes of in-depth analysis of budgetary items. Zero-Based Budgeting is, in principle, the analysis of expenditure on the assumption that all existing expenditure has to be justified. One starts from a zero base. In practice it has meant the arrangement of packages of expenditure at various specified levels of increase or decrease below existing expenditure, with information on the impact of the proposed levels in relation to their objectives.

Reform movements have taken different forms at different times and in different countries. These movements have been subject to a critique developed by a wide range of authors who have challenged them on two related grounds. They have argued that the movements are based on the assumption that budgeting is a rational process, which should be determined through analytical processes, rather than by political processes. They have also argued that these processes assume information, knowledge and analysis which is not available and whose assembly and use would put unmanageable burdens on organisations and on political processes. They have argued that these reforms are not only unrealistic, but wrong in principle. Wildavsky in particular has argued that:

> traditional budgeting makes calculations easy precisely because it is not comprehensive. History provides a strong base on which to rest a case. The present is made part of the past, which may be known, instead of the future, which cannot be comprehended. Choices that might cause conflict are fragmented so that not all difficulties need to be faced at one time. Traditional budgeting lasts, then, because it is simpler, easier, less stressful than modern alternatives like ZBB or PPB. (Wildavsky, 1984, p. 221)

In reality the choice is not necessarily between comprehensive budgeting and incremental budgeting which could be described as involving: single-year budgets; separation of consideration of capital and revenue expenditure; input or financial data only; focus on incremental change; arrangement according to organisational structure, rather than purpose. The budgetary reform movement has had an impact even if its full requirements are not always realistic. The Public Expenditure Survey process in central government means that ministers are presented with multi-year projections of expenditure, covering both capital and revenue expenditure. Budgets in local authorities naturally vary in format from authority to authority, but medium-term financial plans and output data are found in a growing number of authorities.

Reform is possible if it is recognised that the management role in budgeting is to support the political process. The fact that the budgetary process necessarily involves advocacy, bargaining and negotiation does not mean that the process cannot be strengthened. Caiden has argued:

> Between these two positions – the neutral technician and the Machiavelli of the budget process – a middle ground is needed. Undoubtedly those responsible for the financial well-being of their organisations need the capacity to justify their positions. The budget advocate must be able to write good justifications, to

argue a case convincingly, to take advantage of favourable circumstances, and to assist priority where it is necessary. The
budget rationer must be capable of insisting upon fiscal sound-
ness, making cuts where and when necessary, questioning claims
and grappling with uncertainties. But justification and arguments, strategies and tactics should rest upon genuine assessment of costs, benefits, alternatives, program ability, efficiency
of operations, and future plans. (Caiden, 1985, p. 498)

She concludes by quoting Allen Post who had been for many
years legislative analyst for the State of California as seeing 'his
role as trying to make the political system work at its best not its
worst' (ibid.). That is the task for management in the public
domain. Budgetary reform has to work with the grain of political
processes, because those express the purposes and conditions of
the public domain. There is no point in presenting information
that will not be used. The structure of the budgetary process can
influence the nature of the political process, but only if that structure meets political requirements. The Public Expenditure Survey
process in central government was a major change, but can now
be seen as part of the basic pattern of working of central government because it meets political requirements.

A significant change in budgetary processes has been brought
about by the less favourable political climate for public expenditure. There has been a marked growth internationally in the use
of target budgeting in which guidelines are laid down for the
preparation of departmental estimates. Schick who has described
this tendency has written:

The purpose of the macro norms is to exert downward pressure
on spending demands ... As political statement the norms must
be simple and straightforward; they cannot get entangled in the
complications of economic policy or the particular limits of
individual programmes. (Schick, 1987, pp. 124–33)

When advance limits are imposed the government must have
the capacity to make important budget decisions before agencies prepare estimates. Despite not being derived from agency
requests or detailed program analysis, ceilings and targets must,
if they are to be useful, be grounded in realistic notions of what
is attainable through the budgetary process. (ibid., p. 129)

The development of advance limits in the budgetary processes expresses a political imperative of expenditure constraint. Schick argues that this change altered the dynamics of the budgetary process and strengthened the position of the 'guardians' concerned with budgetary constraints as opposed to the advocates of increased expenditure.

Changing the structuring of the budgetary process changes the process itself and hence the outcome. This budgetary change reflected political priorities and used established organisational practices. In effect budgetary reform worked with the grain of the organisation. The Medium Term Financial Strategy was designed to play this role in Britain, but did not entirely succeed.

> At the most basic level there were two reasons. First, the Treasury was unable to cut those programmes intended to contribute most to the savings set out in the 1980 plan ... However at a deeper level the Treasury's failure is explained by its inability to gain the compliance of Whitehall in achieving compensatory cuts to allow for rising expenditure due to the recession. Essentially the failure was political. (Colin Thain, 1985, pp. 280–1)

Or perhaps rather than a failure, a political judgement was made.

The requirement of the MTFS did not work with the grain of the organisation, even though it was expected to do so. To work with the grain is not to accept the status quo, but to understand the working of the organisation. Budgetary reform in the public domain must not be imposed on the political process. Budgetary reform cannot by itself change organisational reality, but can influence it. If organisational change is sought, then that should be faced directly and not through budgetary reform alone. Budgetary change can influence the organisational structure, but cannot run counter to the whole working of the organisation. Budgetary change:

● can help to clarify the choices before the decision-makers if it arranges information in a way that assists decision-makers
● can add more relevant information on the consequences of various levels of expenditure and on the allocation of expenditure
● can clearly identify, as in target-setting, the distinction between the choice on the level of expenditure and on the

allocation of expenditure, although recognising the interrelationship between them

• can highlight the revenue effects of capital expenditure, so that politicians are aware of its longer-term consequences

• can be supported by analyses of existing expenditure which open up options

Each of these changes may meet the needs of the political process, is feasible and does not necessarily meet overwhelming organisation resistance. To work with the grain is not to avoid change, but to increase the likelihood of achieving change.

Managing priorities. Budgets once made and resources once allocated have still to be managed. Public organisations will normally have systems of budgetary control which ensure that financial allocations are maintained, although they are less likely to focus on whether the intended output is achieved, because the budgets themselves are input-focused rather than output-focused. Resource management is not, however, limited to the centre of the public organisation but to all those who have responsibility for them. It is the manager responsible for a unit, or the fieldworker responsible for a case-load, who faces the immediate pressures of demand for services.

The dilemma which lies at the heart of resource management in the public domain is that the demand for services is not limited to the resources available and that there is no automatic mechanism for relating need or demand to the resources available. In the market, demand and supply are brought into balance by price. In the public domain, fees and charges are used and it is part of the budgetary process to set those fees and charges, but they will not normally be set by reference to the market alone. Demand and need have to be matched to the resources available and the budgetary process will have set the resources available, but it has not necessarily determined how that matching is achieved. Need is contestable and contested, while demand may vary unrelated to need. The services provided have to be rationed and the management of rationing is therefore a key task in the public domain, although not always recognised as such. Recognition is necessary if rationing is to reflect priorities tested in discourse and determined through political processes.

Prioritising can be achieved in a wide variety of ways. Resources can be allocated according to a set of rules laid down, of which archetypes are the points systems devised for housing and the formulae used for allocating grants by central government to local authorities or to health authorities. This was carried out by the RAWP process: 'For to Health Authorities RAWP is the policy of allocating budgets to regions on the basis of their populations and a crude assessment of health needs ... RAWP is a mechanism for sharing a budget, no matter how small or big that budget' (West, 1988, p. 120). From 1992/93 a new formula was introduced for the funding of regional health authorities, but it again reflects the size, age and health of their resident population.

These mechanisms are not open-ended. The housing allocation system defines priorities in relation to the houses available, that is, orders the queue. The formulae used for allocating grants to health authorities and local authorities allocate the resources available. The social security system is, on the other hand, in principle open-ended. The amount of resources required will vary with the level of unemployment or the extent of need, although in allocating resources and determining the level of benefits, regard will be had to the likely level of need and of expressed demand. In many services however, rationing is not determined by the priorities of a formal allocation process. Reality is set in a world of pressure and protest, and of demand and need, meeting limited resources. Thus: 'hospital management is really the art of juggling and rationing the available services to meet the constant pressure from patients, doctors and other staff' (West, 1988, p. 99).

There are many mechanisms of rationing, conscious or unconscious. Failure to publicise a service is an act of rationing. Language that is not easily understood can limit the number of clients. Difficulty of gaining access because of remote offices or unhelpful reception arrangement rations services. None of these approaches should be tolerated in the public domain, since they challenge its basic values. The values of public service are denied in any act that deters the public. The values of equity remain unrealised by actions that ration services by ignorance or difficulty, rather than by need. Price can be used as a means of rationing, but the issue for management in the public domain must be the impact of price upon the demand for the service, not merely in total, but on demand by differing groups. The question to be faced is whether the results of rationing in practice are in accordance with collective choice.

Much resource rationing is carried out by those who are immediately responsible for providing the service. Discretion is inherent in any organisation. It is beyond organisational capacity to control all actions taken. Discretion even if not acknowledged will still exist. Policemen, the epitomy of rule observance as the representatives of law and order, will exercise a discretion in action taken on offences. They may caution rather than prosecute. The 'street-level bureaucrat' described by Lipsky, is a key allocator of resources facing immediate pressures:

> Clients of street-level bureaucracies respond angrily to real or perceived injustices, develop strategies to ingratiate themselves with workers, act grateful and elated or sullen and passive in reaction to street-level bureaucrats' decisions. It is one thing to be treated neglectfully and routinely by the telephone company, the motor vehicle bureau, or other government agencies whose agents know nothing of the personal circumstances surrounding a claim or request. It is quite another thing to be shuffled, categorised and treated 'bureaucratically' (in the pejorative sense), by someone to whom one is directly talking and from whom one expects at least an open and sympathetic hearing. (Lipsky, 1980, p. 9)

The street-level bureaucrats face the immediate pressures of demand and need upon resources. Inevitably they make their own choices, which are not necessarily in accordance with collective choice. The public organisation faces the issue of how discretion is controlled. Rationing is a task in which individual members of the staff will inevitably be given or will use discretion. The management of rationing has to be grounded in that reality, but has to ensure that as far as possible it is conditioned by priorities determined by collective choice and open to public discourse. The first requirement is to ensure that there is understanding of how choices are actually made. Discretion can have an impact beyond the intentions of the authority. Investigations in local authorities showed racial discrimination in housing allocation despite the existence of a formal allocation scheme and a commitment to equal opportunities. Housing allocation systems may determine that a house is offered, but not which house is offered. Management needs information on how resources are actually allocated, the impact of that allocation and how that allocation comes about.

Much information lies within the organisation. The need is to use it and appraise it. Who is actually using the services? Does the pattern vary between different parts of the organisation? Are those differences expected and intended? The differences between expectation and intention can be investigated in a variety of ways. Surveys can provide information as can the operation of appeals procedures as with the allocation of children to schools, complaints procedures or disciplinary procedures constituted by professional bodies. In addition appeals can lie to the ombudsman on grounds of maladministration leading to injustice, which can involve the denial of a service to which an individual is entitled. It is characteristic of the public domain that such appeal procedures exist. The customer as citizen should have rights beyond the customer in the market.

The more subtle understanding is how the rules or working of the organisation actually determine the allocation. This is less likely to be learnt by formal survey or inspection than through discussion. Rationing has to be acknowledged as a key dilemma for staff – in which there are few medals to be won. In discussion of that issue management can learn. Once understanding is gained, the issue may not be so much how to control discretion, but how to ensure that discretion achieves collective choice. The responsiveness that can develop through the use of discretion is an asset to be realised. The issue is whether that discretion is being used in accordance with collective choice on priorities and the values of the public domain. Collective choice is not realised by endless elaboration of rules. The important requirement is to ensure that the conditions in which discretion is exercised encourage the achievement of collective choice and access for public discourse.

Discretion may be formally given. The surgeon can have discretion not merely on how a patient is operated on, but on the priority given to patients. The doctor is a resource allocator. In giving discretion, the need for organisational control is not necessarily overlooked. Reliance is placed on other mechanisms than direct control. In acknowledging the responsibility of a doctor for allocating resources, reliance is placed upon professional training, to secure both that resources are allocated in accordance with need and are used in the most effective manner. Reliance on professionalism has been dominant in the management of rationing in many activities in the public domain. Where reliance is placed on professionals in rationing services, professional judgement can be strengthened if informed by an understanding of the resources involved. Thus development in resource management in the NHS seeks to improve patient care by:

- giving doctors and nurses a bigger role in the management of resources
- devolving budgetary responsibility to clinical teams within hospitals
- enabling managers to negotiate work-load agreements with these clinical teams
- improving information systems to provide staff with better data about their services (Ham, 1991, p. 31)

Public organisations can develop other forms of socialisation that are designed to control the use of discretion. In the police service a heavy emphasis is laid upon training, but also upon the shared culture of a uniformed force. The processes of socialisation in any organisation can set the parameters for the use of discretion more effectively than the formal rules.

Review in Action

Policy as experienced is policy as it is implemented, which may not correspond to intention. Even if implemented as intended its impact may not be as expected. Even if impact is as intended, views on that impact can change as public discourse reflects societal learning.

Effective public management requires that there be regular processes for the review of policy, but that they are politically guided. Strategic management may highlight certain issues; the manifesto can be taken on board, but policy review may be required in areas outside the strategic or the political priority as stated in the manifesto. A focus on where review is required should bring together the political process inside the organisation, public discourse and organisational awareness of policy stress. The agenda for review should not be determined by the normal working of the organisation. It requires an organisational pause and strategic management can protect that pause.

Public management can develop systematic procedures of policy review. Such reviews can be cyclical as when an organisation reviews all its policies over a five-year period. A cycle is, however, liable to routinisation. It means 'one's turn has come'. It is review for the sake of review. Routinisation within the organisation can be countered, if review is also triggered by public discourse. The timetable of review is then set by public debate and discussion. Policy review processes cannot be isolated from political priorities or the pressure of public discourse, the impact of both of which can be sudden or immediate.

Judgement is also involved in policy review, as well as in choosing policy alternatives, for in any policy, objectives, values and interests have to be weighed in action as well as in intention.

> If the Forest Service for example managed to achieve its timber sales goal but achieved only 80 per cent of its grazing and 60 per cent of its wild life objectives in a year would that have been as good as attaining 80 per cent of all goals ...? No amount of information would automatically have answered these questions, they were matters of judgement. (Kaufman, 1981, p. 32)

Indeed policy review can be described as bringing the ongoing activities of public organisations into the arena of public discourse as a basis for political judgement.

Conclusion

The organising principle of the public domain is public discourse leading to collective choice based on public consent. It is that principle that constitutes public choice, which rests on political judgement informed by discourse. The task of management in the public domain is to enable that judgement. Strategic management can be the process that supports that task, but it will only be effective if grounded in the nature of the public domain. That requires processes for learning from the public, interpretive analysis, informing political judgement and assisting collective choice, prioritising resources and learning through review.

10
Enabling Public Accountability

Action in the public domain rests upon public consent, for without consent collective choice is deprived of legitimate authority. The learning society requires a continuous and continuing relationship of accountability within the polity. The management task within the public domain is to enable an account to be made to the public about performance, but also to enable the variety of interests within the public to engage in discourse about what counts as performance in the pursuit of public policy. The management of public accountability is thus central to the vitality of the public domain ensuring relations of control and consent ('holding to account') and also of discourse within the polity ('the giving of accounts').

Accounting for Performance

The demand for services to become more accountable was a demand for public managers and professionals to look beyond their boundaries to the world beyond. The effect has been to extend and multiply the number of accounts that are now expected to be provided to a diverse range of audiences. Schools are now expected to account in various ways to industry and commerce, to elected members and communities, as well as to governors and parents. Some of the linkages have been formalised, while others have remained more tentative with the understanding that an audience's expectations (interpretive schema) will be taken into account.

Accountability is usually conceived as an institution of control, being 'held to account'. It implies formal ties between parties one of whom is answerable to another for the quality of their actions and performance in the stewardship of public funds and service. There is a bond in the accountable relationship: 'to say that an agent is accountable for his actions to another is not merely to say that he is *able* to deliver an account but to assert that he is *obliged* to do so'(Sockett, 1980, p. 10). Evaluation of performance as a basis for holding to account forms an essential element of the accountable relationship:

> Being accountable may mean ... no more than having to answer questions about what has happened or is happening within one's jurisdiction ... But most usages require an additional implication: the answer when given, or the account when rendered, is to be evaluated by the superior or superior body measured against some standard or some expectation, and the differences noted: and then praise or blame are to be meted out and sanctions applied. It is a coupling of information with its evaluation and application of sanctions that gives accountability or 'answerability' or 'responsibility' their full sense in ordinary usage. (Dunsire, 1978, p. 41)

Discovering a language in which public services can be held to account is not straightforward. Whereas clear quantitative criteria exist to judge the performance of organisations in the private sector such evaluation is rarely available in the public domain. Even judging what is to count as an output is sometimes difficult, let alone measuring it.

Nevertheless, if accountability is a defining quality of the public domain, then an essential task for management is to develop an appropriate language and process of accountability. We will argue that processes of performance review have a part to play, but that they must develop from the simplicities of performance measurement towards processes that enable political judgement on what counts as good performance.

The Development of Performance Review for Public Accountability

Performance review can provide the processes required to sustain accountability in the public domain if it is grounded in the organisational principles of the public domain. To enhance public accountability, performance review has to be open to public discourse. Review has to cover:

- the unanticipated as well as the anticipated
- the extent of public pressure and protest
- the nature of learning for the manager and for the organisations
- needs unmet as well as needs met
- concerns for the political process, present and future

Space for learning through performance review has to be protected, whether the review is of the individual manager, of a service or of an organisation. The aim of review is to enhance understanding of performance, both in action and in impact as a necessary part of both organisational and public learning. Performance assessment should be the basis of performance review. In performance assessment, understanding is sought of what has been done and what has been achieved not merely to record success or failure, but to learn of change and the need for change. Performance assessment in the public domain extends beyond the organisation because performance has in the end to be judged in the arena of public discourse.

Performance assessment is normally seen as applying performance measures. Performance measures have the strength of commanding attention. They permit comparison within an organisation (between schools, between hospitals, between old people's homes) and between organisations (between health authorities and between local authorities) and in comparisons, questions can be found even if answers prove more difficult. But performance measures cannot by themselves provide an adequate basis for performance assessment, because they are necessarily limited for the public domain.

CRUX

The Limitations of Performance Measures

Even performance measures specifically designed for the public
domain have a limited contribution to public understanding. The
Audit Commission has set out a set of indicators for local authority services as required by the Local Government Act 1992 to provide information on the performance of local authorities for the
general public. Measures are set out for the provision of an educational service:

Education before Statutory School Age
1.   a.   The number of children under five in maintained
         schools
     b.   These children as a percentage of all three and four
         year olds
2.   The cost of educating these children.

School Places and Admissions
3.   The percentage of unfilled places in admission classes in:
     a.   primary schools
     b.   secondary schools.
4.   The percentage of pupils admitted in excess of schools'
     nominal capacity:
     a.   primary schools
     b.   secondary schools.

(There then follow measures 5–9 related to special schools and
student awards.)

Expenditure on Education
10. The net expenditure per pupil in LEA maintained schools,
     as follows:
     a.   Nursery and primary schools – pupils under five
     b.   Primary schools – pupils five and over
     c.   Secondary schools – pupils under 16
     d.   Secondary schools – pupils over 16. (Audit
         Commission, 1993, pp. 21–2)

Such limited measures can hardly enhance understanding, but
in defence it can be urged that the Audit Commission was pressed

by local authorities themselves to restrict the number of indicators. Thus the Audit Commission had previously suggested a more extended list of indicators for use by auditors and by local author- ities (Audit Commission, 1988b) rather than by the public. However extended the indicators were, there would remain problems. In the different field of hospital beds, John Yates identified five problems which also apply to the performance measures set out above:

1. The need to ensure that measurements are correct ...
2. The necessity to make value judgement, in interpreting results ...
3. Some measurements may indicate that something is wrong but not what is wrong ...
4. Information is required not merely of the result but also of the conditions under which the measurement was made ...
5. The volume and range of results available can confuse rather than clarify the problems (Yates, 1982, p. 35)

Yates has pointed out that waiting lists 'not only under-estimate true need, but actually help to suppress need because patients and general practitioners, aware of the long waiting lists, fail to refer themselves or their patients to hospital' (Yates, 1987, p. 20). Often measures used do not measure outcomes, but intermediate output.

A case covering the Department of the Environment's Urban Programme Management Initiative lists as 'key output meas- ures' such items as number of workshop units provided and number of loans and grants made. If the objective of the ini- tiative is to provide jobs, improve the environment and society, the workshops and grants are not outputs. (Flynn *et al.*, 1988, p. 179)

It is common when discussing performance measures in the public domain to recognise that there are limits to the extent to which adequate measures have been developed, but not to deny the hope that they will be. Flynn *et al.*, summing up Treasury Working Papers, say they 'suggest that, though some progress is being made, the day of the comprehensive, output-oriented, per- formance indicator (in other words the true performance indica- tor) is still some way off, particularly for the "mainstream" operations of central government' (ibid.). The implication is that the problem to be faced is one of devising appropriate measures, and that the problem can in principle be overcome. For many of the activities of public organisations it may seem that they can be overcome. Activities are not, however, pursued for their own sake but to achieve public purposes, the outcome of which can only be fully tested in the public domain through public discourse.

There are limits to the extent to which adequate performance indicators can ever be derived in the public domain for the overall impact of activities undertaken. That overall uncertainty affects the role of measures for particular activities. It is for that reason that in discussing the limits of performance measures, we focus not on performance measures for individual managers, but for organisations, since those limits have an impact on the whole organisation.

The Necessary Limits on Performance Measurement in the Public Domain

There are practical problems in finding adequate performance measures. For services, measures are inherently more difficult to find than for products, because the output of services is determined in interaction in which the customer, client or consumer contributes to and determines the quality of the output. It is not however with these practical problems that we are concerned. The limitations we focus on are fundamental in the public domain.

Weisbrod has argued 'that certain activities are in the public or non-profit sector largely because of the complexity of assessing them. Because these activities are not easily monitored and therefore rewarded (the strength of the private sector), society turns to other sectors to carry them out' (Weisbrod, 1988, p. 14).

The private sector organisation can in principle, as well as in practice, measure performance by sales. Of course the private sector organisation will be concerned with public satisfaction and many other factors because they affect sales. They are, however, intermediate measures. It is 'sales' that are the measure of final output. A sale is essentially a private transaction between buyer and seller. Wider interests are not involved, and if wider interests are affected by the sale then that is not necessarily of concern to the buyer and seller. Because of those wider interests, regulations may be introduced to secure, for example, that the production process does not create environmental problems, but that decision and the application of the regulations lie not with the private sector but in the public domain.

"It is, however, a condition of the public domain that the provision of a service (or even the sale of a good) is not in itself an adequate indicator of satisfactory performance." The actual provision does not measure the extent to which collective purpose is met. The provision of a public service is not a private act, of concern only to the organisation that provides the service and to the person receiving it. It is an act carried out in the public domain, in which concerns are in principle unbounded. In the realm of public discourse, all can draw attention to effects of the service which have wider implications, and those wider effects can become part of the public purpose, determined by collective choice. What is an appropriate performance indicator can itself be a legitimate subject for political argument and often is – as when there is argument about the extent to which social factors should be taken into account in assessing educational performance, or environmental factors in assessing a highways programme. The appropriate performance measure will vary according to who is concerned with performance and there can be no boundaries excluding citizens from concern. Sir Peter Middleton said in evidence to the Committee on Public Accounts:

> Information on final output measures over a large area is not actually going to be attainable but that seems to me to be a perfectly reasonable procedure. In a way, when we talk about the effectiveness of policies in central government we are using an intermediate measure anyway because we are assuming the Government is the person whose objectives we are trying to meet. I suppose that if you are applying a philosophical concept you would see that the needs are the needs of the people out there and they have not necessarily got it right. (HC 61, 1987, Evidence Q 171)

Thomas and Lynda Dalton argue that the criteria of performance in the public domain are wider than in the private sector: 'while some of our ways of appraising private sector performance find expression in public sector contexts (for example, productivity, innovations and others), we may characterise an organisation's implementation of public policies as just or unjust, equitable or non-equitable, coercive or non-coercive, or representative or non-representative' (Dalton and Dalton, 1988, p. 30).

The values realised in the public domain are necessarily different from those realised in the private sector – that after all is part of the rationale for the public domain.

> One important reason why some service organisations are located in the public sector is that they cannot be solely concerned with efficiency but must also attempt to guarantee certain minimum levels of equity, access and so on. While market forces provide very effective incentives to greater efficiency, without carefully designed countervailing measures, they can encourage public sector managers to buy increased efficiency at the cost of other aspects of performance such as equity of access. (Best, 1987, p. 12)

These many dimensions of performance mean that the reason why adequate performance measures cannot be found in the public domain is not a technical problem. This was recognised in a Treasury publication:

> There are inherent difficulties in measuring the impact of all programmes in particular, their aims are usually broad and progress towards them is not directly measurable. Many individual programmes have multiple objectives. Although achievement of particular objectives can, in many cases, be measured, interpretation is a problem when policy trade-offs have to be taken into account. Another common problem is distinguishing the effect of the programme from other factors. Some indicators of final output are available but most use is made of intermediate indicators. (Lewis, 1986, p. 6)

No set of indicators can ever be assumed to be complete, since in the public domain no relevant issues can be excluded. The indicators, the weight to be attached to them and the form given to them can be and indeed should be the subject of public discourse.

Performance is a dynamic concept – it has a time perspective. Furthermore, it is possible to trade off one element of performance against another. For example, short-run gains in economy (budget cutting) can be purchased at the expense of longer-term effectiveness and excellence. Cutting capital maintenance expenditure is a case in point. Extending the scope of equity is often traded off against a reduction in efficiency. Trade-offs of this kind are the substance of public sector management. (Jackson, 1990, p. 11)

In Sweden there have been attempts to establish a broader concept of effective performance in the public domain:

A government agency performs effectively if it reaches its objectives

– whilst husbanding its resources
– with due regard to demands for public service, public disclosure and due process
– and with regard to the employees' good working environment, job security and possibility of codetermination and personal development. (Arvidsson, 1986, p. 630)

But even that concept cannot be allowed to close the debate, as Arvidsson recognises. Once performance is recognised as having many dimensions, then measures can be seen as competing or reflecting different value systems:

It seems appropriate to distinguish between the following major dimensions – or ethics – or performance

(1)   economic ethic
(2)   democratic ethic
(3)   legal ethic
(4)   professional ethic.

A battery of indicators for each ethic is needed. Some examples are

Economic ethic: cost per product, time per case handled, variance from budget, criticism by audit
Democratic ethic: treatment in political assemblies and public debate, new 'movements', legitimacy crises
Legal ethic: complaints, appeals, verdicts by administrative courts, criticism by ombudsmen and legal inspectors

Professional ethic: opinions expressed by leading professionals, research findings, statement by professional association, violations of professional standards.

These examples of 'indicators' illustrate a general problem of
performance evaluation of public activities, the difficulty in
finding indicators which are both relevant and operational. This
concerns all four ethics but especially the democratic and professional ethics. The consequence is that performance can seldom
be expressed in a meaningful way by quantitative data only. To a
great extent, analysis of performance has to be based on qualita-
tive descriptions and statements. (Arvidsson, 1986, p. 631)

Different ethics reflect different values sought in the public
domain and contested for in public discourse. Performance
assessment is at the heart of the political process and is a proper
subject of public discourse: 'opponents involved in the dispute
may advance different interpretations of productivity' (Dalton
and Dalton, 1988, p. 34).

EXHIBIT 10.1

Sentencing in magistrates' courts

Studies have shown considerable variation in sentencing policy in magistrates' courts.

> [In] Bournemouth magistrates' court in 1986, 12 per cent of adult males
> received a custodial sentence, while in Brighton the figure was 25 per cent.
> Similarly, while Liverpool magistrates' court used a custodial sentence in
> 13 per cent of cases, Hull magistrates sentenced 28 per cent of their de-
> fendants in this way. Moreover, the official Criminal Statistics also indicate
> the existence of variations of hardly lesser magnitude between courts in
> close proximity to one another ... In Hereford and Worcester for example
> in 1986, the custody rate for Malvern was 10.4, while for neighbouring
> Worcester it was 22.1 per cent. (Raine, 1989, p. 91)

It is difficult to say whether this represents unacceptable variation or the
proper exercise of judgement by magistrates and if unacceptable variation,
what is acceptable variation?
The *issue raised* is the contestability of performance measures.

These problems in developing adequate performance measures are inherent in the public domain. They are in summary:

- no set of measures can ever be regarded as complete and the case for any measure can be made and can be disputed in the arena of public discourse
- performance in the public domain has many dimensions and no dimension can be considered irrelevant
- the difficulty of integrating different measures is that values are at stake in the weights to be given
- many of the apparently technical difficulties reflect the impossibility of regarding provision in the public domain as the equivalent of sale in the private sector
- the final output lies beyond the boundaries of the organisation and can only be judged in the quality of life in society through public discourse
- different groups have different emphases and it cannot be assumed that all have the same requirements of performance

Judgement, Not Measurement

While the arguments above suggest that it is unrealistic in the public domain to expect to develop fully satisfactory measures of performance, that does not mean that performance measures have no role in performance assessment. They can have a role provided their limitations are appreciated. If perfect performance measures are not available, then the alternative is not to abandon performance measures, but to use imperfect or uncertain performance measures in full awareness of their limitation. That means using the measures but not placing total reliance on them, rather seeing them as one means of informing and judging. The Council of Civil Service Unions has argued that

> in pursuit of what may be a fool's errand of trying to develop batteries of proxy measures for the immeasurable, Departments have neglected to develop procedures for the evaluation of their activities which recognise the judgmental nature of the process. (Council of Civil Service Unions, 1987, para. 18)

Judgement can be informed by measures, but not by measures alone. Judgement rests upon political processes tested in public discourse. The danger of measures is that they can too easily substitute for discourse. The language of measures can drive out the language of discourse. The task is to find a vocabulary (or way of talking) that can encompass performance measures but can also encompass: the softer views of opinion; the pattern of complaints; the experience of inspectors; the understanding of officers; the views of politicians; the processes of pressure and protest. For all of these can inform judgement as they can test it. That vocabulary is more likely to be found and performance measures are more likely to be useful

- if they are seen as relevant but not decisive
- if the need for a set of measures is recognised, even if necessarily incomplete
- if conflict between measures is seen as desirable in informing judgement rather than as confusing
- if the problem of weighing measures is recognised
- if measures are seen as having a political content (as when the health of the economy is challenged in arguments over the relevant measures)
- if measures reflect the political process – who gains and who loses is a possible performance measure

and if it is recognised that in the end performance assessment in the public domain rests upon judgement. That judgement will be made through political processes, informed and tested by public discourse. It is the public who know directly the quality of life, which activities in the public domain sustain. Their voices inform and test the judgement that underlies assessment and guides performance review as a key element in performance management.

It has to be recognised that effective performance at all levels cannot escape from the values to be realised in the public domain. Effective performance cannot be achieved if justice is denied, citizenship ignored and equity confounded. Effective performance depends upon the realisation of values, even when the meaning of those values is contested – which is why effective performance has to be judged and the judgement tested in discourse. Performance assessment should be seen as dependent on public accountability – itself dependent upon public discourse.

Rediscovering Public Accountability

Those held to account are drawn to communicate why they have been doing what they have been doing and how they have gone about it. Accountability is a court of judgement which distributes praise and blame, but it must in the public domain institution-alise a discourse about purposes, practice and performance.

> Our starting point is that accountability is all about the con-struction of an agreed language or currency of discourse about conduct and performance, and the criteria that should be used in assessing them. It is a social and political process. It is about per-ceptions and power. It can be expected to vary in different con-texts, depending on the nature of the policy arena and the power of the different organisational actors. (Day and Klein, 1989, p. 2)

The management challenge is to enable the public dialogue which can realise Habermas's notion of 'communicative ration-ality', whereby actors in an unfettered setting can explore the integrity of the reasons which have informed action and reach common understanding about future progress.

Learning new languages of account is a major step forward. Accountability forms a process of communication, of discourse between polity and public. It creates an understanding of com-munication as reciprocation: of speaking to, but also listening to, the public. But there is a need, in the analysis, to attend further to the conditions for communication. This can place the focus of change upon structures and upon power.

Simey has made a short but invaluable contribution to our understanding of public accountability. Her trenchant analysis provides some of the answers to these questions, principally to explicate the political theory underlying public accountability. Simey's study was written as an attempt to make sense of the Toxteth riots and an alienated community, where the loss of trust was, seemingly, exacerbated by the actions of professionals and the local bureaucracy. Simey perceives the roots of the problem as lying deep in the perfunctory neglect of accountability which, she argues, is the principle that stands at the heart of our institutions of government. There is an urgent need, she proposes, to sharpen our understanding of the theory of accountability which, ostens-ibly, underlies the working of democratic government:

The theory is simple enough: In a democracy it is only by the consent of the people that authority to govern can be delegated. And that consent is given on one condition, that all those who then act on our behalf will hold themselves accountable for their stewardship. This holds good whether they be elected members or officials. Accountability is thus the solid plank on which our whole political system rests.

... the urgent need to grasp the fact that accountability is not a mechanism or a routine but a principle. More than that, it is a principle which services a specific purpose. In a democracy, that purpose is to provide the basis for the relationship between society and its members, between those who govern and those who consent to be governed. The word consent provides the significant clue. (Simey, 1985, pp. 17, 20)

It is only by consent of the people that authority can be delegated. Simey argues cogently that what happened with the police force in Toxteth illustrated a more general problem:

that lesson is a universal one in the society of today. By and large 'government' has been taken over by the bureaucracy. We the people have allowed ourselves to all intents and purposes to be excluded from the practice of politics. Ours is not an accountable society. (ibid., p. 33)

This shift of power from elected representatives to officials represents for Simey a major retreat from the 'political and moral vision', which inspired the postwar settlement and the creation of the welfare state:

The ideal of the welfare state was not just to set people free from deprivation but to do so in order that they might be enabled to play their proper part as members of the community. Instead we have permitted the development of a system of imposed government which reduces whole sections of the population, especially in the inner areas of our cities, and the outer housing estates, to the status of dependent colonies. (ibid., p. 5–6)

Public accountability articulates a theory of political authority grounded in the consent of society. That authority resides with the public and is delegated to representatives and officials on condition that they, in turn, account to the public. The structuring of the institution implies that consent has continually to be tested and reaffirmed. The traditional form of holding to account and of testing consent has been the periodic election.

The demand for greater accountability, therefore, arguably challenges not only the insularity of the professionals and their inability to account to the public, but also this ongoing political tradition of accountability because of the assumptions which it embodied of:

- a passive electorate: expressing its political vote every three to five years before returning to their respectful place leaving government to the experts
- a disregarded electorate: the low status of the public in the political order caused the public authorities to neglect their duty to communicate with the public and generate understanding of the policies and practices being developed

Our current form of public accountability is inadequate or, more precisely, incomplete. It offers members of the public a particularly exiguous form of participation (periodic voting) which has been used to distance them from the polity. It establishes the polity as something out there, not something *we* as citizens are members of or believe we have any responsibility for.

Accountability for Citizenship in a Learning Society

Public accountability needs to reach beyond existing forms. A form of public accountability needs to be developed which maintains the authority of the public as electors but more importantly as citizens. To the citizen as elector is given the right and the means to hold government to account. The active citizen retains that right and that means, but is informed by the giving of an account as part of the continuing process informing the arena of public discourse. For the giving of an account only has sufficient meaning to those to whom it is given, if it is given in the interaction that is a condition of understanding. The agency of the public as citizens presupposes a more active participation of the public in the government of their own affairs. This form of public accountability finds its legitimacy both in reaching an under-

standing and in discourse as the basis of consent between government and people. It presupposes an active citizenry.

A number of important characteristics would define such a citizenship. To be a citizen is *to be a member*, and thus to possess
value, status and dignity intrinsically but also by *participating
actively* in:

● community and society: sharing a way of life, enacting and
   developing its values and culture
● wealth production of the economy: as a worker contributing
   energy, ideas and knowledge
● the polity: sharing rights (of well-being, health, education and
   income); sharing duties and responsibilities, the most important being sharing in power (in the distribution and control of
   power, in decision-taking, and in taking responsibility for decisions); and, finally, in sharing in the resourcing of the polity
   (through taxes)

Analysis of the changing forms of public accountability reflects
the changing polity. The challenge to the professions to become
more accountable to their publics reflects these changes. In the
neo-liberal polity, legislation has enacted a distinctive form of
market accountability with the public defined as consumers whose
informed preferences would improve the effectiveness of services.

In the learning society the assumptions of the market are seen
as inadequate since they deny the notion of publicness as expressing a community of interest in the welfare of all. That leads on to
the need for forms of public accountability to express that community of interest.

Discussion of accountability for a learning society focuses analysis
on the foundation of public action on public consent. Yet this
understanding of the condition of public accountability highlights
the dilemma of the polity: the need to reconcile the idea of political control resting on elected representatives with the idea of their
authority deriving from citizens who need to inform representative
institutions. While holding to account may require representative
institutions and a clear line of accountability, those representative
institutions will only meet the requirements of a learning society if
informed by fully developed public discourse. That requires the
giving of accounts through many channels. While there can be a

single line of accountability to hold to account, there must be many channels by which accounts are given.

The Management Requirements of Accountability

The development of public accountability for a learning society places its own requirements on management in the public domain. Many of those requirements will be met by the development of the arena of public discourse. The strength of that arena and of the political processes related to it ensure channels for giving accounts that can be understood in interaction.

But more is required of management. The development of public accountability requires a culture of *stewardship*. Management in the public domain has to take many actions in giving expression to collective choice. Those actions cannot always assume public consent, although such public consent is more likely the more public discourse is enhanced. What is required is that management action is taken with a sense of stewardship. This means that power is exercised not in its own right, but on behalf of the citizens from whom that power is derived. This is closely related to the position finally reached by Simey in her search for the accountable society:

> Accountability is not about control but responsibility for the way in which control is exercised. The distinction is a fine one but it is of fundamental importance. In other words accountability is not an administrative tool but a moral principle. Of those to whom responsibility is given, an account of their stewardship shall be required. It is a principle whose purpose is to govern the relationship between those who delegate authority and those who exercise it. (Simey, 1988, p. 118)

The moral principle required expresses the learning society:

> The way we understand our values, individualistically or communally, determines our identity as citizens and sets the limit of our community. As atomistic individual one is a consumer of goods and services; as a citizen, one is accountable to other citizens in the public realm. Accountability means that all must count, they must be included as free and equal citizens in the civil community – and the community has a stake in each citizen. (McCullough, 1991, pp. 106–7)

Organisational values based on a sense of stewardship have deep implications for the staffing policies of public authorities to which we turn in the next chapter. Recruitment, promotion, training and communication are powerful instruments for reinforcing organisational values. These values must however influence behaviour. Stewardship, as Simey makes clear, requires accounts to be given. These accounts can be given to any or indeed all who have in McCullough's words 'a stake in the civil community'.

Many Forms of Account

A variety of requirements have been placed, or are being placed, on public bodies to produce accounts, but often they are restricted accounts as was shown in the discussion of performance measures. Understanding comes from discourse through interaction; without that these requirements do not by themselves provide an adequate account.

Accounts can be given in many ways and many forms. There are many languages of account that have to be learnt by management, if they are to reach all the stakeholders, for words or statistics that are easily assimilated by some are not understood by others. Statistics are one form of account, but so are actions. Accounts can be given to the many or to individuals. What is required is a habit of accounting even when the account is to an individual or to a small group, because it reinforces a sense of stewardship.

The director of social services who spends a night in an old persons' home, the general manager who sits on the reception desk of a hospital, the civil servant who uses services on which he or she prepares legislation, the chief executive of a Next Steps agency who follows up individual complaints personally, are all giving an account themselves and signalling the need for an accountable organisation to their staff.

Management informed by stewardship reviews the many forms in which it gives accounts and the many stakeholders in the community to which accounts are given. The tests to be applied can include:

● does the account enhance understanding?
● how is the account used?
● does the accounting permit interaction?

- what stakeholders are neglected in the accounting?
- what forms and languages of account are required for understanding?

In the learning society, accounting has to follow many channels and use many forms. Accounts should not just depend on public organisations accounting for themselves, but should depend as much on those to whom the account is given, if the danger of distorted discourse is to be avoided. A role can be played by external scrutiny. The scrutineers have grown in number and in responsibilities. The Audit Commission has responsibilities for scrutiny of the health service and for local government. The National Audit Office has responsibilities for scrutiny of central government departments and of Next Steps agencies as well of the health service. Select Committees of the House of Commons can scrutinise the performance of central government departments. Inspectorates play a role in scrutiny as do ombudsmen.

Such scrutinies provide instruments to be used. They do not however by themselves ensure public accountability. Each particular institution of scrutiny has its own limitations set by its terms of reference – the very proliferation of such bodies indicates the limitations of each. They can distort the account, if read in isolation. After all, they provide their own account which represents a particular view and which can be narrower than that of management in the public domain. Their impact can be limited, except where their views reinforce those already held within the organisation.

Although such scrutiny is valuable, it is no substitute for a sense of stewardship within organisations. Indeed it is when there is that sense of stewardship that such scrutiny will be welcomed by management as enhancing public accountability, although recognising too that such scrutiny has itself to be tested in public discourse.

The main guarantee of accounts and accounting lies not in external scrutineers but in open, democratic government. Active citizenship implies a right to know, a right to explanation, but also a right to be involved, to be heard and to be listened to. Those rights imply open government for public discourse. Open government provides its own account, by providing direct access. A sense of stewardship is necessary for its full development. It involves an acceptance not that information *can* be available but that it *should* be; it involves open discussion with the public so as to accommodate policy to the variety of their perspectives and needs. That requires attitudes in management for which private sector models provide no guide. The publicness of action in the public domain is a condition for its full development.

Holding to Account

While public accountability requires many means of accounting, holding to account requires a clear line of accountability. This is an issue for the design of institutional frameworks, but management requires an understanding of what those frameworks mean for accountability.

In recent years, lines of accountability in the public domain have become less clearly defined, due to growth of new forms of organisation. Appointed boards such as district health authorities, training and enterprise councils are accountable in the final resort to ministers. Next Steps agencies are similarly accountable. The accountability for grant-maintained schools and health service trusts is less clear. The development of government by contract or partnerships between the public and the private sector introduces new stages in the lines of accountability and raises issues about what activities the client and what activities the contractor is accountable for.

Institutional issues are posed where lines of accountability become overextended, as they are by the requirement of public accountability placed on private organisations charged with tasks in the public domain. At its very simplest the issue is whether those private organisations have the same requirement for accounting for their work as public organisations since they have taken over responsibilities in the public domain with its conditions for openness for public discourse.

In practice a private firm will claim that its accountability is limited to the terms of the contract. Salaman has argued that similar developments in America 'continually place federal officials in the uncomfortable position of being responsible for programmes they do not really control ... Instead of hierarchical relationship between the federal government and the agents therefore what exists in practise is a far more complex relationship in which the federal government has the weaker hand' (Salaman, 1981, p. 260).

While clarification depends upon institutional development of a more active public domain, the task for management is the development of understanding of the line of accountability and what it requires, for that line provides the conditions for public management action. Stewardship implies not merely giving an account by the steward but also that the steward can be held to account and that how that can be done is known to the public to whom accountability is due. There is a danger in the new uncertain institutions of indirect government and of appointed boards that those lines are hidden from the public. An unknown government cannot be readily held to account. Management as stewardship has a responsibility to make the unknown into the known within the public domain.

Conclusion

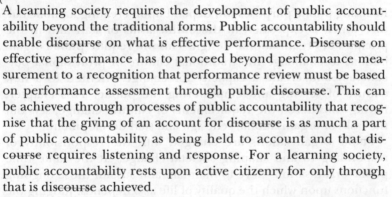

A learning society requires the development of public accountability beyond the traditional forms. Public accountability should enable discourse on what is effective performance. Discourse on effective performance has to proceed beyond performance measurement to a recognition that performance review must be based on performance assessment through public discourse. This can be achieved through processes of public accountability that recognise that the giving of an account for discourse is as much a part of public accountability as being held to account and that discourse requires listening and response. For a learning society, public accountability rests upon active citizenry for only through that is discourse achieved.

In the diversity of a learning society, public accountability requires many channels by which accounts are given and received and a clear line by which those who exercise collective choice are held to account. That will only be achieved if management is informed by the moral sense of stewardship on behalf of all the citizens of the community.

11

Empowering a Public Culture

Challenging the Dominance of Organisational Continuity

Realising public purposes will depend upon creating a public culture which is expressed in the enthusiasms of staff and in the priciples of organisational design. This will require public organisations to challenge the traditional culture of professional bureaucracy and create a capacity for change oriented to a new culture of serving and empowering the public. This chapter, having considered the requirements of cultural change, sets out the tasks of organisational redesign and staff development.

Public organisations are charged with the responsibility of responding to and shaping societal change. At the same time public organisations have to maintain and sustain those ongoing functions upon which the quality of life also depends. Judging the balance of change and continuity, what has to be jettisoned and what maintained, and assessing how what is carried forward needs to be reformed are the distinctive challenges facing the public domain.

In any organisation the requirements of continuity will tend to dominate, unless countervailing processes develop to protect other modes. Kaufman (1981) has stressed the extent to which bureau chiefs in American federal government are constrained by the continuities built into the workings of the organisation.

All the same, it would not be surprising if bureau chiefs were to express feelings of helplessness. In any large organisation, so much momentum has built up and so many routines have already been formed that the prospects of having a profound effect in anything short of a lifetime of concentrated effort must seem dim, especially in the early months. The programming of the members of the agency, whatever the benefits of this process, is sure to feel to the chiefs like a crushing burden of constraints much of their time. (Kaufman, 1981, p. 124)

Management can become absorbed in the requirements of operational management for continuity. Past history and present experience build organisational inertia.

The reasons for organisational inertia are obvious. The members of an organisation have developed a set of skills useful only for doing particular jobs. The organisation itself has an institutional memory for only certain matters. It has standard procedures, established internal jurisdiction and routines. The personnel have been socialised to a certain view of the problems in the area and how they should be handled. Relations have been built with powerful legislators and interest groups. Other government agencies and political figures all feel entitled to rely on expectations of what the agency will do and those expectations have been engendered by a history of past actions. (Heymann, 1987, pp. 6–7)

To be effective, organisations need continuity, but also a capacity for change. Organisational change requires processes that look beyond existing activities and provide time and space to highlight issues, to set directions and to review current practice. It involves a capacity to break out of the rhythms of routine. The danger is that the immediate pressures of operational management limit the capacity for strategic change, enclosing the organisation, rather than opening it for public discourse where the need for change can be expressed.

The capacity for reorienting and reforming organisations in the public domain lies in embodying a new public culture within staff development and organisational design (see Metcalfe and Richards, 1987; Golembiewski, 1985).

Towards a Public Culture

An effective public organisation will have a culture that supports
its values:

> Culture represents the understandings that we live by as mem-
> bers of an organisation; these are carried as symbols which act
> as vehicles for meaning. In addition to specific meanings, we
> also absorb other things characteristic of the culture such as
> attitudes and ways of thinking about the world. Culture is some-
> thing that is lived, and the lived reality may not always coincide
> with statements about the culture. One image of culture is that
> it represents a web of understanding that we need in order to
> make sense of and cope with the complexity and confusion of
> organisational life. This web then gives shape to what we do and
> the ways in which we do it. (McLean and Marshall, 1988, p. 11)

Most organisations have a dominant culture, although there
can be subcultures, some of which may strive to resist and subvert
the dominant values. Individuals can come to accept organisational values as part of getting by, but culture may need to change
in a changing environment. In effect the Fennell Inquiry into the
Kings Cross fire called for not only specific organisational and
policy changes by London Transport but also the creation of a
culture that put a high value on safety, for without the change in
culture, other changes could be in form rather than in reality.

Particular institutions will have their own values. Health authorities can give expression to values of positive health and of caring.
Local authorities can give expression to values of community.
Departments within both central and local government have their
own values built up around the services for which they are
responsible. The test for management must be whether those
cultures support the values of the public domain.

The values of democracy, justice and citizenship should inform
the organisational culture of the public domain. Professional
values, in the working of local authorities and of health authorities, can be developed to express and celebrate the value of
public participation. The dominance of the traditional values of
the higher civil service gives too little regard to the values of citizenship. The result can be a limited approach which only stresses

the minister's responsibility for collective choice and has too little concern for the wider arena of public discourse.

> High quality intellectual fire-power rather than managerial drive was the primary requirement for devising such frameworks. What developed was an organisational culture which stressed some elements at the expense of others ... At the core of the administrative culture, therefore, is the notion of personal service to ministers, inherited from service to the Crown, rather than impersonal service to the state or the public. (Richards, 1988, p. 2)

The development of public management requires a shift in organisational culture to express the purposes and conditions of the public domain. If the challenge facing the public domain is to be met, public organisations need to create a capacity for cultural change: the central code of the culture is *think public.* The values of the public domain need to be embodied in the working of public organisations: in their policy-making and decision-taking, in their principles of staff development and organisational design.

The importance of developing a public culture within public organisations has increasingly been acknowledged. In the polity of the welfare state the public was seen as a client, not as an active participant in the polity. In the neo-liberal polity the public culture is a marketing culture based on the public as customer. We argue for the development of a public culture based on an active citizenry.

Marketing Orientation

In private sector organisations, the marketing function provides a means of breaking out of the enclosed organisation, linking it to the public as customer. Kotler and Andreason have argued that the marketing function has developed through stages:

> The starting point for an effective marketing strategy is the proper orientation toward the marketing function. Historically, marketing has passed through four stages: a product orientation stage, a production orientation stage, a selling orientation stage, and finally, today's customer orientation stage. The first three stages are characterised by management putting the organisation's own needs and desires at the centre of the strategic process. It is only when management realises that it is the

customer who truly determines the long-run success of any strategy that the non-profit firm can join the ranks of the sophisticated marketing strategies found in the private sector. (Kotler and Andreason, 1987, p. 64)

Marketing in the private sector encompasses the relationship of the organisation to its customers. It is concerned with much more than promotional or advertising activities, which can reflect a 'selling orientation' but not a customer orientation. Marketing is often presented as seeking the right mix of product, price, place and promotion – the four Ps – although others have argued that for services, people, physical evidence and process should be added (Cowell, 1984, p. 70) because in services, staff behaviour, the physical surroundings and the way the service is delivered are part of the service as experienced by the customer.

Marketing based on the private sector model has a role to play and has been adopted where public services are supplied in a market governed by price and demand, such as in colleges of further education selling their courses to industry. There are limits, however, upon its wider adoption in the public domain. Public services have to recognise that the direct user of the services cannot be regarded as the only consumer of the service. Marketing approaches that focus on the customer alone are not adequate in the public domain.

In the public domain, services are provided not to meet demand, but to meet need as determined by criteria established in the political process. Marketing approaches that are directed at identifying and stimulating demand can therefore be inappropriate for public services where the task is to identify need. If marketing has a role it has to be marketing for equity for which the private sector model gives little guidance. The private sector model presupposes a model of customer behaviour. It is by no means certain that even the direct consumers of a public service, if they can be identified, behave in the same way as in the market. The customer will have different expectations and follow different patterns of behaviour because the public are citizens as well as customers:

- the public may consider that they have a right to a service and will pursue that right – in the market they will merely buy the service

- the public may argue that they have not been fairly treated – although that claim will rarely be urged in the market
- the public may demand to know the policies of the organisation – although few would express that right in the market
- the public will accept the right of the state to compel – they will deny that right to the market

A model is needed of behaviour in the public domain, if marketing approaches are to develop. The private sector model cannot encompass the complexities of relationships in the public domain. In the public domain the public are more than customers or consumers: 'such "consumers" are not beings who rule and are ruled in turn, they do not take part in reasoned judgements for the common good, nor take part in authoritative action; they simply consume and demand more' (Walmsley, 1990, p. 133)

The public are citizens with the right to a voice in the arena of public discourse and the right to be heard, whether or not they are consumers of the service. If marketing is concerned with the relationship between an organisation and the public, then in the public domain it has to encompass the relationship with citizens as well as consumers and for that the private sector model gives no guidance. Kotler has argued for a wider definition of the role of marketing – a societal marketing orientation: 'The key tasks of the orientation are to determine the needs, wants and interests of target markets, and to adapt the organisation to delivering the desired satisfactions ... in a way that preserves or enhances the consumer's and the society's well-being' (Kotler, 1980, p. 10) Goodrich has pointed out that this concept is

> directly relevant to public administrators who must rationalize their activities in terms of serving the public interest. Certainly regulatory activities of government as well as direct services provision could readily be included in this 'societal marketing' concept which is concerned with overall public welfare and the quality of life. At the same time, this array of management philosophies is helpful in defining the marketing orientation more broadly and avoiding the normal tendency to equate marketing with advertising or public relations. (Goodrich, 1983, p. 92)

This involves the application of marketing in new ways:

> While most marketing experts are in the business of encourag-
> ing and building up demand for an organization's products or
> services, a major task of public managers in these times of
> scarcity is often to stretch their meagre resources, trying to make
> sure that there is enough left of the shrinking pie to give their
> clients some amount, however reduced. They are not trying to
> attract customers for their programs. In some other cases (e.g.
> energy or water conservation ... or emergency calls) the aim is
> to dampen public demand or limit usage to only 'essential' cus-
> tomers and activities as a matter of public policy. Demarketing –
> the use of marketing strategies to reduce demand or channel it
> to appropriate uses – can be helpful here. (ibid., p. 101)

The development of marketing for the public domain would
require a language appropriate to that domain. It will have to be
capable of encompassing the variety of relationships between
public organisations and their public as customer or citizen, consumer or client, voter or protester. If marketing is to encompass
that variety, the issue must be whether the nature of such marketing is not so different from marketing in the private sector that it
is inappropriate to use a word grounded in the market and hence
in conditions that do not apply to public services.

The Public Service Orientation

Clarke and Stewart argued that rather than a marketing culture, a
public service orientation was required. Too many public organisations, paradoxically, had taken the public for granted, so that:
'A public service can easily become service *to* rather than *for* the
public. The organisation knows best. The public service orientation stresses that services are only of real value if they are of value
to those for whom they are provided' (Clarke and Stewart, 1986,
p. 1). A public organisation that put service for the public first
would stress:

- closeness to the customer and the citizen
- listening to the public
- access for the public
- seeing service from the public's point of view

- seeking out views, suggestions and complaints
- the public's right to know
- quality of service
- the public as the test of quality

This meant that a public organisation

> had to recognise that: its activities exist to provide services for the public; it will be judged by the quality of service provided within the resources available; the service provided is only of real value if it is of value to those for whom it is provided; those for whom services are provided are customers demanding high quality services and citizens entitled to receive it; quality of service demands closeness to the public as customer and citizen. (Clarke and Stewart, 1990, pp. 25–6)

There was a recognition in the public service orientation that the public was both a customer and a citizen. The dual emphasis rejected both the model of the public as client dominant in the polity built by the welfare state and the model of the public as customer sought by the neo-liberal polity. It recognised that public organisations required both learning from customers and learning from citizens. Citizens 'have an interest in the services provided; the services not provided; the level of expenditure; the use of resources; the distribution of resources; the use of the powers of the authority. They have a concern with whatever is done in their names. Each citizen has a right to express her views and to have those views respected and attended to' (Stewart, 1988, p. 61).

Approaches developed for a public service orientation have a significant role to play in improving the quality of public services. There is a need to improve access to services, to learn from the users of services, and to inform them about the services. All these considerations, however, flow mainly from the requirements of the public as customers. More is required if the public as citizen is primary.

A Culture of Active Citizenship for the Learning Society

A learning society requires an active citizenship as the basis for action in the public domain. Citizenship is given expression in the arena of public discourse. It requires therefore a development built upon, but going beyond, the public service orientation in which the public is both customer and citizen and these are posed together in some uneasy equality. That assumption of equality does not resolve the dilemma, but poses it in another form as to how the views of the citizen and the interests of the customer are reconciled.

In a learning society citizenship is primary. The public is also a customer, as the public is also a client, a user, an applicant, a patient, a defendant or even a prisoner, for there are many forms of relationships between the organisation in the public domain and its publics, which are imperfectly caught by the word 'customer'. To say the public as citizen is primary, however, means that the relationship with citizens is not just another relationship, but that it underlies all other relationships. The relationship as citizen is the determining relationship in the public domain.

Recognition of the primacy of the citizen does not predetermine the extent to which the service received is decided by collective choice or by the recipient of the service, since citizenship is involved at both levels. This dilemma has to be resolved in public discourse, where the extent of required uniformity or requisite variety can be discussed as an issue of how citizenship is best expressed.

Thus the issue to be discussed need not be whether there is a National Curriculum or not, but where a choice has to be made at national level, where at local level, where at school level and where at the level of the individual – for citizenship is not restricted to one level. The role of the professional expert as a participant in the choice can also be discussed. The dilemma is resolved, as it should be resolved, in the public domain through the organising principle – public discourse leading to collective choice based on public consent. That involves the active participation of citizens not merely in public discourse as the basis for collective choice, but also at the point of service delivery.

Services both in the public domain and in the private sector have characteristics that differentiate the management task from that required in the production of goods. Normann highlights three characteristics of service organisations:

> One is the basic intangibility of services (as opposed to the concreteness of manufactured goods). This immediately suggests several related properties; services cannot be stored; they cannot easily be demonstrated; and while they can be sold,

there is not necessarily any transfer of ownership ... Secondly, most services actually consist of *acts*, and *interactions* are typically social events. The control and management of social events call for certain special skills. (Normann, 1984, p. 7)

But the critical characteristic is his third point that 'the production and consumption of a service cannot always be clearly kept apart, since they generally occur simultaneously and at the same place' (ibid., p. 7)

Services are normally produced at the point of consumption. In services, producer and consumer meet. Indeed, it has been argued that service production is an act of co-production involving both consumer and staff.

A feature of many state-organised services is that in the course of their production the distinction between 'consumption' and 'production' is blurred. The 'production' carried out by schools, hospitals, prisons but also welfare systems and transportation systems, is in principle completed through the *collaboration* of agents with users. (Offe, 1985, pp. 310–11)

The simultaneous process of production and consumption of services has implications for management. Because both staff and the public are involved in the production of the service, it is difficult to standardise it and also to control its delivery. 'Technology does not determine organisation in service where the client/customer is an integral part of the service operations activities because he or she provides information that is essential for the input, conversion and export processes ... and therefore is ... not amenable to a closed system logic' (Mills, 1988, p. 75)

Normann has described services as involving the moment of truth:

Most services are the result of social acts which take place in direct contact between the customer and representatives of the service company. To take a metaphor from bullfighting, we could say that the perceived quality is realized at the moment of truth, when the service provider and the service consumer confront one another in the arena ... At that moment they are very much on their own. What happens then can no longer be directly influenced by the company. It is the skill, the motivation and the tools employed by the firm's representative and the expectations and behaviour of the client which together will create the service delivery process. A large service company may well experience tens of thousands of 'moments of truth' each day. (Normann, 1984, pp. 8–9)

In the public domain there are millions of moments of truth each day. The teacher and the child, the doctor and the patient, the social security officer and the claimant each have their moment of truth. A sense of citizenship can transform those moments of truth. The provision of public services can be seen as co-production in which the citizen participates as well as the customer. For a citizen participating as a customer in the act of co-production, there is a right to explanation and a right to be listened to. Service delivery in the public domain can be informed by discourse at the individual level, as collective choice is informed by the arena of public discourse. The service as delivered develops in that discourse. The citizen as customer can develop individual choice, which need not challenge collective choice, since it is made within the limits set by that choice; the customer as citizen is exploring the meaning of collective choice. Choice can be made individually as people can choose furniture for their rooms in an old persons' home, the method of childbirth in hospitals, or collectively as when tenants on an estate make decisions on its management. In doing so they act as citizens as well as customers and from their choices collective choice can be informed and developed. The citizen can be involved as quality monitor of the services, provided the standards of quality are stated, in for example a service contract specifying the frequency and method of street cleansing: 'when, however, one focuses on the effectiveness of the service delivery system, clients assume the role of "supervisor" evaluating the performance (that is the quality of the service) of the public employee' (Riddle, 1988, p. 202).

There is scope for management innovation to involve the public as citizen as well as customer in the co-production of public services. Seen as participation by the citizen in service delivery, the moment of truth can be transformed into an element in the building of a learning society through active citizenship. That transformation with its emphasis on discourse can itself help to open up the arena of public discourse. Participation in that wider arena can build upon the habit and expectation of discourse at the point of service delivery. The requirements upon management are then the management of co-production for citizenship as well as support for public discourse as citizenship. In that way a culture of and for citizenship can be expressed, but to achieve that the culture must be supported in organisational design and built by staffing policy.

Designing the Public Organisation

To build a culture of citizenship for a learning society is a strategic choice and strategic choice is effected through organisational change. Organisational development is the instrument of implementation in strategic management. Strategic management works through changing the organisational framework and the pattern of working within it. This can involve changing structure, building new management processes or working with and through organisational culture. Development can take place within an organisation or amongst a set of organisations. Thus for central government, organisational development can involve setting the conditions for other organisations, requiring an understanding of organisational design *and* of organisational development. Organisational design by itself is not enough. Changes in organisational structures and procedures are unlikely by themselves to lead to major strategic change unless given continuing support by wider processes of organisational development. Strategic organisational development involves:

- an understanding of organisational strengths and weaknesses
- a capacity to translate strategic choice into organisational change
- skills in organisational design and the avoidance of over-design
- communication skills: listening as well as telling
- space for staff involvement in organisational change
- training policies grounded in the process of organisational development
- development opportunities for staff
- recruitment, promotion and incentives geared to organisational change

The art of strategic organisational development lies not in the elements but in the way they are used together. Thus training by itself is an inadequate response to the need for strategic organisational development.

> Sometimes training is put forward as a major inducer of change. Training is a valuable and necessary adjunct to other mechanisms to support an overall strategy, but as a change process has little success in its own right. The civil servant newly trained in innovative techniques and imbued with new values, returns to his or her work situation and usually has little choice but to readjust rapidly to the existing procedures and processes. (Wilenski, 1986, p. 26)

What has been written about strategic organisational development could apply to organisations both in the private and in the public domain. The special feature of strategic organisational development in the public domain is that the public are part of the organisation as citizens. Strategic organisational development involves the public and should be tested in the arena of public discourse. But more is required. The public are themselves part of the process of strategic organisational development, participating in the determination of activities and in the activities themselves.

The structuring of a public organisation – how it specialises functions, encourages integration, and distributes authority – should be shaped by the organising assumptions that carry the dominant values and functions of the public domain into the working practice of an organisation. These are:

- to convene the public discourse, the debate about need and thus to constitute the public as a critical public; to enable the public to be a public
- to listen, interpret and articulate the expressed needs
- to enable collective choice about provision to meet need by mediating and seeking to reconcile differences of interest
- to promote the public interest
- to provide effectively the services and priorities which have been collectively chosen, but in discourse with those for whom they are provided
- to support the public in managing the delivery of those services, and in making use of those services

- to coordinate the diverse services to realise the presumption of cooperation in the experience of delivery
- to account to the public about the effectiveness of performance
- to serve the public, but in doing so to recognise that the organisation itself represents and involves the public

In effect, the structuring of the organisation should support the culture of active citizenship for the learning society. Such organising assumptions key, as Goffman (1974) puts it, public values and institutional conditions into the working of the organisation. Three processes of organisational design are central to the task of realising the characteristics and culture of a public organisation.

Public Priorities in the Structure of Public Organisations

One of the most significant ways in which organisational designers can support key values is in the way they define and specialise the major functions of the organisation; in defining what are to be the central divisions and therefore limits/boundaries of work and activity. The differentiating of functional activity defines and specialises the focus of knowledge, skill and practical competence.

The public organisation can seek to constitute the division of functional activity according to the values of the learning society. The implications of publicness for structuring is to take the public's definition of need and value as the basis of functional differentiation. Thus the values of equal opportunities have led to the constituting of the interests of women or of minority groups in the structure of a number of public organisations. The values of the public are taken up and constituted in the defining of departmental working. Public values are thus taken into the heart of organisational routines and working.

Team-Working and Partnership

Public organisations requiring to open out not only to respond to variety, but also to support public choice need to balance uniformity and flexibility, collegiality and networking. If the public organisation is to accommodate the changing demands and needs of the public, then internal systems have to reinforce flexibility,

---

EXHIBIT 11.1

Equal opportunities

Within the working of public organisations, barriers have been built between groups of staff or against particular groups. These barriers deny the values of the public domain in which citizenship attaches to all and principles of equity and justice require equal opportunities for all. An organisation that denies equal opportunities ·is a flawed public organisation, since it is an organisation that has not realised its own potential, denying the value of many of its own staff or of potential recruits. That reflects a weakness in any organisation, but in the public domain it is a denial of domain values.

For a public organisation, both domain values and the realisation of organisational potential support an equal opportunities policy that is directed against the barriers that lie within. The barriers that lie between manual and non-manual workers are marked out by different terms and conditions of service. Within the staff, barriers can be built against movement. In local authorities professionals can be seen as barring the way for administrators. There is a different position in the Civil Service where the administrative staff have been seen as barring the way for professionals.

Yet beyond the formal barriers of grade are barriers of discrimination which have limited the opportunities for women, for ethnic minorities and for people with disabilities. Those barriers may be built by recruitment and promotion practices, which ensure that the staffing of the past is reproduced in the future. Those barriers can be built by attitudes denied or unrecognised.

The *issue raised* is how public organisations can express domain values in their structure and design.

---

communication and team-working. Organisation theorists have termed such an organisation 'organic' in form. Organic organisations strive to remain open and responsive to the public as citizens by creating a more informal pattern which allows elected representatives and their officials to share their knowledge within flexible work settings that enable team-working in the public interest. Tasks are performed in common, responsibilities are shared, control is located close to the action and communication is continuous. Special roles and project groups may be created to facilitate coordination. Yet managers in public service organisations have to establish some bureaucratic uniformities of rules and procedures that ensure impartiality. The public organisation cannot be wholly organic because it has to act as the vehicle for imposing collective will. The virtues of bureaucracy secure greater certainties of action and implementation of public choice. The challenge for the public manager is to hold uniformity and flexibility in balance. The means are processes which encourage managers to account for the reasonableness of their actions in adapting boundaries and rules to new needs (Lynn, 1981).

Internal collegiality and external networking must also be balanced. The principle of continually keeping in touch with colleagues has to be carried beyond the boundaries of the organisation, if the necessary connections are to be made with many other agencies so that the public can be listened to, served and supported. Yet the organisation needs to retain an internal coherence and integration based upon collegiality of purpose at the same time as being open and responsive to the culture and perspectives of multiple organisations in the public sphere. As we emphasised in Chapter 6, the public domain entails interdependent government of the community that links together related public organisations to ensure coherence of purpose. No one organisation can achieve self-sufficiency of public service provision and there will always be a need to realise the presumption of cooperation in the public domain.

Organic flexibility and networking presuppose considerable decentralisation of authority to those who require discretion in their day-to-day working with the public or other public organisations in the network.

Participation at the Centre and the Periphery

The distinctive management task in the public domain of supporting and enabling the duality of publicness requires specific organisational arrangements. If the duality of active participation together with collective choice is to be achieved, then public organisations need to be arranged in ways which enable the diverse public perspectives to be expressed and consulted and yet also to be drawn together to enable a collective choice to be made and action taken in the common interest. This can be accomplished, we argue, if organisations seek to establish duality in the distribution of authority: that is, to decentralise as much discretion as possible to those working closely with the public while reserving authority for strategic planning and for decision-making at the centre. If public organisations are to be open and responsive to their public, they need to decentralise decision-making in order to support those working with the public, because they will often be the best judge of needs as well as the antennae sensitive to emerging demands. Decentralisation allows public access to the point of decision-making.

A number of strategies are being used by public organisations to devolve decision-making and to encourage participation. Local public service institutions – such as schools, hospitals and social service offices – are granted more financial discretion to allocate resources according to locally defined public need. 'Outreach' workers – such as careers officers, adult tutors and detached community workers – are appointed to counsel, advise and encourage public participation. The creation of local area or neighbourhood offices is another significant organisational innovation for enabling responsive service provision as well as encouraging active community development.

Yet if the public organisation is to retain the necessary coherence for developing and enabling public choice it must retain a strategic centre as well as responsive outreach institutional forms. The role of the centre in the public domain is not to be involved in detailed management. It is to clarify public choice and public purpose. The organisation at the centre is small rather than extensive, concerned with clarifying strategic needs and plans; monitoring and evaluating the quality of public service; and leading to an open accountability of performance to the public.

New forms of organisation, therefore, designed to embody the principles of the public domain will only be effective if they accompany and express a culture of innovation committed to new ways of working on behalf and for the public. A responsive, enabling, public organisation challenges the conventional structures and procedures that support the routinised service delivery. What is needed is not just a simplification of structures and rules, but the transformation of organisational culture so as to enable change for the public domain.

Staffing for Citizenship

A culture of citizenship is required but changes in culture are not easily achieved. They require policies for staff and organisational development that build, sustain and reinforce the changes. Such policies cannot be imposed; they must be built with staff who are themselves citizens and that requires recognition of the barriers to 'citizenship of the organisation'.

The main instruments available to management for building, maintaining and strengthening organisational culture are staffing policies and practices, for in them management shows not merely

---

EXHIBIT 11.2

The Benefits Agency programme – *Towards the Core Values*

The Benefits Agency has four core values:

 Customer Service
 Caring for Staff
 Bias for Action
 Value for Money

It has adopted a programme called *Toward the Core Values*, comprising eight parts each led by a member of the management team. This programme shows the importance of staff policies and how they relate to a wider strategy.

– *A framework for managers* establishing an empowering, rather than a controlling environment
– *Redefining the role of junior and middle management* ensuring that management within the operational network is responsive to both the needs of our customers and emerging technology
– *Caring for staff* a more flexible and motivated workforce, enabling staff to give their best
– *Serving the customer better* raising the standard of service by improving behaviours as well as delivery systems
– *Developing the relationships between Districts, Benefit Directorates and Central Services* to ensure that the operational network is free to deliver services with a supportive, rather than prescriptive, emphasis from the Centre
– *A better basis for resourcing* to ensure that the operational network resources and planning systems fully reflect their needs, in addition to the corporate requirements of the Agency, the Department and Ministers
– *Simplify processes and systems* to develop a framework and systems for future business, taking full advantage of the technology to reduce forms and paper work
– *Improving communications* to ensure that all staff are committed to the same aim, and that each level understands their role in communication (Benefits Agency, 1992, p. 19)

The *issue raised* is how values translate into action. The Benefits Agency programme shows the importance of staff policies in resolving that issue.

the values it proclaims, but the values it practises. Communication should show the values; staff training and development should reinforce them; promotion and recruitment should be guided by them. Above all management show staff by their own actions the organisational values they espouse as opposed to those they profess. Management may stress 'close to the public' in words, but if in practice they are isolated from concerns for the public, the statement will be seen for what it is – words rather than commitment.

Development

Staff development is a means of building organisational culture but is also a necessary condition of a learning society. If the public domain is the setting for societal learning through which organisations in that domain change and are changed, then that requires a learning staff. Staff development has to encompass the needs of the present and the potential of the future.

Four primary needs can be identified. The first is for all those who work in the public domain to be aware of its purposes and conditions. It would be commonplace for an effective organisation in the private sector to seek to build staff commitment to the organisation and its products. The task in the public domain is to combine commitment to service with an understanding of the public domain. The professional can be committed to the service provided and that should not be undermined, but the professional, as other members of staff, may lack commitment to or even understanding of the organisation in which he or she works and of its role in the public domain. The starting point for staff development must be to build that commitment and understanding, without weakening the commitment to service.

The second is for continuing development as a necessary condition of the learning society. Much of training has been built upon the model of basic training acquired at the start of the career – indeed that is the professional model – that assumes that knowledge stands still and the environment demands no change. Continuing professional education is advocated but may be little more in practice than attendance at an occasional short course.

The third is for career patterns that extend experience to match the concerns of the public domain by movement that extends across and beyond the boundaries of the public sector. Staff development has been limited by careers, experience and training to particular parts of the public sector. The development of public management should not be limited to particular organisations. The presumption of cooperation would be better realised by careers that crossed organisational boundaries in the public domain.

The fourth is the recognition that management development in the public domain has its own curriculum. The argument of this book has been that management must be grounded in the distinctive values, conditions and tasks of the public domain. That should guide the curriculum of management development by which we mean the skills, attitude and knowledge it is designed to build. As well as content common to management development in other organisations, it should encompass some or all of the following:

- *Managing in a political–management system.* Management in the public domain is intertwined with the political process. If management does not understand the political process, it cannot be effective. Management development can cultivate skills in organisational analysis that encompass the interrelationships between political and management processes.
- *Working with public pressure and protest.* Both learning from and managing pressure and protest can be part of the management task in the public domain. Management development should recognise pressure and protest as necessary elements in public discourse.
- *A sense of accountability.* Management development can help to build a sense of accountability. Management in the public domain is in the public arena. Special skills and attitudes are required not merely to accept openness, but to build openness for accountability.
- *Understanding public behaviour.* Citizens, customers, consumers and clients are all words used to describe the public. Management in the public domain requires an understanding of public behaviour not in the one but in the many relationships.
- *The management of rationing.* A public service organisation has to ration services. The manager needs understanding of how rationing actually takes place and of the ways in which it could take place.

- *The management of influence.* In the public domain organisations interact not in necessary competition, but to realise the presumption of cooperation. The management of interaction requires skills in the management of mutual influence, as much as in the management of action.
- *Assessing a multi-dimensioned performance.* In the public domain, performance can rarely be reduced to a simple measure. Assessment of a multi-dimensioned performance as an aid to judgement is the required skill.
- *Understanding a wider responsibility to a changing society.* Built into the working of the organisation should be a sense of responsibility that goes beyond the particular services provided. Management in the public domain needs an understanding of societal change as necessary to a learning society.

This list is designed to suggest rather than to define the distinctive issues for management development for the public domain.

Motivation

In the past it has been assumed that established procedures are their own guarantee of performance and that if motivation is required, it will come from the public service ethic or from professional commitment. Yet the continuities of administration can limit motivation.

> At the same time, the novelty of the job and the sense of achievement that people feel when they start in an agency diminish over the years for those who reach their respective career ceilings, as many do after a while in any large organisation. The annual cycles repeat. Things change and then change back again. The old problems persist. The rhetoric stays the same. Few people can sustain much enthusiasm under these conditions.
>
> And with it all comes the drum fire of criticism and complaint, denunciation and derision aimed at civil servants. (Kaufman, 1981, p. 32)

These are not conditions for effective management in a changing environment. Motivation becomes an issue and motivation may not be easily achieved within traditional staffing policies and practices. For example there is a need to ensure that 'the public enterprise managers/bureaucrats will take attitudes towards risk which are appropriate from the standpoint of the community' (Jackson, 1982, p. 205).

There are, of course, special problems in motivating staff for effective performance in the public domain – because effective performance cannot be readily defined when there are multiple criteria of success. That means that effective performance rests upon judgement, but that is only a problem if it is not recognised. It is still possible to reward performance.

Performance-related pay is one, but only one, form of reward but motivation need not depend upon payment alone, any more in the public sector than in the private sector. Sir Derek Rayner said in evidence to the Select Committee on Expenditure:

> I often do not believe that they are encouraged to take the cal-
> culated risk – and it is not much of a risk – that a businessman
> will take in dealing with certain problems. How do we encour-
> age it? I think that we have to reward people ... by acknowledg-
> ing their success. I have never heard of the Committee of
> Public Accounts sending for people who did an excellent job.
> (HC 535, 1977, Evidence Q313)

Motivation can derive from understanding and recognition – the need for which is too often ignored, but which is of particular importance in the public domain, because actions taken can be and often are the subject of criticism in public discourse. The motivation for promoting the values of the public domain can reside in the understanding that professional and public service values of serving the public and the domain values of involving the citizen are not incompatible. Professional values and public service can be secured more effectively if the public share those values and are motivated by them, 'owning' the purposes which the professionals and the public service espouse.

Communication

Reliance on the procedures of bureaucracy and on the folkways of the professional culture limits communication with staff. Bureau-cracy defines and limits the extent of communication to pre-scribed tasks. Professionalism has its own enclosed patterns of communication. Staff communication should have a special role in public management since the public domain is the domain of public discourse. That discourse should involve the staff themselves as citizens. Effective management of a public organisation requires communication not merely for the effective internal working of the organisation, but also to achieve the requirements of the public domain.

The staff are the main means of communication between a public authority and its public as customer and as citizen. On staff who provide service for the public falls not merely the responsibility for action, but also for explanation. Public relations are formed not at the centre of the organisation alone or by the activities of public relations departments in handling the media, but in the many points of interaction between the public authorities and the public. Those interactions depend upon and are formed by the understanding and knowledge of staff which depend on communication. It is also through the staff that at least, in part, the authority learns. Staff have the direct experience of policy in action, that must form a basic element in the learning authority, but that again requires effective communication.

The changing nature of the political process places special demands upon communication within public organisations. As policies change with political change so grows the need to build communication as a means of understanding that change.

Communication can use the channels laid down by bureaucratic hierarchies, but can also bypass them. The chief executive of a local authority who invites different staff from all levels each week to a discussion of the work of the authority or the Permanent Secretary who has similar meetings is creating alternative channels of communication.

Redundancy of channels is required for effective communication. Each channel carries its own distortion upwards or downwards:

● staff newspapers, newsletters
● briefing groups linking levels of the organisation
● informal seminars to explore problems
● staff meetings
● visits by senior staff and politicians for communication and learning
● official consultation procedures
● active involvement of trade unions

The modes of communication used are themselves part of the message. Communication is most effective in public organisation when it gives expression to the values and organising principles of the public domain and recognises that staff are part of and are involved in public discourse. Communication should itself be part of discourse, listening and learning as well as telling.

Dilemmas Faced

There are however tensions in and between these requirements for staff. Thus it cannot be simply assumed that staffing policies and procedures should themselves express the values of the public domain or be structured upon the organising principle. Democratic values are expressed in collective choice based on a political process, and in public discourse as a condition of public consent. Both imperatives can appear to override staff's own needs and requirements. Thus industrial democracy in the public domain is subject to political democracy. Waldo in arguing for a democratic theory of public administration pointed out that the accepted maxim was that 'Autocracy during hours is the price of democracy after hours' (Waldo, 1952, p. 86). Mosher has argued:

> There has already developed a great deal of collegial decision making in many public agencies, particularly those which are largely controlled by single professional groups. But I would point out that *democracy within administration*, if carried to the full, raises a logical dilemma in relation to political democracy. All public organisations are presumed to have been established and to operate for public purposes – i.e. purposes of the people. To what extent, then, should 'insiders', the officers and employees, be able to modify their purposes, their organisational arrangements and their means of support? It is entirely possible that internal administrative democracy might run counter to the principles and objectives of political democracy in which the organisations of government are viewed as instruments of public purpose. (Mosher, 1968, pp. 18–19)

This argument can however be carried too far. If the values of justice and equity are to be realised in the public domain, then they have implications for staff policies and procedures. Public organisations cannot expect domain values to be realised by staff unless they are applied to staff. The staff are after all citizens. Indeed, Stivers (1990) has described them as 'citizens of the organisation', with implications for their involvement in collective choice.

There can be tensions within the requirement to support and express the organising principle. Staff are engaged in discourse with citizens as customers. The requirements of collective choice can lead to an emphasis on hierarchical control over staff, limiting discretion, while the citizenship relationship in service provision can suggest a degree of responsiveness which requires freedom from overdetailed control. The openness required for public discourse may conflict with the imperatives of collective choice achieved through party control. The flow of information necessary for discourse may conflict with a political party's interests. This conflict can present staff with a dilemma in which loyalty to the Government is opposed to domain values.

The conditions under which staff work can make it difficult to realise the domain values of openness to and for discourse. For a clerical officer on the counter of a supplementary benefits office, the issue may be necessary protection against attack at the counter, yet that protection can be a symbol not of open government but of an enclosed organisation. Openness may seem an abstract concept to the officer in a housing department being abused by a tenant. Staff have to face the tensions implicit in public services between public purpose which enforces rationing and responsive service. What is a dilemma in theory becomes for them pressure and protest in the reality of the working situation.

The same staff can be called upon both to express the coercive power of the state and to provide a service. The social worker in dealing with a child abuse case moves from enforcement to advice in a single act. The tension that is inherent in the combined role of government and of service is enacted at the point where the organisation meets the public. The diversity of interests, the conflict of values, the pressures of needs and demands upon limited resources are everpresent in the public domain. The act of balancing and reconciling but, if necessary, imposing is inherent in the public domain. The necessities extend beyond management and involve staff at all levels.

The tensions and the dilemma inherent in them can never be finally resolved. Those tensions constitute the dynamic necessary for a learning society. To deny a role to staff in collective choice, in response to discourse, in balancing values, would be not only an unrealistic limitation on discretion but would be to deny their own citizenship and their participation in discourse. Discretion is not merely necessary but can itself enable the attainment of domain values, provided it is governed by those values and by the organising principles.

Discretion was implicit in our discussion of performance management; staff discretion is and should be discretion governed by collective choice, itself the product of public discourse in which staff have a role to play, although not so dominant a role that it excludes other voices. Collective choice is expressed in laws, policies and procedures, but such superordinate rules need not and should not totally limit discretion for staff. Such rules can never specify the variety of conditions in which they are applied – although the degree of specification can and should vary with the nature of collective choice. They have to be applied in understanding of the collective choice and informed by the public discourse inherent in the nature of service delivery. Above all they have to be governed by the values of the public domain expressed in organisational culture.

The Ethics of Domain Values

Ethical issues have to be faced by management in the public domain. They reflect these dilemmas. There can be a conflict between values sustaining public discourse and the requirements of collective choice as expressed through the political process. The requirements of public discourse demand public access to information which it can be in the political interests of government to deny. Leaks in government reflect the ethical dilemma and its resolution by individuals in favour of the values sustaining public discourse.

In the Ponting prosecution the Government argued that the dilemma should be resolved by the requirements of collective choice. The memorandum issued in 1985 by Sir Robert Armstrong, Secretary of the Cabinet, on the duties and responsibilities of civil servants stated: 'it is the Minister who is responsible, and answerable to Parliament, for the conduct of affairs and the management of its business'. He concluded that 'The civil service as such has no constitutional personality or responsibility separate from the duly elected Government of the day' (HC 92, Vol. II, 1986, pp. 7–9). This implies that the Government can take action that denies the organising principles, which govern the public domain. The same principles are not necessarily applied to other organisations in the public sector. The Local Government (Access of Information) Act 1985 gives the public rights of access to information which they can enforce against the local authority. Such legislation protects domain values.

Staff in the public service have a responsibility to sustain domain values. In some countries domain values will be given constitutional expression and are binding on public servants in both central and in local government:

> Is it not possible to accept ministerial responsibility to Parliament as an essential of the British constitution and yet allow civil servants the right to their own voice? It is said that this would weaken ministerial responsibility but at best that is a practical argument, not one of constitutional principle. And it is hard to see why, with some adaptation of constitutional conventions (said to be flexible anyway), the two could not co-exist as they do in other democracies. (Ridley, 1987, p. 83)

It is a condition of management for a learning society that there should be limits set to organisational requirements by domain values.

Conclusion

The management of the public domain has to be realised through the staff and the organisations that inhabit that domain. This requires that the activities of staff are governed by a culture that supports the values of the public domain. The public domain for the learning society can be expressed through a culture of citizenship. That culture can guide organisational design, but organisational structure and processes have to be given life by staffing policies for citizenship.

Conclusion

The Challenge for Public Management

The social and economic changes since the early 1970s revealed a polity which had been atrophying over time, increasingly cut off from the well-springs of its authority – the consent of the public. If the postwar period began with a 'settlement' between the estates of the realm (the state, capital and labour) to create a fairer and prosperous modern society for all its citizens, then thirty years later, although much had been achieved, society was becoming increasingly fragmented. Accelerating long-term unemployment brought into question the status of many citizens as full members of the community participating in the development of their community. The public life of the community has been eroding over time to the point where it is uncertain whether our society has the social resources to resolve those problems – for example, environmental pollution – which can only be resolved through collective action, informed by an understanding of the public good that is widely shared throughout the community.

Yet a society which can hold in balance the public and private good, so as to flourish as a community as well as through strong individuals, is unlikely to be a spontaneous process occurring naturally without a public domain which develops those institutions and a style of management which can nurture the quality of life for the public as a whole. It is the responsibility of the polity to establish the framework which provides the conditions for society to flourish (Nussbaum, 1990; Nussbaum and Sen, 1993). It is the neglect of this principal purpose of renewing the quality of the public domain – the processes of democratic citizenship nourishing collective and individual well-being – that now threatens the future of society. Part II set out the purposes and institutional

269

conditions for the reconstituting of the public domain as necessary for the development of society.

The challenge for public management is to discover its distinctive task in enabling the public domain to flourish. The challenge
for management is to regenerate the public domain. Realising this
will require public management to move beyond the traditional
management of the social democratic period with its emphasis
upon the delivery of uniform and expanding services, defined
according to the prevailing professional paradigm. Public support
was taken for granted. Management was structured for the stability
and uniformity of service provision: stability was ensured by continuing economic growth while uniformity was based upon the ethos
of professionalism and sound public administration. Traditional
management was structured for continuity and growth. The new
public management will have to challenge the organising assumptions of the era of traditional social democratic management and
go beyond the enclosed polity that excluded a passive public dominated by a professional culture, within organisations managed
according to the bureaucratic principles of hierarchical control.
The new public management will challenge the inappropriateness
of private management within the public domain: a reliance on
market competition as the organising principle can only corrode
the public in favour of private advantage and thus deny the discourse which alone can resolve the collective problems experienced by society. The new public management must develop its
tasks, informed by the distinctive purposes and conditions for
renewing and sustaining the public domain. If public management
is to realise its purposes, it must develop a capacity for internal
renewal in order to regenerate the public domain.

The Nature of Public Management

The nature of management in the public domain must reflect the
purposes, conditions and tasks of that domain. That theory has
shaped the approach set out in this book. It denies that there is
only one way of managing: a generic approach to management
applicable to all organisations. That denial would be readily
accepted if one were concerned with differences in technology or
tasks. It is well-understood that one does not manage a service

industry in the same way that one manages manufacturing processes, and that within each of these categories the nature of management varies. If such variations are accepted, then it is hardly surprising that it is argued that the nature of management in the public domain is, and should be, different from the nature of management in the private sectors. Activities are placed in the public domain in order to be organised and delivered according to fundamentally different purposes and conditions.

There are, it is acknowledged, some generic processes of management which are common to all organisations – clarifying strategy, communicating policy, developing staff, evaluating performance. But the purposes to which these processes are put and the ways in which they are expressed is very different according to the domain and its defining purposes. While strategy can in the private sector be grounded in instrumentally rational analyses of accumulation and efficiency, in the public domain strategy has to emerge from a political process of mediating and reconciling in a judgement of common purpose for the public good.

Grounding the study of management in the public domain in its distinctive purposes, conditions and tasks is therefore inescapably grounded in a theory of the polity rather than an economic theory of production. The purpose of management in the public domain is to serve the needs of the learning society. Only if learning is placed at the centre can individuals continue to develop their capacities, institutions be enabled to respond openly and imaginatively to change and the differences between communities become a source for reflective understanding. The challenge for the polity is to promote the purposes and conditions for such a learning society. Only a public domain which can support the public in developing the powers and capacities to make sense of the changes and to shape them according to shared purposes can flourish. It requires the diversity of interests to enter into dialogue to learn from the alternative ways of interpreting experience and the meanings which inform cultures.

A learning society cannot be expected to develop automatically. Understanding will need to emerge from the contending forces. But that understanding cannot emerge without considerable reform to democratise the polity so that the conditions are provided to enable different communities and perspectives to articulate their purposes and needs. The task for public management is to support the development of a reformed public domain. Management cannot itself bring about the learning society but unless public management is itself reformed, jettisoning inappropriate concepts of the private sector, then it will frustrate the needs of the public domain.

The organising principle for the reformed public domain depends upon regenerating the arenas of public discourse. The social democratic polity held the public at a remove, while the neo-liberal polity only involved the public as consumers, denying them as much as the previous tradition a 'voice' in public affairs. The argument that the public does not want to be involved is denied by experience of strong minorities which have struggled to be involved so as to press their rights and to influence the reform of public policy. Wants have in any event been shaped by institutional forms that can be changed and which, in the light of social change, must alter if individuals and their communities are to flourish into the future.

Public discourse can take many forms and does not assume any particular form. It is not restricted to particular settings. The media, the voices of interest groups, pressure and protest are part of discourse, but so is the testing of opinions through surveys of citizens, the dialogue between staff and the public, the messages to councillors and MPs, and the use of citizens' panels. Discourse can lead directly to action in the field, or in user control, or can help to give meaning to participation in a representative democracy.

The organising principles of the public domain provide the purposes, conditions and tasks for public management. The purposes present the criteria by which the practice of public management in enabling the democratic process for the learning society can be judged. We have explored their meaning for:

• public learning
• public choice
• public accountability
• empowering a public culture

The exploration of these themes has revealed a key underlying idea – the critical nature of judgement in the public domain. Judgement grounded in practical reason is the indispensable task that lies at the centre of public management, since judgement is the condition of action in the public domain. Because that domain is unbounded, judgements have to be made to determine the scope of action. Because any voice has access, judgements have to be made on the response. In that domain objectives do not predetermine action, because in a plural community objectives can compete and conflict. Values and interests in society have to be balanced. In the public domain the public interest is sought, but can never be finally determined. A judgement has to be based on public discourse, the role of which is to involve all within the polity in developing an understanding of and contributing to those judgements that are to shape public policy.

The task of management in the public domain is to enable political judgement. This requires understanding of the nature of judgement. Judgement, as Beiner (1983) has argued, offers the faculty which requires deliberation to reach reasonable decisions. The issues that we face in everyday public life are then opened to reflection and discussion.

The world of the political involves everyone and is everyone's responsibility. An expert can advise but not appropriate that responsibility. It requires of citizens a recognition of that responsibility and a willingness to learn about and to exercise the faculty of intersubjective deliberation. Judgement gains importance in a learning society as learning grows with judgement. Vickers illuminates the nature of that society and, therefore, management in the public domain:

> For if my analysis is remotely right, the future of our society depends on the speed with which it can learn; learn not primarily new ways of responding, though these are needed, but primarily new ways of appreciating a situation which is new and new through our making; and thus of finding a basis to combine in securing, so far as we still may, what belongs to our peace.
>
> To 'our' peace – but who are we? How wide are 'our' frontiers? How remote are the unborn whom we already include among 'us'. This is one of the things we have to learn. (Vickers, 1965, p. 233)

References

Adams, G. B., P. U. Bowerman, K. M. Dolbeare and C. Stivers (1990)
'Joining Purpose to Practice: A Democratic Identity for the Public
Service', in H. D. Kass and B. L. Catrow (eds), *Images and Identities in
Public Administration* (London: Sage).

Archer, M. (1979) *Social Origins of Educational Systems* (London: Sage).

Arendt, H. (1958) *The Human Condition* (Chicago, Ill.: University of
Chicago Press).

Arendt, H. (1973) *Crisis in the Republic* (Harmondsworth: Pelican).

Argyris, C. (1993) *On Organisational Learning* (Oxford: Blackwell).

Argyris, C. and D. Schon (1978) *Organisational Learning: A Theory of Action
Perspective* (London: Addison-Wesley).

Aristotle, *The Politics* (Harmondsworth, Penguin).

Arvidsson, G. (1986) 'Performance Evaluation', in F. X. Kaufman,
G. Majone and J. Ostrom (eds), *Guidance, Control and Evaluation in the
Public Domain* (Berlin: de Gruyter).

Attwood, M. and N. Beer (1988) 'Development of a Learning Organisation', *Management Education and Development*, 19 (3).

Audit Commission (1984) *Improving Economy, Efficiency and Effectiveness*
(London: Audit Commission).

Audit Commission (1986) *Making a Reality of Community Care* (London:
HMSO).

Audit Commission (1988a) *The Competitive Council* (London: HMSO).

Audit Commission (1988b) *Performance Review in Local Government: Action
Guide* (London: Audit Commission).

Audit Commission (1993) *Citizen's Charter Indicators Charting a Course*
(London: HMSO).

Barbalet, J. (1988) *Citizenship* (Milton Keynes: Open University Press).

Barber, B. (1984) *Strong Democracy: Participatory Politics for a New Age*
(Berkeley, Calif.: University of California Press).

Barr, N. (1983) *The Economics of the Welfare State* (London: Weidenfeld).

Barry, B. (1965) *Political Argument* (London: Routledge).

Barry, B. (1967) 'The Public Interest', in A. Quinton (ed.), *Political
Philosophy* (Oxford University Press).

Barry, B. (1989) *Theories of Justice: Volume 1: A Treatise on Social Justice*
(London: Harvester Wheatsheaf).

Bateson, G. (1973) *Steps to an Ecology of Mind* (London: Paladin).

Bauman, Z. (1988) *Freedom* (Milton Keynes: Open University Press).

274

Beer, S. (1965) *Modern British Politics* (London: Faber).
Beetham, D. (1987) *Bureaucracy* (Milton Keynes: Open University Press).
Beiner, R. (1983) *Political Judgement* (London: Methuen).
Bell, D. (1974) *The Coming of Post-Industrial Society* (London: Heinemann).
Benefits Agency (1992) *Benefits Agency Annual Report 1991/2* (Leeds: Benefits Agency).
Benn, S. and G. Gaus (1983) *Public and Private in Social Life* (London: Croom Helm).
Benson, J. K. (1982) 'A Framework for Policy Analysis', in P. Rogers, D. Whitter and Associates (eds), *Inter-organisational Co-ordination* (Ames, Iowa: Iowa State Press).
Berlin, I. (1969) *Four Essays on Liberty* (Oxford University Press).
Best, G. (1987) *The Future of General Management* (London: King's Fund).
Birmingham City Council (1992) *City Strategy Report 1992/3* (Birmingham: Birmingham City Council).
Bittner, E. (1965) 'The Concept of Organisation', *Social Research*, 32.
Blau, P. (1964) *Exchange and Power* (Chichester: Wiley).
Blau, P. and R. Schoenherr (1971) *The Structure of Organisations* (London: Basic Books).
Blumenthal, W. H. (1983) 'Candid Reflections of a Businessman in Washington', in J. K. Perry and K. L. Kraemer (eds), *Public Management: Public and Private Perspectives* (Palo Alto, Calif.: Mayfield).
Blunkett, D. and K. Jackson (1987) *Democracy in Crisis: The Town Halls Respond* (London: Hogarth Press).
Bogdanor, V. (1986) *Electoral Systems in Local Government* (University of Birmingham: Institute of Local Government Studies).
Boston, J., J. Martin, J. Pallot and P. Walsh (1991) *Reshaping the State: New Zealand's Bureaucratic Revolution* (Auckland: Oxford University Press).
Brown, C. and P. Jackson (1986) *Public Sector Economics* (Oxford: Blackwell).
Brown, R. (1978) 'Bureaucracy as Praxis: Toward a Political Phenomenology of Formal Organisations', *Administrative Science Quarterly*, 23.
Brundlandt Report (1987) *Our Common Future*, Report of the World Commission on Environment and Development (Oxford University Press).
Bryson, A. (1988) *Strategic Planning for Public and Nonprofit Organisations* (San Francisco: Jossey-Bass).
Buchanan, J. (1975) *The Limits of Liberty: Between Anarchy and the Leviathan* (Chicago: University of Chicago Press).
Burns, T. (1977) *The BBC: Public Institution and Private World* (London: Tavistock).
Butler, Sir R. (1988) *Government and Good Management – Are They Compatible?* (London: Institute of Personnel Management).
Cabinet Office (1984) *Public Purchasing* (London: HMSO).
Caiden, N. (1985) 'The Boundaries of Public Budgeting: Issues for Education in Tumultuous Times', *Public Administration Review*, 45 (4).
Callinicos, A. (1993) 'Socialism and Democracy', in D. Held (ed.), *Prospects for Democracy* (Oxford: Polity Press).
Cawson, A. (1978) 'Pluralism, Corporatism and the Role of the State', *Government and Opposition*, 13.

Cawson, A. (1985) *Corporatism and Welfare* (London: Heinemann).
Central Policy Review Staff (1977) *Relations Between Central Government and Local Authorities* (London: HMSO).
Challis, L., S. Fuller, M. Henwood, R. Klein, W. Plowden, A. Webb, P. Whittingham and G. Wistow (1988) *Joint Approaches to Social Policy: Rationality and Practice* (Cambridge University Press).
Chambers, D. (1987) 'Assessing Public Performance', in B. Stocking (ed.), *In Dreams Begins Responsibility* (London: King's Fund).
Chandler, A. D. (1962) *Strategy and Structure* (Cambridge, Mass; MIT Press).
Chase, G. and E. C. Reveal (1983) *How to Manage in the Public Sector* (Reading, Mass.: Addison-Wesley).
Child, J. (1972) Organisation Structure, Environment and Performance: the Role of Strategic Choice', *Sociology*, 6.
Christopher, M. G., S. H. Kennedy, M. M. McDonald and E. S. Wills (1980) *Effective Marketing Management* (Aldershot: Gower).
Clarke, M. and J. Stewart (1986) *The Public Service Orientation: Developing the Approach* (Luton: Local Government Training Board).
Clarke, M. and J. Stewart (1990) *The General Management of Local Government* (Harlow: Longman).
Cmnd 1599 (1992) *The Citizen's Charter* (London: HMSO).
Cmnd 2911 (1992) *The Next Steps Agencies Review '92* (London: HMSO).
Cmnd 9058 (1983) *Financial Management in Government Departments* (London: HMSO).
Cohen, M. D., J. G. March and J. P. Olsen (1972) 'A Garbage Can Model of Organisational Choice', *Administrative Science Quarterly*, 17.
Common, R., N. Flynn and E. Mellor (1992) *Managing Public Services* (Oxford: Butterworth Heinemann).
Coombs, R. and D. Cooper (1992) 'Accounting for Patients: Information Technology and the Implementation of the NHS White Paper'
Council of Civil Service Unions (1987) Memorandum submitted to the Committee of Public Accounts, printed in HC 61, Report of the Committee 1986/7.
Cowell, D. (1984) *The Marketing of Services* (Oxford: Heinemann).
Crick, B. (1964) *In Defence of Politics* (Harmondsworth: Penguin).
Crosby, N., J. M. Kelly and P. Schaefer (1986) 'Citizens' Panels: A New Approach to Citizen Participation', *Public Administrative Review*, 46 (6).
Dahrendorf, R. (1987a) 'Liberal Helpings', *Times Higher Educational Supplement* (14 August) p. 9.
Dahrendorf, R. (1987b) 'The Erosion of Citizenship and the Consequences for Us All', *New Statesman* (12 June).
Dahrendorf, R. (1988) *The Modern Social Conflict: An Essay in the Politics of Liberty* (London: Weidenfeld & Nicolson).
Dahrendorf, R. (1990) 'Decade of the Citizen' (interview with J. Keane), *The Guardian* (1 August).
Dalton, T. C. and L. C. Dalton (1988) 'The Politics of Measuring Public Sector Performance', in R. M. Kelly (ed.) *Promoting Productivity in the Public Sector* (London: Macmillan).
Davies, A. and J. Willman (1992) *What Next? Agencies, Departments and the Civil Service* (London: IPPR).

Day, P. and R. Klein (1987) *Accountabilities: Five Public Services* (London: Tavistock).

Day, P. and R. Klein (1989) 'Interpreting the Unexpected: The Case of AIDS in Policy Making in Britain', *Journal of Public Policy*, 9.

Day, P. and R. Klein (1990) *Inspecting the Inspectorates* (York: Joseph Rowntree Memorial Trust).

Departmental of Health (1983) *NHS Management Inquiry: Report of the Griffiths Inquiry* (London: DHSS).

Department of the Environment (1983) *Property Service Agency: Final Report of the Wordale Inquiry* (London: HMSO).

Dewey, J. (1915) *Democracy and Education* (New York: Free Press).

Dewey, J. (1939) 'The Modes of Societal Life', in J. Ratner (ed.), *Intelligence in the Modern World* (New York: Random House).

Douglas, J. (1971) *Understanding Everyday Life* (London: Routledge).

Dreze, J. and A. Sen (1974) *Hunger and Public Action* (Oxford: Clarendon Press).

Drucker, P. (1974) *Management: Tasks, Responsibilities and Practices* (London: Heinemann).

Dunn, J. (1984) 'Who Should Own What?', *London Review of Books* (18–31 October).

Dunn, J. (ed.) (1992) *Democracy: The Unfinished Journey: 508 BC to AD 1993* (Oxford University Press).

Dunsire, A. (1978) *Control in a Bureaucracy: The Execution Process* (Oxford: Martin Robertson).

Dunsire, A. (1982) 'Challenges to Public Administration in the 1980s', *Public Administration Bulletin*, 39 (August).

Dunsire, A. (1986) 'A Cybernetic View of Guidance, Control and Evaluation', in F. X. Kaufman, G. Majone and V. Ostrom (eds), *Guidance, Control and Evaluation in the Public Domain* (Berlin: de Gruyter).

du Parq, L. (1987) 'Neighbourhood Services: The Islington Experience', in P. Willmott (ed.), *Local Government Decentralisation and Community* (London: Policy Studies Institute).

Durkheim, E. (1964) *The Division of Labour* (New York: The Free Press, Collier-Macmillan).

Dworkin, R. (1977) *Taking Rights Seriously* (London: Duckworth).

Echols, F., A. McPherson and D. Willms (1990) 'Parental Choice in Scotland', *Journal of Education Policy*, 5 (3).

Eden, C. and S. Cropper (1992) 'Coherence and Balance in Strategies for the Management of Public Services', *Public Money and Management*, 12 (3).

Edwards, T. and G. Whitty (1992) 'Parental Choice and Educational Reform in Britain and the United States', *British Journal of Educational Studies*, 40 (2).

Efficiency Unit (1988) *Improving Management in Government: The Next Steps* (London: HMSO).

Ellis, A. and K. Kumar (eds) (1983) *Dilemmas of Liberal Democracies: Studies in Fred Hirsch's 'Social Limits to Growth'* (London: Tavistock).

Elshtain, J. (1982) *Public Man, Private Woman* (Oxford: Martin Robertson).

Elster, J. (1979) *Ulysses and the Sirens* (Cambridge University Press).

Elster, J. (ed.) (1987) *Rational Choice* (Oxford: Blackwell).
Elster, J. (1983) *Sour Grapes* (Cambridge University Press).
Elster, J. (1992) *Local Justice: How Institutions Allocate Scarce Goods and Necessary Burdens* (Cambridge University Press).
Elster, J. and K. Moene (1989) *Alternatives to Capitalism* (Cambridge University Press).
Estrin, S. and J. Le Grand (1989) *Market Socialism* (Oxford: Clarendon Press).
Evans, T. (1987) 'Strategic Response to Environmental Turbulence', in B. Stocking (ed.), *In Dreams Begins Responsibility* (London: King's Fund).
Farnham, D. and S. Horton (eds) (1993) *Managing the New Public Services* (London: Macmillan).
Finley, M. (1985) *Democracy Ancient and Modern* (London: Hogarth).
Flynn, A., A. Gray, W. I. Jenkins and B. A. Rutherford with W. Plowden (1988) 'Accountable Management in British Central Government: Some Reflecting on the Official Record', *Financial Management and Accountancy*, Vol. 4, No. 3.
Flynn, N. (1990) *Public Sector Management* (Brighton: Wheatsheaf).
Foster, C. D., R. Jackman and M. Perlman (1980) *Local Government Finance in a Unitary State* (London: Allen & Unwin).
Foster, P. (1983) *Access to Welfare: An Introduction to Welfare Rationing* (London: Macmillan).
Friedman, M. (1962) *Capitalism and Freedom* (Chicago: University of Chicago Press).
Friedmann, J. (1987) *Planning in the Public Domain: From Knowledge to Action* (Princeton, NJ: Princeton University Press).
Gadamer, H. G. (1975) *Truth and Method* (London: Sheed & Ward).
Galbraith, J. (1973) *Economics and the Public Purpose* (New York: Mentor Books).
Gamble, A. (1981) *Britain in Decline: Economic Policy, Political Strategy and the British State* (London: Macmillan).
Garfinkel, H. (1967) *Studies in Ethnomethodology* (Englewood Cliffs, NJ: Prentice-Hall).
Gellner, E. (1979) *Spectacles and Predicaments* (Cambridge University Press).
Gellner, E. (1983) *Nations and Nationalism* (Oxford: Blackwell).
Gershuny, J. (1978) *After Industrial Society: The Emerging Self-Service Economy* (London: Macmillan).
Giddens, A. (1976) *New Rules of Sociological Method* (London: Heinemann).
Giddens, A. (1982) *Profiles and Critiques in Social Theory* (London: Macmillan).
Giddens, A. (1984) *The Constitution of Society* (Oxford: Polity Press).
Gilligan, C. (1986) 'Remapping the Moral Domain' in T. Heller, M. Sosna and D. Wellbury (eds), *Reconstructing Individualism: Autonomy, Individuality and the Self in Western Thought* (Stamford, NY: Stamford University Press).
Goffman, E. (1974) *Frame Analysis* (Harmondsworth: Penguin).
Goldsworthy, D. (1991) *Setting Up Next Steps* (London: HMSO).
Goldthorpe, J. (1980) *Social Mobility and the Class Structure in Modern Britain* (Oxford: Clarendon Press).

Golembiewski, R. (1985) *Humanizing Public Organisations* (Maryland: Lomond).

Goodman, E. (ed.) (1983) *Non-Conforming Radicals in Europe: The Future of Industrial Society* (London: Macmillan).

Goodrich, J. A. (1983) 'Marketing for Managers', in B. H. Moore (ed.), *The Entrepreneur in Local Government* (Washington, DC: ICMA).

Gough, I. (1979) *The Political Economy of the Welfare State* (London: Macmillan).

Gould, C. (1988) *Rethinking Democracy: Freedom and Social Cooperation in Politics, Economy and Society* (Cambridge University Press).

Gouldner, A. (1955) 'Metaphysical Pathos and the Theory of Bureaucracy', *American Political Science Review*, 49.

Gouldner, A. (1971) *The Coming Crisis of Western Society* (London: Heinemann).

Grant, W. (1985) *The Political Economy of Corporatism* (London: Macmillan).

Gray, A. and B. Jenkins (1985) *Administrative Politics in Britain* (Brighton: Wheatsheaf).

Gary, A. and B. Jenkins (1991) 'The Management of Change in Whitehall: The experience of the FMI', *Public Administration*, 69 (1).

Green, P. (1985) *Retrieving Democracy: In Search of Civic Equality* (London: Methuen).

Greenway, U. R. (1988) 'The Civil Service Mandarin Elite', in R. Fieldhouse (ed.), *The Political Education of Servants of the State* (Manchester: Manchester University Press).

Greenwood, R. (1987) 'Management Strategies in Local Government', *Public Administration*, 65 (3).

Griffiths, Sir R. (1988a) 'Does the Public Service Serve? The Consumer Dimension', *Public Administration*, 66 (2).

Griffiths, Sir R. (1988b) *Community Care: Agenda for Action*, Report to the Secretary of State (London: HMSO).

Grunow, D. (1991) 'Customer-Oriented Service Delivery in German Local Administration', in R. Batley and G. Stoker (eds), *Local Government in Europe* (London: Macmillan).

Gunn, L (1987) 'Perspectives on Public Management', in J. Kooiman and K. Eliassen (eds), *Managing Public Organisations* (London: Sage).

Gustaffson, G. and J. Richardson (n.d.) *Concepts of Rationality and the Policy Process* (Umea: University of Umea).

Gyford, J. (1987) 'Decentralisation and Democracy' in P. Willmott (ed.), *Local Government Decentralisation and Community* (London: Policy Studies Institute).

HC 535 (1977) *Report on the Civil Service, Vol. 1: Committee on Expenditure* (London: HMSO).

HC 61 (1987) *The Financial Management Initiative, Committee of Public Accounts* (London: HMSO).

HC 92 (1986) *Report on Civil Servants and Ministers: Duties and Responsibilities, Treasury and Civil Service Committee* (London: HMSO).

Habermas, J. (1972) *Knowledge and Human Interests* (London: Heinemann Educational Books).

Habermas, J. (1974) 'The Public Sphere', *New German Critique*, 3.

Habermas, J. (1976) *Legitimation Crisis* (London: Heinemann).

Habermas, J. (1984) *The Theory of Communicative Action: Volume 1: Reason and the Rationalization of Society* (London: Heinemann Educational Books).

Hall, S. and M. Jacques (1989) *New Times: The Changing Face of Politics in the 1990s* (London: Lawrence & Wishart).

Halsey, A. H. (1986) *Change in British Society* (Oxford University Press).

Ham, C. (1986) *Managing Health Services* (Bristol: School of Advanced Urban Studies).

Ham, C. (1991) *The New National Health Service: Organisation and Management* (Oxford: Radcliffe Memorial).

Ham, C. (1992) *Locality Purchasing* (Birmingham: Health Services Management Centre).

Hampshire, S. (1989) *Innocence and Experience* (London: Allen & Unwin).

Handy, C. (1984) *The Future of Work* (Oxford: Blackwell).

Handy, C. (1989) *The Age of Unreason* (London: Arrow).

Harman, M. (1981) *Action Theory for Public Administration* (New York: Longman).

Harman, M. and R. T. Mayer (1986) *Organisation Theory for Public Administration* (BOston, Mass.: Little, Brown).

Harrow, J. and L. Willcocks (1990) 'Public Services Management: Activities, Initiatives and Limits to Learning', *Journal of Management Studies*, 27 (3).

Harrow, J. and L. Willcocks (1992) 'Management, Innovation and Organisational Learning', in L. Willcocks and J. Harrow (eds), *Rediscovering Public Services Management* (London: McGraw-Hill).

Harvey, D. (1989) *The Condition of Postmodernity* (Oxford: Blackwell).

Haydon, G. (ed.) (1987) *Education for a Pluralist Society*, Bedford Way Papers 30 (University of London Institute of Education).

Hayek, F. A. (1976) *Law, Legislation, and Liberty, Vol. 2: The Mirage of Social Justice* (London: Routledge & Kegan Paul).

Heald, D. (1983) *Public Expenditure* (London: Martin Robertson).

Hedberg, B. (1981) 'How Organisations learn and Unlearn', in P. Nystrom and W. H. Starbuck (eds), *Handbook of Organisational Design* (Oxford University Press).

Held, D. (1984) *Political Theory and the Modern State* (Oxford: Polity Press).

Held, D. (1993) *Prospects for Democracy* (Oxford: Polity Press).

Heseltine, M. (1980) 'Ministers and Management in Whitehall', *Management Services in Government*, 35.

Heymann, P. (1987) *The Politics of Public Management* (New Haven, Conn.: Yale University Press).

Hillgate Group (1986) *Whose Schools? A Radical Manifesto* (London: The Hillgate Group).

Hinings, C. R., S. Leach, S. Ranson and C. Skelcher (1983) 'Implementing Policy Planning Decisions', *Long Range Planning*, 18 (2).

Hirsch, F. (1977) *The Social Limits to Growth* (London: Routledge & Kegan Paul).

Hirschman, A. O. (1970) *Exit, Voice and Loyalty: Responses to Decline in Firms, Organisations and States* (Cambridge, Mass.: Harvard University Press).

Hirst, P. (1990) *Representative Democracy and its Limits* (Oxford: Polity Press).

Hobsbawm, E. (1981) 'Observations on the debate' in M. Jacques and F. Mulhern (eds) *The Forward March of Labour halted?* (London: New Left Books).

Hoggett, P. and R. Hambleton (1987) *Decentralisation and Democracy: Localising Public Services,* Occasional Paper 28 (School for Advanced Urban Studies, The University of Bristol).

Hogwood, B. W. and G. B. Peters (1983) *Policy Dynamics* (Brighton: Wheatsheaf).

Hogwood, B. and B. G. Peters (1985) *Policy Dynamics* (Brighton: Wheatsheaf).

Holly, P. and G. Southworth (1989) *The Developing School* (London: Falmer).

Hood, C. (1983) *The Tools of Government* (London: Macmillan).

Hood, C. (1986) *Administrative Analysis* (Brighton: Wheatsheaf).

Hood, C. (1990) 'Beyond the Public Bureaucracy State', *Public Administration,* 67.

Hood, C. (1992) 'A Public Management for All Seasons', *Public Administration,* 69 (1).

Hood, C. and M. Wright (1981) *Big Government in Hard Times* (Oxford: Martin Robertson).

Hudson, R. and A. M. Williams (1989) *Divided Britain* (London: Belhaven Press).

Ignatieff, M. (1984a) *The Needs of Strangers* (London: Hogarth).

Ignatieff, M. (1984b) 'Caring Just Isn't Enough', *New Statesman and Society* (3 February).

Ignatieff, M. (1989) 'Citizenship and Moral Narcissism', *Political Quarterly,* 60 (1).

Jackson, P. (1982) *The Political Economy of Bureaucracy* (Oxford: Philip Allan).

Jackson, P. (1990) *Measuring Performance in the Public Sector* (Leicester: University of Leicester).

Jennings, B. (1987) 'Interpretation and the Practice of Policy Analysis', in F. Fischer and J. Forester (eds), *Confronting Values in Policy Analysis* (Newbury Park: Sage).

Jessop, B., K. Bonnett, S. Bromley and T. Ling (1988) *Thatcherism* (Oxford: Polity Press).

Johnson, G. and K. Scholes (1984) *Exploring Corporate Strategy* (Englewood Cliffs, NJ: Prentice-Hall).

Jonathan, R. (1990) 'State Education Service or Prisoners' Dilemma: The "Hidden Hand" as a Source of Education Policy', *Educational Philosophy and Theory,* 22 (1).

Jones, G. (1979) 'Central–Local Relations, Finance and Law', *Urban Law and Policy,* 2 (1).

Jönsson, S. (1984) 'Budget Making in Central and Local Government', in A. Hopkins and C. Tomkins (eds), *Issues in Public Sector Accounting* (Oxford: Philip Allan).

Jordan, B. (1989) *The Common Good: Citizenship,* Morality and Self-Interest (Oxford: Blackwell).

Kanter, R. M. (1989) *When Giants Learn to Dance* (London: Routledge).

Kaufman, H. (1981) *The Administrative Behaviour of Federal Bureaucracies* (Washington, DC: The Brookings Institution).

Kay, J. (1989) 'Research and Policy: The IFS Experience', *Policy Studies*, 9 (3).

Keane, J. (1984) *Public Life and Late Capitalism: Towards a Socialist Theory of Democracy* (Cambridge University Press).

Keane, J. (1988) *Democracy and Civil Society* (London: Verso).

Keeling, D. (1972) *Management in Government* (London: Allen & Unwin).

King, D. (1987) *The New Right: Politics, Markets and Citizenship* (London: Macmillan).

Kolb, D. (1973) *Organizational Psychology* (Englewood Cliffs, NJ: Prentice-Hall).

Kolb, D. (1984) *Experiential Learning* (Englewood Cliffs, NJ: Prentice-Hall).

Kooiman, J. and K. Eliassen (eds) (1987) *Managing Public Organisations* (London: Sage).

Kotler, P. (1980) *Principles of Marketing* (Englewood Cliffs, NJ: Prentice-Hall)

Kotler, P. and Andreason, A. R. (1937) *Strategic Marketing for Non-Profit Organizations* (Englewood Cliffs: NJ: Prentice-Hall).

Lane, J.-E. (ed.) (1985) State and the Market: The Politics of the Public and Private (London: Sage).

Lane, J.-E. (ed.) (1987) *Bureaucracy and Public Choice* (London: Sage).

Lane, J.-E. (1993) *The Public Sector: Concepts, Models and Approaches* (London: Sage).

Lash, S. and J. Urry (1987) *The End of Organised Capitalism* (Oxford: Polity Press).

Latimore, J. (1980) 'Indirect Provision of Government Services', in C. H. Levine (ed.), *Managing Fiscal Stress: The Crisis in the Public Sector* (Chatham: Chatham House).

Laver, M. (1983) *Invitation to Politics* (Oxford: Martin Robertson).

Laver, M. (1986) *Social Choice and Public Policy* (London: Blackwell).

Le Grand, J. (1989) 'Markets, Welfare and Equality', in S. Estrin and J. Le Grand (eds), *Market Socialism* (Oxford: Clarendon Press).

Lessem, R. (1993) *Business as a Learning Community* (London: McGraw-Hill).

Levitas, R. (ed.) (1986) *The Ideology of the New Right* (Oxford: Polity Press).

Lewis, S. (1986) *Output and Performance Measurement in Central Government Departments* (London: The Treasury).

Lindblom, C. (1977) *Politics and Markets* (New York: Basic Books).

Lipsky, M. (1980) *Street Level Bureaucracy: Dilemmas of the Individual in Public Services* (New York: Public Services).

Locke, J. (1967) *Two Treatises of Government*, ed. P. Lasleth, 2nd edn (Cambridge: Cambridge University Press).

Local Government Training Board (1988) *Going for Better Management* (Luton: Local Government Training Board).

Lord Chancellor's Department (1992) *The Courts Charter* (London: Lord Chancellor's Department).

Lukes, S. (1974) *Power: A Radical View* (London: Macmillan).

Lukes, S. (1984) 'The Future of British Socialism?' in B. Pimlott (ed) *Fabian Essays in Socialist Thought*, (London: Heinemann).

Lynn, J. (1981) *Managing the Public's Business* (London: Basic Books).

Lyotard, J-F (1984) *The Postmodern Condition: A Report on Knowledge* (Manchester University Press).

McCullough, T. (1991) *The Moral Imagination and Public Life* (London: Chatham House).

MacIntyre, A. (1981) *After Virtue: A Study in Moral Theory* (London: Duckworth).

McLean, A. and J. Marshall (1988) *Cultures at Work* (Luton: Local Government Training Board).

MacMurray, J. (1953) *The Self as Agent* (London: Faber & Faber).

McPherson, C. (1973) *Democratic Theory: Essays in Retrieval* (Oxford University Press).

McPherson, C. (1977) *The Life and Times of Liberal Democracy* (Oxford University Press).

Majone, G. (1989) *Evidence, Argument and Persuasion in the Policy Process* (New Haven, Conn.: Yale University Press).

Mann, M. (1987) 'Ruling Class Strategies and Citizenship', *Sociology*, 21 (3).

March, J. G. and J. P. Olsen (1989) *Rediscovering Institutions* (New York: Free Press).

Marquand, D. (1988) *The Unprincipled Society: New Demands and Old Politics* (London: Jonathan Cape).

Marquand, D. (1990) 'Citizens', *London Review of Books* (20 December) pp. 8–9.

Marquand, D. (1991) 'Civic Republicans and Liberal Individualists: The Case of Britain', *European Journal of Sociology*, 32.

Marshall, T. (1977) *Classes, Citizenship and Social Development* (Chicago, Ill.: Chicago University Press).

Marshall, G., D. Rose, H. Newby and C. Vogler (1988) *Social Class in Modern Britain* (London: Unwin Hyman).

Massey, D. and R. Meegan (1982) *The Anatomy of Job Loss* (London University Press).

Maxwell, R. (1984) 'Quality Assessment in Health', *British Medical Journal*, 288.

Maxwell, R. (1987) 'Unfinished Business, A Progress Report on Griffiths' in B. Stocking (ed.), *In Dreams Begins Responsibility* (London: King's Fund).

Metcalfe, L. and S. Richards (1987) *Improving Public Management* (London: Sage).

Miller, D. (1989) *Market, State and Community: Theoretical Foundations of Market Socialism* (Oxford University Press).

Miller, J. (1962) *The Nature of Politics* (Harmondsworth: Penguin).

Millett, J. (1961) *Organisation for the Public Service* (Wokingham: Van Nostrand Rheinhold).

Mills, C. Wright (1959) *The Sociological Imagination* (New York: Oxford University Press).

Mills, P. (1988) *Managing Service Industries* (Cambridge, Mass.: Ballinger).

Mintzberg, H. (1983) *Structure in Fives: Designing Effective Organisations* (Englewood Cliffs, NJ: Prentice-Hall).

Mishra, R. (1984) *The Welfare State in Crisis: Social Thought and Social Change* (London: Wheatsheaf).

Moore, Barrington (1985) *Privacy: Studies in Social and Cultural History* (New York. M. E. Sharpel).

Morrison, C. (1988) 'Consumerism – Lessons from Community Work', *Public Administration*, 66 (2).

Mosher, F. C. (1968) *Democracy and the Public Service* (New York: Oxford University Press).

Mouffe, C. (1992) *Dimensions of Radical Democracy: Pluralism, Citizenship, Community* (London: Verso).

Mueller, Dame A. (1987) 'Foreword' in *Getting the Best Out of People* (London: HMSO).

Murphy, R. (1988) 'Great Education Reform Bill Proposals for Testing – A Critique', *Local Government Studies*, 14 (1).

Murray, R. (1989) 'Fordism and Post Fordism' and 'Benetton Britain' in S. Hall and M. Jacques (eds) *New Times: The Changing Face of Politics in the 1990s* (London: Lawrence & Wishart).

Nagel, T. (1990) 'Freedom Within Bounds', *Times Literary Supplement* (16–22 February).

Nagel, T. (1991) *Equality and Partiality* (Oxford University Press).

Natchez, P. B. and I. C. Bupp (1973) 'Policy and Priority in the Budgetary Process', *American Political Science Review*

National Audit Office (1986) *The Financial Management Initiative* (London: HMSO).

National Audit Office (1988) *Department of Health and Social Security: Quality of Service to the Public at Local Offices* (London: HMSO).

National Health Service Training Authority (1986) *Better Management, Better Health* (Bristol: NHSTA).

Nichol, D. K. (1986) 'Action Research and Development', in G. Parston (ed.), *Managers as Strategists* (London: King's Fund).

Niskanen, W. (1971) *Bureaucracy and Representative Government* (Chicago, III.: Aldine Atherton).

Niskanen, W. (1973) *Bureaucracy: Servant or Master?* (London: Institute of Economic Affairs).

Niskanen, W. (1975) 'Bureaucrats and Politicians', *Journal of Law and Economics*, 18 (4).

Normann, R. (1984) *Service Management* (Chichester: Wiley).

Nozick, R. (1974) *Anarchy, State and Utopia* (Oxford: Blackwell).

Nussbaum, M. (1990) 'Aristotelian Social Democracy', in G. Mara and H. Richardson (eds), *Liberalism and the Good* (New York: Routledge).

Nussbaum, M. (1993) 'Non-relative Virtues: An Aristotelian Approach', in M. Nussbaum and A. Sen (eds), *The Quality of Life* (Oxford University Press).

Nussbaun, M. and A. Sen (1993) *The Quality of Life* (Oxford University Press).

O'Connor, J. (1973) *The Fiscal Crisis of the State* (London and New York: St Martin's Press).

Offe, C. (1975) 'The Theory of the Capitalist State and the Problem of Policy Formation', in L. Lindberg, R. Alford, C. Crouch and C. Offe,

Stress and Contradiction in Modern Capitalism (London: Lexington Bootes, D. C. Heath and Company).

Offe, C. (1984) *Contradictions of the Welfare State* (London: Hutchinson).

Offe, C. (1985) *Disorganised Capitalism* (Oxford: Polity Press).

Okin, S. M. (1991) 'Gender, the Public and the Private', in D. Held (ed.), *Political Theory Today* (Oxford: Polity Press).

O'Neill, O. (1984) 'Private Lives and Public Affairs', *London Review of Books* (18–31 October).

Ossowski, S. (1963) *Class Structure in the Social Consciousness* (London: Routledge).

Pahl, R. (1977) 'Collective Consumption and the State in Capitalist and State Socialist Societies', in R. Scase (ed.), *Industrial Society: Class Cleavage and Control* (London: Allen & Unwin).

Panitch, L. (1980) 'Recent Theorisation of Corporatism', *British Journal of Sociology*, 31 (2).

Parekh, B. (1973) *Bentham's Political Thought* (London: Croom Helm).

Parekh, B. (1988) 'Good Answers to Bad Questions' (review of R. Dahrendorf, *The Modern Social Conflict*), *New Statesman and Society* (28 October).

Parfit, D. (1984) *Reasons and Persons* (Oxford: Clarendon Press).

Parq, L. du (1987) 'Neighbourhood Services: The Islington Experience', in P. Willmott (ed.) *Local Government Decentralisation and Community* (London: Policy Studies Institute).

Pateman, C. (1970) *Participation and Democratic Theory* (Cambridge University Press).

Pateman, C. (1987) 'Feminist Critiques of the Public/Private Dichotomy', in A. Phillips (ed.), *Feminism and Equality* (Oxford: Blackwell).

Paton, C. (1992) *Competition and Planning in the National Health Service* (London: Chapman & Hall).

Pedler, M., J. Burgoyne and T. Boydell (1991) *The Learning Company* (London: McGraw-Hill).

Perkin, H. (1989) *The Rise of Professional Society: England Since 1880* (London: Routledge & Kegan Paul).

Perrin, J. (1988) *Resource Management in the NHS* (Wokingham: Van Nostrand Reinhold).

Perry, J. C. and K. L. Kraemer (eds) (1983) *Public Management: Public and Private Perspectives* (Palo Alto, Calif.: Mayfield).

Perry, J. and Rainey H. G. (1988) 'The Public Private Distinction in Organisation Theory: A Critique and Research Strategy', *Academy of Management Review*, 13 (2).

Pettigrew, A. (1973) *The Politics of Organisational Decision-Making* (London: Tavistock).

Pettigrew, A., E. Ferlie and L. McKee (1992) *Shaping Strategic Change: Making Change in Large Organisations: The Case of the National Health Service* (London: Sage).

Pfeffer, J. (1981) *Power in Organisations* (Marshfield: Pitman).

Pfeffer, J. and G. Salancik (1978) *The External Control of Organisations* (London: Harper & Row).

Phillips, A. (1991) *Engendering Democracy* (Oxford: Polity Press).

Phillips, A. (1993) *Democracy and Difference* (Oxford: Polity Press).

Pirie, M. (1992) *Blueprint for a Revolution* (London: Adam Smith Institute).

Plant, R. (1988) 'Citizenship and Social Class', *New Socialist*, 58 (December).

Plant, R. (1990) 'Citizenship and Rights', in R. Plant and N. Barry (eds), *Citizenship and Rights in Thatcher's Britain: Two Views* (London: Institute of Economic Affairs).

Plant, R. and N. Barry (1990) *Citizenship and Rights in Thatcher's Britain: Two Views* (London: Institute of Economic Affairs, Health and Welfare Unit).

Pollitt, C. (1980) Performance Measurement and the Consumer: Hijacking a Bandwagon?', in *National Consumer Council's Performance Measurement and the Consumer* (London: National Consumer Council).

Pollitt, C. (1990) *Managerialism and the Public Services: The Anglo American Experience* (Oxford: Blackwell).

Pollitt, C. and S. Harrison (eds) (1992) *Handbook of Public Services Management* (Oxford: Blackwell).

Pollitt, C., S. Harrison, D. J. Hunter and G. Marnoch (1991) 'General Management in the NHS: The Initial Impact 1983–88', *Public Administration*, 69 (1).

Potter, J. (1988) 'Consumerism and the Public Sector: How Well Does the Coat Fit?', *Public Administration*, 66 (2).

Prince, M. J. (1983) *Policy Advice and Organisational Survival* (Farnborough: Gower).

Putnam, R. (1993) *Making Democracy Work: Civic Traditions in Modern Italy* (Princeton, NJ: Princeton University Press).

Quinn, J. B. (1980) *Strategies for Change: Logical Incrementalism* (Homewood, Ill.: Irwin).

Raine, J. W. (1989) *Local Justice* (Edinburgh: T. & T. Clark).

Raine, J. W. and I. R. Scott (1982) *The Hampshire Magistrates' Courts: Planning for the Future* (Birmingham: Institute of Local Government Studies and Institute of Judicial Administration).

Ranson, S. (1988) 'From 1944 to 1988: Education, Citizenship and Democracy', in S. Ranson, R. Morris and P. Ribbins (eds), 'The Education Reform Bill', *Local Government Studies*, 14(1).

Ranson, S. (1992) 'Towards the Learning Society', *Educational Management and Administration*, 20 (1).

Ranson, S. (1993) 'Markets or Democracy for Education', *British Journal of Educational Studies*

Ranson, S. (1994) *Towards the Learning Society* (London: Cassell).

Ranson, S. and J. Stewart (1989) 'Citizenship and Government: The Challenge for Management in the Public Domain', *Political Studies*, 37 (1).

Ranson, S., B. Hinings and R. Greenwood (1980) 'The Structuring of Organisation Structures', *Administrative Science Quarterly*, 25 (March).

Rawls, J. (1971) *A Theory of Justice* (Oxford: Clarendon Press).

Rawls, J. (1982) 'Social Unity and Primary Goods', in A. Sen and B. Williams (eds), *Utilitarianism and Beyond* (Cambridge: University Press).

Rawls, J. (1993) *Political Liberalism* (Columbia, Ohio: Columbia University Press).

Raz, J. (1986) *The Morality of Freedom* (Oxford University Press).

Revans, R. (1982) *The Origins and Growth of Action Learning* (Bromley: Chartwell Brett).

Rhodes, R. A. W. (1981) *Control and Power in Central–Local Government Government Relations* (Westmead: Gower).

Rhodes, R. A. W. (1986) *The National World of Local Government* (London: Allen & Unwin).

Rhodes, R. A. W. (1988) *Beyond Westminster and Whitehall: The Sub-Central Governments of Britain* (London: Unwin Hyman).

Richards, S. (1988) *Turning Civil Servants into Managers: Strategies for Cultural Change*, paper to Royal Institute of Public Administration Conference.

Riddle, D. (1988) 'Public Sector Productivity and Role Conflicts', in R. M. Kelly (ed.), *Promoting Productivity in the Public Sector* (London: Macmillan).

Ridley, F. F. (1987) 'What Are the Duties and Responsibilities of Civil Servants?', *Public Administration*, 65 (1).

Robbins, C. (1991) 'Our Manufactured Diet', in P. Draper (ed.) *Health Through Public Policy* (London: Green Print).

Roche, M. (1987) 'Citizenship, Social Theory and Social Change', *Theory and Society*, 16.

Roche M. (1992) *Rethinking Citizenship: Welfare, Ideology and Change in modern Society* (Oxford: Polity Press).

Rochefort, D. A. and C. A. Boyer (1988) 'Use of Public Opinion Data in Public Administration Health Care Polls', *Public Administration Review*, 48 (2).

Roemer, J. (ed) (1986) *Analytical Marxism* (Cambridge. Cambridge University Press).

Rorty, R. (1989) *Contingency, Irony, and Solidarity* (Cambridge:

Rosenbloom, D. (1986) *Public Administration: Understanding Management, Politics and Law in the Public Sector* (New York: Random House).

Ryan, A. (1984) *Property and Political Theory* (Oxford: Blackwell).

Salaman, L. M. (1981) 'Rethinking Public Management: Third-Party Government and the Changing Forms of Government Action', *Public Policy*, 29 (3).

Saltman, R. B. and C. Van Otter (1992) *Planned Markets and Public Competition* (Buckingham: Open University Press).

Saner, M. (1992) 'Learning to Improve Quality of Service' in D. Wilkinson (ed.), *Working and Learning Together: Development as a Strategic Activity* (London: Association of Management Education and Development).

Saunders, P. (1979) *Urban Politics: A Sociological Interpretation* (London: Hutchinson).

Schick, A. (1987) 'Macro-Budgeting Adaptation to Stress in Industrial Democracies', *Public Administration Review*, 46 (2).

Schon, D. (1971) *Beyond the Stable State* (New York: Norton).

Schutz, A. and T. Luckmann (1973) *The Structures of the Life World* (London: Heinemann).

Self, P. (1965) *Bureaucracy and Management* (London: Bell & Sor).

Self, P. (1985) *Political Theories of Modern Government* (London: Allen & Unwin).

Self, P. (1987) *Redefining the Role of Government*, paper at the National Conference, Royal Australian Institute of Public Administration (November).

Sen, A. (1982) *Choice, Welfare and Measurement* (Oxford: Blackwell).

Sen, A. (1987) *On Ethics and Economics* (Oxford: Blackwell).

Sen, A. (1990) 'Individual Freedom as Social Commitment', *New York Review of Books* (14 June).

Sen, A. (1992) 'On the Darwinian View of Progress', *London Review of Books* (5 November).

Shearer, A. (1991) *Who Calls the Shots?* (London: King's Fund).

Shepherd, C. (1987) 'The Middlesbrough Community Councils', *Local Government Policy Making*, 14 (2).

Simey, M. (1985) *Government by Consent: The Principles and Practice of Accountability in Local Government* (London: Bedford Square Press).

Simey, M. (1988) *Democracy Rediscovered: A Study in Police Accountability* (London: Pluto Press).

Skidelsky, R. (ed.) (1988) *Thatcherism* (Oxford: Blackwell).

Skinner, Q. (1992) 'On Justice, the Common Good and Priority of Liberty', in C. Mouffe (ed.), *Dimensions of Radical Democracy: Pluralism, Citizenship, Community* (London: Verso).

Smith Ring, P. and J. Perry (1985) 'Strategic Management in Public and Private Organisations', *Academy of Management Review*, 10 (2).

Smith, M. J. (1991) 'From Policy Community to Issue Network: Salmonella in Eggs and the New Politics of Food', *Public Administration*, 69 (2).

Sockett, H. 'Accountability: The Contemporary Issues', in H. Socket (ed.), *Accountability in the English Educational System* (London: Hodder and Stoughton).

Solesbury, W. (1986) 'Dilemmas of Inner City Policy', *Public Administration*, 46 (4).

Steele, K. (1992) 'Patients as Experts: Consumer Appraisal of Health Services', *Public Money and Management*, 12 (4).

Stewart, J. (1988) *Understanding the Management of Local Government* (Harlow: Longman).

Stewart, J. and S. Ranson (1988) 'Management in the Public Domain', *Public Money and Management*, 89 (1/2).

Stewart, J. and G. Stoker (1989a) *The Future of Local Government* (London: Macmillan).

Stewart, J. and G. Stoker (1989b) 'The Free Local Government Experiments and the Programme of Public Service Reform', in C. Crouch and D. Marquand (eds), *The New Centralism* (Oxford: Blackwell).

Stewart, J. and G. Stoker (1994) *Local Government in the 1990s* (London: Macmillan).

Stewart, J. and K. Walsh (1990) 'Change in the Management of Public Services', *Public Administration*, 70 (4).

Stewart, J. and K. Walsh (1994) 'Performance Management When Performance Can Never be Finally Defined', *Public Money and Management*

Stewart, M. (1987) 'Ten Years of Inner City Policy', *Town Planning Review*, 58 (2).

Stinbrunen, J. D. (1974) *The Cybernetic Decision* (Princeton, NJ: Princeton University Press).

Stivers, C. (1990) 'Active Citizenship and Public Administration', in G. Walmsley (ed.) *Refounding Public Administration* (Newbury Park: Sage).

Stoker, G. (1987a) 'Decentralisation and Local Government', *Social Policy and Administration*, 21 (2).

Stoker, G. (1987b) 'Decentralisation and the Restructuring of Local Government in Britain', *Local Government Policy Making*, 14 (2).

Susskund, L. and J. Cruikshank (1987) *Breaking the Impasse* (New York: Basic Books).

Tawney, R. N. (1931) *Equality* (London: Unwin).

Taylor, C. (1984) *Philosophy and the Human Sciences: Philosophical Papers 2* (Cambridge University Press).

Taylor, C. (1986) Discussion on 'Modernity and its Discontents', *The Listener*, 1 May 1986, Reprinted in M. Ignatieff (ed.) (1987) *Modernity and its Discontents* (Nottingham: Spokesman/Hobo Press).

Taylor, C. (1991) *The Ethics of Authenticity* (Cambridge, Mass.: Harvard University Press).

Taylor, C. (1992) *Multiculturalism and 'The Politics of Recognition'* (Princeton, NJ: Princeton University Press).

Taylor-Gooby, P. (1985) *Public Opinion, Ideology and State Welfare* (London: Routledge).

Thain, C. (1985) 'The Education of the Treasury', *Public Administration*, 63 (3).

Thucydides (1954) *History of the Peloponnesian War* (London: Penguin).

Titmuss, R. M. (1971) *The Gift Relationship: From Human Blood to Social Policy* (London: Allen & Unwin).

Turner, B. (1986) *Citizenship and Capitalism: The Debate over Reformism* (London: Allen & Unwin).

Turner, B. (1990a) 'Outline of a Theory of Citizenship', *Sociology*, 24 (2).

Turner, B. (ed.) (1990b) *Theories of Modernity and Postmodernity* (London: Sage).

Turner, B. (ed.) (1993) *Citizenship and Social Theory* (London: Sage).

Vickers, Sir G. (1965) *The Art of Judgment* (London: Chapman & Hall).

Vickers, Sir G. (1972) *Freedom in a Rocking Boat* (Harmondsworth: Penguin).

Wainwright, H. (1987) *Labour: A Tale of Two Parties* (London: Hogarth Press).

Waldo, D. (1952) 'Development of Theory of Democratic Administration', *American Political Science Review*, 46 (1).

Walmsley, G. (1990) 'The Agency Perspective – Public Administrators as Agential Leaders' in G. Walmsley (ed.) *Refounding Public Administration* (Newbury Park: Sage).

Walsh, K. (1989) *Marketing in Local Government* (Harlow: Longman).

Walsh, K. (1991) *Competitive Tendering for Local Authority Services: Initial Experiences* (London: HMSO).

Walton, J. and J. Evans (1966) 'Special Education Policy', *Public Administration*, 64 (2).

Walzer, M. (1989) 'The Good Life: The Civics Argument', *New Statesman and Society* (6 October).

Walzer, M. (1992) 'The Civil Society Argument', in C. Mouffe (ed.), *Dimensions of Radical Democracy: Pluralism, Citizenship, Community* (London: Verso).

Webb, A. and G. Wistow (1986) *Planning, Need and Scarcity* (London: Allen & Unwin).

Weber, M. (1978) *Economy and Society* (Berkeley, Calif.: University of California Press).

Weiner, M. (1981) *English Culture and the Decline of the Industrial Spirit* (Cambridge University Press).

Weisbrod, B. A. (1988) *The Non-Profit Economy* (Cambridge, Mass.: Harvard University Press).

Weiss, H. L. (1983) 'Why Business and Government Exchange Executives', in J. G. Perry and K. L. Kraemer (eds), *Public Management: Public and Private Perspectives* (Palo Alto: Mayfield).

Wells, R. (1992) 'Change – As Good as Arrest', in D. Wilkinson (ed.), *Working and Learning Together: Development as a Strategic Activity* (London: Association for Management Education and Development).

West, P. (1988) *Understanding the NHS* (London: King's Fund).

Wildavsky, A. (1984) *The Politics of the Budgetary Process* (Boston, Mass.: Little, Brown).

White, J. (1990) 'Images of Administrative Reason and Rationality: the Recovery of Practical Discourse', in H. D. Kass and B. L. Catron (eds), *Images and Identities in Public Administration* (Sage, London).

Wilenski, P. (1986) 'Administrative Reform – The Australian Experience', *Public Administration*, 64 (1).

Willcocks, L. and J. Harrow (eds) (1992) *Rediscovering Public Services Management* (London: McGraw-Hill).

Williamson, O. E. (1975) *Markets and Hierarchies* (New York: Free Press).

Williamson, O. E. (1983) *The Economic Institutions of Capitalism: Firms, Markets, Relational Contracting* (New York: Free Press).

Willmott, P. (ed.) (1987) *Local Government Decentralisation and Community* (London: Policy Studies Institute).

Winkler, J. (1977) 'The Corporate Economy: Theory and Administration' in R. Scase (ed.), *Industrial Society* (London: Allen & Unwin).

Winter, G. (1970 'Toward a Comprehensive Science of Policy', *Journal of Religion*, 50.

Wirth, W. (1986) 'Control in Public Administration: Plurality, Selectivity and Redundancy', in F. X. Kaufman, G. Majone and V. Ostrom (eds),

Guidance, Control and Evaluation in the Public Domain (Berlin: de Gruyter).

Yates, G. (1987) 'Management Accounting in the Public Service', in F. Terry and P. Jackson (eds), *Public Domain 1987* (London: Public Finance Foundation).

Yates, J. (1982) *Hospital Beds: A Problem for Diagnosis and Management* (London: Heinemann).

Yates, J. (1987) *Why Are We Waiting? An Analysis of Hospital Waiting Lists* (Oxford University Press).

Zimmerman, D. (1971) 'The Practicalities of Rule Use', in J. Douglas (ed.), *Understanding Everyday Life* (London: Routledge).

Index